STUDENT MISSION POWER

Report of the First International Convention of the Student Volunteer Movement for Foreign Missions

Held at Cleveland, Ohio, U.S.A.
February 26, 27, 28 and March 1, 1891.

William Carey Library

1705 N. SIERRA BONITA AVE. • PASADENA, CALIFORNIA 91104

Library of Congress Catalog Card Number 79-92013
International Standard Book Number 0-87808-736-2

Published by the William Carey Library
1705 N. Sierra Bonita Avenue
Pasadena, California 91104
Telephone (213) 798-0819

Contents

Foreword

The Student Volunteer Movement watchword, "The Evangelization of the World in this Generation," is as relevant for us today as it was at the First International Convention in 1891. We therefore can learn much from this report.

First we are reintroduced to the spiritual giants of that time. Dr. Adoniram Judson Gordon, who was a close friend and co-worker of Dwight L. Moody, gives the opening address on "The Holy Spirit in Missions." He used to describe the work of completing Christ's commission by saying, "Our task is not to bring all the world to Christ, our task is unquestionably to bring Christ to all the world." Robert and Grace Wilder, a brother and sister team, were powerful in prayer. They took seriously Christ's command to interceed for laborers. And they saw God answer with thousands signing the Student Volunteer pledge stating, "God helping me, I purpose to become a foreign missionary." John R. Mott founded and ministered to Christian associations all around the world which in turn became the bases for the ecumenical movement. When Woodrow Wilson asked him to become the United States Ambassador to Russia, he declined stating that he already was an ambassador for Christ the King of Kings. Robert E. Speer became Secretary of the Presbyterian Board of Foreign Missions and saw it grow ten times larger in the number of missionaries sent, from 150 to over 1500. Dr. John L. Medius from China also spoke and developed the mission strategy being successfully used in Korea to encourage Christians to become self-governing, self-supporting, and self-propagating.

Secondly, we see that the natural outcome of the revivial is mission expansion. Even as the Holy Spirit brought the Student Volunteer Movement Missionary Revival on the crest of the wave of the awakening under Dwight L. Moody, so today God has brought a renewed interest in world evangelization on the part of many, along with the spiritual renewal which is taking place in this generation.

Thirdly we come to realize that this missionary conference became the prototype for the Student Volunteer Movement quadrennials which were held every four years so that students in every college generation would be challenged to become missionaries. It also became the model for the Inter Varsity Student Foreign Missions Fellowship Urbana Conventions and the Campus Crusade for Christ Explos and Christmas Conferences.

Fourthly, we see that the topics were practical. Questions are considered of how to apply to the mission socieites, how to get to the field, how to volunteer, and also what those planning to go could do to help the cause before leaving. One receives marching orders in these pages.

Fifthly this report brings out the fact that the movement was beginning to appreciate the importance of women in missions. Not only did twelve women speak and participate on the program, but also a workshop conference on "Woman's Work for Woman" was held and representatives from the outstanding Women's Missionary Societies were in attendance.

Sixthly, by the time of this first convention, the Student Volunteer Movement was only four and a half years old, yet one cannot help but be amazed at the plethora of publications on missions listed in the back of this book. Most of these are out of print yet it shows the tremendous number of publications which were produced in the early years of this movement. Dr. Samuel Zwemer, who was one of the first volunteers, used to say, "Just as Martin Luther threw the inkwell at the devil, so we need to use ink in opposing Satan around the world today by writing, publishing, and distributing Christian literature."

Finally, one is impressed with the basic evangelical doctrines which were the foundation of this convention. These include the primacy of prayer, the exposition of the Scriptural teaching concerning Christ's great commission, the goal of accomplishing world evangelization, the honoring of the Holy Spirit in His work of extending missions, the close association with churches, and the instruction in soul winning which assumed the lostness of humanity without Christ. The love of Christ was to be put into action. Ways were considered of meeting the world's need evangelistically, educationally, medically, industrially, and editorially.

The William Carey Library is to be congratulated for republishing this book "for such a time as this" so that many today may benefit from the challenge and spirit and that they may "go and do likewise."

J. Christy Wilson, Jr.
Gordon-Conwell Theological Seminary
November 1, 1979

Preface

As I write this preface in California this morning, before leaving for South Africa tomorrow, it strikes me that I have been most fortunate to have seen anew the value, enduring to the demanding days in which we live, of the remarkable principles held by leaders of the early Student Volunteer Movement for Foreign Missions. Last evening I was with a small gathering of students and soon-to-be missionaries, staff-members of the U.S. Center for World Mission, at the home of Dr. & Mrs. Ralph Winter. Dr. & Mrs. Donald McGavran were the special guests on this occasion, and our dinner conversation excitedly ranged across the many miles, peoples, and years of Dr. McGavran's remarkable missionary life. After dinner we turned to questions of the future, matters of consuming and mutual concern to all present from the eldest to the youngest, from the most experienced to the least. "How will we play the most effective part possible in reaching the as yet unreached peoples for Christ?" and "how will young people in particular best enter the stream of God's plan for the completion of the Great Commission, Christ's last command?"

Dr. Winter produced a book containing John R. Mott's own description in 1892 of the first six years of the Student Volunteer Movement (see appendix), that unprecedented and as yet unparalled movement of the Holy Spirit among American students beginning in 1886 which so dramatically changed the world. Dr. Winter asked me to read, and I did so, stopping after practically every paragraph to allow for the brimming discussion, reflections of the heartfelt yearnings of every one present.

There we were, three generations of missions-minded people, Dr. & Mrs. McGavran, members of the old S.V.M., delegates to the 1920 quadrennial student missions conference before marrying and going out to service in India; Dr. & Mrs. Winter, one generation younger than the McGavrans, delegates to the first "Urbana" held in Toronto in 1946 before entering a life together of missionary committment that has been so instrumental in focusing the attention of the Christian world today on the 2.5 billion "Hidden" people without Christ; and several other younger people who, like myself and my wife Debbie are the "younger generation," with the majority of our missionary career years still before us.

At one point in my reading of John R. Mott's review of the S.V.M.'s potent teachings and "watchwords," Dr. McGavran interrupted. "You know," he said, "I've just returned from a school in the midwest where I spoke to the students on missions. It was my third trip out there, but I wish I'd had the material for my addresses that you're reading." Dr. McGavran was responding in particular to a statement by Dr. Wm. Ashmore, returned missionary from China, addressing students at the original Mt. Hermon Conference in 1888.

His question to the vocationally undecided students before him: "Show me, if you can, why you should not obey the last command of Jesus Christ?"

Here in the *Report of the First International Convention of the Student Volunteer Movement for Foreign Missions* held in Cleveland, in 1891, are recorded the burning concepts and the motivating material that the Holy Spirit used to fuel the fires of the career missionary commitments of 100,000 U.S. college students in an era when the student population in America was only 1/37th of what it is today. Is it dated, sentimental, "quasi-Christian manifest destiny" jingoism of the gay nineties? Perpetrated on a naive, unsuspecting U.S. student population by a few Princetonians who knew how to organize? Hardly. The material is just as up-to-date, just as applicable as anything one could find in 1979 on the subject. I doubt that in recent years the S.V.M. has in academic circles even rated that much of an evaluation. During my undergraduate years at Princeton in the late '60's I heard much about Woodrow Wilson's foreign policy and that of our other noted alumnus, John Foster Dulles, but not once did I hear even a mention about the work of Robert Wilder and Robert Speer, two Princeton students whose words are contained dramatically in this volume. Together with other, older spirit-filled saints like A. J. Gordon, these student leaders gave scriptural motivation and direction to a "foreign policy" which sent 20,000 young men and women out to live and sometimes die in nations around the world, supported by an amazingly active clergy and lay backing made up of 80,000 other "student volunteers" who preached the gospel of God's salvation in Jesus Christ while establishing educational and medical facilities for whole nations, the results of which has changed the world in an enduring, continuing way. Contrast that "foreign policy" contribution to that which millions of students, Christian students, study dutifully, year in and year out at Princeton and thousands of colleges across the land, the work of Wilson and Dulles, now for the most part just period pieces, in need of overhaul or replacement, kicked along like a fraying football with each succeeding American political administration .

Here in the recorded speeches of the 1891 First International Convention, the first for the S.V.M., we hear the characteristics of the vibrant undertaking propounded over and over again, the characteristics that would to prove so enduring, so valuable in the world-wide growth of the Church of Jesus Christ. It demands from its members first of all a total, personal, and disciplined commitment to Jesus Christ as Savior, based on a daily, private walk with Christ in personal Bible reading and prayer. Read, for instance, Wilder's record of how prayer was the foundational element for the launching of the movement. Certainly the data was there too, "the accusing map", as Hudson Taylor used to say, the facts about the unreached people, and this too will be seen as elemental to the success of the S.V.M., but listen again to A. J. Gordon as he alerts those gathered to another foundational principle: that it is only through the power of the Holy Spirit that true missionary work can be undertaken and sustained.

Furthermore, and most unavoidably, you will see in Wilder, Speer, and others a personal and consuming concern for the lost, for people without Christ as Savior, for people without the opportunity to call upon Christ for salvation even if they wanted to. Theirs was a compassion that parallels the concern of

Jesus Himself as he looked at the multitudes in Matthew 9:36, where it is recorded that Jesus was so moved that he was literally torn up inside. The S.V.M. leadership had that kind of concern, and they conveyed it to others, saying in effect, "The fate of the unreached peoples is in large measure *your* responsibility."

Was this a "guilt trip?" An impossible burden laid upon young, unsuspecting minds? Absolutely not, for as Speer himself indicates in his great speech entitled, "The Evangelization of the World in the Present Generation—A Possibility," "It is not a human issue, God is in it." Speer closed that historic address (included herein) by asking, basically, "What are you going to do about it?" May the same question penetrate your mind and heart as you read these pages. Speer had an answer, and it is the same answer we need today. "It is high time," he said, "to awake out of sleep and, banding ourselves with new and deeper devotion, to swing out on the currents of God's purpose, to accomplish our mission in the world." He goes on to ask, just as we need to ask today, "Are you ready then, fellow students, to throw your lives in with this watch-cry: 'Christ to the world before we die?' Can you endure the thought of anything else in the presence of the thorn-crowned One, who died not for our sins only but for the sins of the whole world?"

Facing the facts of the 2.5 billion "Hidden people" of the world, hidden in 16,750 peoples without a church, and looking at the next twenty years of forecasted population growth particularly in the areas where there are the most unreached, I am convinced that we must have a new Student Volunteer Movement, this time for *Frontier* Missions, to cross the cultural barriers into the areas where the "Hidden People" are to be found, cut off from a viable Christian witness even though they may in fact live within a country that has a Christian Church. I believe this new movement must co-operate with any and all who would wish to raise up an international force of career, cross-cultural missionaries prepared to give their lives if necessary to plant churches amidst the over 16,000 sub-cultures of the world still waiting for the chance to learn of God's plan of salvation in Christ Jesus, in a way they can understand.

If such a new student movement arises, complete with watchword and declaration, as I believe it will, may it be based as solidly on the word of God, the enabling of the Holy Spirit and the consuming passion for the lost as was the Student Volunteer Movement as represented here in the springtime of its vigor and Holy Spirit Power.

Dave Bliss
17 March, 1979

PREFATORY NOTE.

The first International Convention of the Student Volunteer Movement for Foreign Missions was held February 26 to March 1, 1891. Since the inception of the Movement, five years ago, at Mt. Hermon, there had never been held a student convention for volunteers,— there had never been even a rallying point for any considerable number of the 6,000 men and women enrolled upon our lists. The rapidly increasing membership and consequent establishment of mission bands in numerous educational institutions which are geographically too widely separated to be in touch with one another, or to receive help from the central organization, made it desirable that a large number of representative volunteers assemble in conference.

The key-note of the Convention was the key-note of the Movement: "The Evangelization of the World in this Generation." The object of the Convention was: 1. To afford an opportunity for the free discussion of many problems confronting the Movement. 2. To secure for the volunteers the advantages coming from intimate contact with Missionary Board secretaries and returned foreign missionaries. 3. To enlighten Board secretaries and others in regard to methods and aims of the Student Volunteer Movement for Foreign Missions. 4. By a closer union in prayer and purpose on the part of volunteers, secretaries, and missionaries, to give a new impetus to the great cause of world-wide evangelization in the present generation.

Cleveland, Ohio, was selected as the place of meeting, because geographically the center of the volunteer population of the United States and the Dominion of Canada. The new and commodious building of the Young Men's Christian Association was thrown open for this purpose from February 26 to March 1.

It was feared that the selection of time — in the midst of a college term's work — would prevent a good attendance. But, contrary to the most sanguine expectations, a larger student body assembled in Cleveland, Ohio, than ever assembled on a similar occasion in the world's history of foreign missionary effort. Every State east of the Missouri River and north of the Gulf line of States, save one, was represented. In all, 558 students, representing 151 educational institutions, were present, besides 32 Board representatives and 31 returned foreign missionaries. Fully 20 denominations were represented.

The results of the Cleveland Convention have been well marked, abundant, and blessed. A more intimate and intelligent relation has been established between volunteers and denominational Boards than ever before existed. Hundreds of students have gained enthusiasm and devotion in the purpose to evangelize the world in this generation; in many instances dispirited or half-hearted volunteers have been moved to resolve to go to their chosen fields as soon as the way opens; one secretary alone received 17 applications at Cleveland for appointment to the foreign work.

In order that the pamphlet be of proper length and not too bulky, the editors have been obliged to condense freely, and in some instances to omit entire addresses. This has been done with reluctance, since many topics treated in an able and helpful way have had to be spared.

God's presence was manifested in so real and extraordinary a manner at the sessions of the Convention that the hope is cherished that the record of the sessions of the Convention, may in some degree bring to others the abundant blessings enjoyed by the privileged ones who were in attendance.

OFFICERS

OF THE

STUDENT VOLUNTEER MOVEMENT FOR FOREIGN MISSIONS.

Executive Committee.

JOHN R. MOTT, College Young Men's Christian Association.
Miss NETTIE DUNN, College Young Women's Christian Association.
ROBERT P. WILDER, American Inter-Seminary Missionary Alliance
and the Canadian Intercollegiate Missionary Alliance.

Advisory Committee.

Rev. GEO. ALEXANDER, D.D.	Pres. MERRILL E. GATES.
Bishop M. S. BALDWIN, D.D.	Rev. A. J. GORDON, D.D.
Miss ABBIE B. CHILD.	Rev. A. T. PIERSON, D.D.

Secretaries.

WILLIAM H. COSSUM,　⎱
Miss LUCY E. GUINNESS, ⎰ Traveling.
MAX WOOD MOORHEAD, Editorial.
WALTER J. CLARK, Corresponding, and Treasurer, 97 Bible House, New York City.

Corresponding Members of the Executive Committee.

Illinois	ROBERT F. LENNINGTON,	Jacksonville.
	IRVING N. MERRIFIELD,	Morgan Park.
Michigan . . .	BERT L. LEE,	Olivet.
Missouri . . .	FRED J. TOWER,	Parkville.
New England .	ARCHIBALD C. HARTE,	Middletown, Conn.
New Jersey . .	ROBERT E. SPEER,	Princeton.
New York . .	WILLIAM L. BRAY,	Ithaca.
	FRED S. RETAN,	Hamilton.
North Carolina,	R. LEE McNAIR,	Davidson College.

Ohio . . . . . William Reed Newell, Wooster.
Tennessee . . . Fletcher S. Brockman, Nashville.
Virginia . . . Cameron Johnson,   Hampden-Sidney.
              John G. Scott,   University of Virginia.
Vermont . . . George F. Pitkin,   Burlington.
Wisconsin . . J. S. Hotten,   619 Francis St., Madison.

OFFICERS OF THE CONVENTION.

John R. Mott . . . . *Moderator.*
Walter J. Clark . . . . *Secretary.*

Assistant Secretaries.

Horace T. Pitkin, Yale.   Alfred L. Shapleigh, Harvard.

Musical Director.

Arthur J. Smith.

Chas. L. Potter . . . . Chairman Committee on Entertainment.
J. C. White . . . . . Chairman Business Committee.
W. W. Smith . . . . . . Chairman Committee on Book Exhibit.
R. J. Kellogg . . . . . Chairman Committee on Chart Exhibit.
Frank H. Wood . . . . Chairman Committee on Ushering.

FIRST DAY, THURSDAY, FEBRUARY 26.

Evening Session.

The Convention was called to order by Mr. John R. Mott, Chairman. Mr. Robert P. Wilder conducted a brief devotional exercise, speaking from Haggai ii. Mr. J. L. Taylor, President of the Young Men's Christian Association of Cleveland, welcomed the delegates as follows : —

"I am very glad to be able to be before you to-night, because I want to tell the delegates and volunteer missionaries, and other workers in the work of the Lord, if I can, how much I appreciate the honor conferred in having you with us. We are glad to welcome you in such a magnificent hall as this, for we feel justly proud of our new building. But we feel a pride far beyond that, in welcoming you in this our new hall,— you who are going forth to carry the Gospel as a witness unto all nations,— thus dedicating our hall to the work of the Lord. And we trust that we, the Christian people of the city of Cleveland, as many days as you are with us, can, by our prayers and by all that lies in our power, help you to glorify Him, in whose name we are gathered together to-night. And while many of us young men in this city may not see our way clear to go forth to the work in the regions beyond, we hope that the Lord will lay it upon our hearts to consecrate what He has given us to help send you to take the Gospel to foreign lands. And so I bid you a most hearty welcome, not only to our new building, but, as a citizen of Cleveland, I welcome you to our city. Again, I want to say that we deeply appreciate the honor of entertaining those of you who are intending to carry out the Master's last command by going to preach the Gospel to all nations."

An account of the extension of the movement and its present status was given by Mr. Mott. The facts stated will be found in the Report of the Executive Committee, which was presented the next morning.

THE HOLY SPIRIT IN MISSIONS.

The Rev. A. J. Gordon, D.D., of Boston, Mass., said : —

"It is one of the great principles of Christianity," says Pascal, "that whatever happened to Jesus Christ should come to pass in the soul and body of every believer." Jesus Christ was the first Great Foreign Missionary. But if He has called us by His Spirit to be missionaries, we are missionaries of the same school as Himself; for He said, "As the Father hath sent me into the world, so have I sent you into the world." And yet I desire to remind you that He did not enter upon His mission until He had Himself sought and obtained the special gracious anointing of the Holy Ghost for His work; and that all through His missions and His ministry He depended upon the Holy Spirit, just as He requires and commands that we should. If we were to ask Him how He cast out devils, we hear Him answer, "I by the Spirit of God do cast out devils." If we ask Him how it was possible that He had power to lay down His life and power to take it up again, that He could yield Himself up to God as a sacrifice for the sins of the world, we read the answer in the Epistle to the Hebrews, that He through the eternal Spirit offered Himself up without spot unto God. And after He rose from the dead, we read, in the opening verses of the Acts of the Apostles, that "He was taken up, after that He through the Holy Ghost had given commandment unto His apostles whom He had chosen." Thus, from the beginning to the very end of His ministry, from His baptism to His ascension, He wrote and spoke and acted under the power and inspiration of the Holy Ghost. I am sure, therefore, it will be very obvious that if He needed the Spirit much more do we need Him. And that is the subject about which I am to speak to-night.

Now, if the sentence I quoted in the beginning be true, that everything which happened to Him is to come to pass in His disciples, we can study this subject no more intelligently than by tracing Jesus Christ's relation to the Holy Spirit, and then see how the same things are predicted and said of us who are to be His missionary co-laborers. Let us begin with the wonderful scene recorded in Luke iii. 21. Jesus had come with the multitude to John the Baptist, to be baptized of him, and now we read that "when all the people were baptized, it came to pass, that Jesus also being baptized, and praying, the heaven was opened." I wonder how many of us ever noticed that word "praying." Though He were the Son of God, yet "He learned obedience by the things which He suffered;" and though He were the Son of God, He Himself prayed, presuming nothing in regard to His relation to the Father.

What is He praying about? Most clearly He is asking for the gift of the Holy Ghost. Is there any promise that He can plead? for the New Testament Scriptures had not yet been written. I think I may say almost without hesitation that I can put my finger upon the promise He would most naturally use; it is recorded in the eleventh chapter of Isaiah, the first verse: "And there shall come forth a rod out of the stem of Jesse, and a Branch shall grow out of his roots."

He has come, He is here. Now what is the promise? "And the Spirit of the Lord shall rest upon Him, the spirit of wisdom and understanding, the spirit of counsel and might, the spirit of knowledge and of the fear of the Lord."

Have you observed that this is a seven-fold Spirit. Turn to the book of Revelation: John says, he saw Him as a Lamb having seven horns and seven eyes, which are the seven Spirits of God; in other words, the complete and full manifestation of the Spirit in Jesus Christ, the fullness of the Holy Ghost. So He was praying for the Holy Ghost in His seven-fold power, because God giveth not His Spirit by measure unto His Son. And while He prays He is heard, and the heavens open, and the Spirit descends like a dove and rests upon Him.

You remember how Noah sent forth the dove out of the ark and it could find no resting place for the soles of its feet, and flew at last wearily back for shelter in the ark. And so I have often thought the dove of the Holy Spirit had gone forth from the ark in heaven and had hovered over many a head of our great human race, but never before had found a single spot where He could alight and rest the soles of His feet, until Jesus emerged from the Jordan, and the Spirit descended like a dove and rested upon Him, and the promise was literally fulfilled. "And I saw and bear record that this is the Son of God." Upon whom thou shalt see the Spirit descending and remaining on Him, the same is He which baptizeth with the Holy Ghost." He had the Holy Ghost in His fullness, coming no longer in casual contact, but to abide with Him; henceforth He is the one that baptizeth with the Holy Ghost.

Now observe that when the disciples on the day of Pentecost came together to pray, they had the definite promise also. They were told to "wait for the promise of the Father which, saith he, ye have heard of me. For John truly baptized with water, but ye shall be baptized with the Holy Ghost not many days hence." And they pleaded the promise, and the Holy Ghost came upon them, and they were all baptized with the Holy Ghost, and began to speak with other tongues as the Spirit gave them utterance. But somebody says : "That was the early church. Does Pentecost need to be repeated?" Certainly not. In one sense, just as at Jesus' birth the second person of the Trinity became incarnate in human flesh, so, on the day of Pentecost, the third person of the Trinity became incarnate in the body of the Church, which is the whole body of believers in all generations — in that sense Pentecost cannot be repeated, because the Holy Ghost had now come to be in office and abide forever. Nevertheless, we observe that when the Gentiles had heard the word the same thing was repeated in a certain sense, because the Holy Ghost descended upon them. And so we believe, down to the present time, if we are to go forth as missionaries of the cross, we need the same thing.

And what promise shall we plead in these days? I think here is one that we may take now and plead, just as Christ had a promise and the first disciples had a promise. This is ours: "If a son shall ask bread of any of you that is a father, will he give him a stone? or if he ask a fish, will he for a fish give him a serpent? or if he shall ask an egg, will he offer him a scorpion? If ye then, being evil know how to give good gifts unto your children, how much more shall your heavenly Father give the Holy Spirit to them that ask him?" That is our promise. Has it not been fulfilled again and again in our day?

When I take up a book on the Holy Spirit, my first question is, does the writer of this book speak of any personal experience? On the cars coming to Cleveland I read an admirable little book by Pastor Topfel, of Geneva, on "The Holy Spirit in Missions." On the 52d page I read this passage, which I repeat from memory: "Not far from the place where I am now writing, many years ago, a teacher had a class gathered about him and was discoursing upon the Holy Spirit, when he came to that memorable promise: 'If ye then, being evil, know how to give good gifts unto your children, how much more shall your heavenly Father give the Holy Spirit to them that ask him?' he paused and said, 'Young gentlemen, it is right that you should take this promise to yourselves, that you should believe it, that you should look to the instant fulfillment of that promise.' One at least that heard that exhortation went away and sought with all diligence the anointing of the Holy Ghost, and very soon the Spirit of God came into him. That young man has now become the teacher and a pastor, but he never reads *one* passage in the Scripture without the deepest emotion, because that passage records what is the most vital experience of his life. 'How much more shall your heavenly Father give the Holy Spirit to them that ask Him.'"

Three weeks ago I read a little book on "The Holy Spirit," by Professor Moule, of Cambridge, a man wonderfully endeared to the students and to the Christian public generally in England for his remarkable spirituality and great tenderness and beauty and simplicity of Christian life. He is now the principal trainer of young men for the ministry in the Established Church of England at Cambridge, England. He writes: "There was a time subsequent to my conversion when I was brought into such relation with the Holy Spirit that for the first time I knew Him as a personal friend and intimate helper. And from that day He has been so wonderfully with me that I cannot describe the constant joy and untroubled peace which I have enjoyed since that day when I was brought into intimate fellowship with the Holy Spirit."

Many years since I met George Mueller, of Bristol, for the first time, having read with great interest the story of his life, and I greatly desired to have a few moments' conversation with him, which was granted. My first question was, " Mr. Mueller, will you kindly tell me when you were converted?" "If you ask when I was born again, it was in such a year, while I was a student in the University of Halle; but if you want to know when I became out and out for God, it was such a year," mentioning a later day. And he went on to tell me how, having lived a barren and fruitless Christian life for many years, he, with a few intimate friends, met together in a room and began to pray that they might receive the gift of the Spirit. " He came to us with such power that at some times it was almost impossible for me to leave Him, His power was so sweet and so entrancing; and I knew what it meant to be baptized with the Holy Ghost."

I have given you these three illustrations from eminent lives to show that we are talking not about something far away and theoretical, but something near at hand and practical. As Jesus Christ prayed that the Holy Ghost might come and He came, so it is our privilege here to-night, in the same way, to ask and to believe, that we may be anointed for the great service of preaching the Gospel to the ends of the earth, to which God has called us.

I read in the fourth chapter of Luke, the first verse: " And Jesus, being full of the Holy Ghost, returned from Jordan." Mark the expression, " being full of the Holy Ghost." Then I turned to the story of the Day of Pentecost and I read: " And they were all filled with the Holy Ghost," — exactly the same statement. And then I turned to Ephesians and I read: " Be not drunk with wine, wherein is excess; but be filled with the Spirit; speaking to yourselves in psalms and hymns and spiritual songs." That is a wonderful metaphor — " Be not drunk with wine." You have seen how an intoxicated man, when he is filled with strong drink, speaks out that which the spirit within him inspires. Well, says the apostle, be like that man; only, instead of the spirit of wine, let it be the Spirit of One that shall control you to speak out what He inspires.

Here is something that is given as a direct duty — " Be ye filled with the Spirit." How can I? some one asks. The answer is often made, You must empty yourself before you can be filled with the Holy Ghost. But who is sufficient to empty himself? I believe God's way is rather the expulsive power of a new affection, throwing off and casting away the old, of which we cannot rid ourselves. There are two ways of emptying a tumbler of water: you can turn it up-side down, or you may drop quicksilver into it drop by drop until all the water will have gone out. Suppose you begin in the same way to seek the Holy Spirit, and see if, in that way, — getting filled with the Holy Ghost, — that which you desire to have cast out is not cast out! The

Spirit of the Lord within us is adequate to cast out the evil spirit that still desires to hold sway.

How was it with the great Apostle? He was told that he was a chosen vessel to bear Christ's name far hence among the Gentiles. How was that vessel prepared? God suddenly, after he had been converted, poured the Holy Spirit into him. Ananias was sent to pray for him and lay his hands upon him, that he might receive the Holy Ghost; and immediately, we have it stated, that being full of the Holy Ghost he said thus and did thus.

Now what do we want, according to that Scripture? You know that memorable phrase used by Novalis about Spinoza, "He is a God-intoxicated man." God wants that kind of men to-day, — men inebriated with the Holy Ghost; men that may be counted insane sometimes because of the tremendous earnestness of their fire and zeal.

You remember that Zinzendorf started one of the most remarkable movements of the Christian era, — that movement which has its center at Herrnhut. There was a time when he came and laid his fortune, his honors, his titles, his property, himself, upon the altar, and said, "Lord I surrender it all up." Immediately after, he said, "I have but one passion — it is He, it is He alone. The world is the field, and the field is the world; and henceforth that country shall be my home where I can be most used in winning souls for Christ." Then came temptation and obloquy, and scorn and hatred from those who said, "He is beside himself." And he said, "The Spirit of God so came upon me after that consecration that it seemed to me, as I went about my missionary service, that rather than walking on earth I was simply swimming in an atmosphere of love and joy."

I think the most sacred spot my feet have ever stood upon was in that little island of Iona on the coast of Scotland. There, one afternoon, with my friend, Dr. Pierson, I looked across to the green banks and fields of Scotland that were visible to the eye, and I was filled with wonder and astonishment that one man in the sixth century, known in history as St. Columba, stormed the whole of Scotland from this little island and won it for Christ,—he had two or three associates, but practically did it alone,—from Inverness on the north to Edinburgh on the south. And if to-day the question were asked who was the greatest of the benefactors of Scotland, it would be answered, St. Columba, who planted the Gospel, and John Knox, who reformed the Church. And as I stood on that spot and thought of what that one man wrought, I wondered if there was any secret that would show where his power lay. I picked up later a history of this man, and found it stated there: "He never spent one hour without study, or writing, or some other holy occupation, so incessantly was he engaged in devotions. Not a day but the burden of his communion seemed almost beyond the endurance of the human soul. But how he was loved by all! For a holy joy ever was beaming from his face, revealing the joy and gladness with which the Holy Ghost filled his inmost soul." So one wrote who associated with him, and who often looked into his face. Is there any wonder that St. Columba alone, single-handed, conquered Scotland for Christ?

There is a missionary whom Dr. Smith, a famous writer on missions, declares in his belief to have been a greater missionary than St. Francis Xavier. I do not speak of Xavier for the results of his work, but for the zeal which he manifested, which was beyond all degree greater than that evinced by any other man. I speak of Raymund Lull. Two hundred years before Columbus discovered America, in 1292, he started to plant the Gospel among the Mohametans of North Africa. What was the certain fate he was to meet? Death was the penalty of making a single convert. But he would go, and when friends pleaded with him he said this : " He who loves not, lives not ; he who lives by the Life cannot die. Let me go." And he went, and when he had won his first convert, was stoned to death, counting it all joy that he was permitted to suffer martyrdom for Christ. These are men who, like their Master, knew what it was to be filled with the Holy Ghost.

Now let us go on just a step farther. In the passage which we have just been reading, we have this phrase : " And he was led by the Spirit into the wilderness." I turn to the Epistles and find : " If ye be led of the Spirit, ye are not under the law ; " and, " as many as are led by the Spirit of God, they are the sons of God." In other words, that is the Christian's prerogative, to be led by the Spirit. To me it is one of the most charming and deeply interesting studies to observe in the Acts of the Apostles the familiarity with which the early disciples speak of the Holy Ghost as an actual, present friend. In that council at Jerusalem, when the question of the new converts is brought in, we hear Peter say : " It seemed good to the Holy Ghost and to us," as though he had said, " James and Peter and John and Paul were there, but there was another person there, and it seemed good to us and to Him." When Ananias and Sapphira committed the sin for which they were struck dead, see how he spoke : " Why hath Satan filled thine heart to lie to the Holy Ghost?" And then we go on and read how, when he hears an inquirer in a chariot, the Spirit said to Philip, " Go near, and join thyself to this chariot." See how perfectly they were under the guidance of the Spirit! And again, " The Holy Ghost said, Separate me Barnabas and Saul for the work whereunto I have called them." " So they being sent forth by the Holy Ghost, departed unto Seleucia." And in the sixteenth chapter of Acts they were forbidden by the Holy Ghost to preach the word in Asia,— now sent and now held back, now told to go and now that they must not go. " They assayed to go into Bithynia; but the Spirit suffered them not." All through the Acts of the Apostles we see this.

Has there been anything like it to-day, you say? If we had an inspired account of the modern missions as of the early missions of the Church, we should find that the Spirit of God is acting in the same way, constantly sending and constantly restraining. Where did William Carey first propose to go, when he marked out that map in his shop on sole leather, studying the geography of the world? To a very insignificant point, and yet his heart was set on it,— Otaheite. But the Spirit said to William Carey that he must not go there. He was wanted in India, with his wonderful linguistic powers; and he, India's first and greatest missionary, went to the home of ancient language and to the very center of that home. The Spirit would not let him go where he proposed to go. Where did Livingstone propose to go when he was studying divinity and medicine in Edinburgh? His ambition was to be a medical missionary to China. But God said no: the Holy Spirit permitted him not to go to China, because He wanted him to go to Africa, that there he might undertake the work of healing the open sore of the world. Where did Adoniram Judson propose to go? His heart was set on India. He landed at Calcutta, but by the jealousy of the East India Company was not permitted to preach the Gospel there, and went to the Isle of France. But he went back, and once more attempted in India to preach the Gospel, and was again driven out to Rangoon. Why did the Holy Ghost send him to Rangoon? Because there was one tribe of the Karens who had a tradition that a white man should come and bring them back to God, and God wanted him among the Karens; and he began his work, and now one-third of the Karens are nominal Christians. And not only are there Christians there of the most consecrated type, but two or three years ago we found that Massachusetts stood first in our contributions for missions, New York second, the Karen Christians third.

And only two years after this — this was in 1813, if I remember rightly — there was a man by the name of Shaw who went to South Africa that he might preach the Gospel in a chosen spot. Through the jealousy of the Dutch settlers he was not allowed to preach the Gospel. With an almost broken heart he took what money he had and bought a yoke of oxen and a new cart, and put his wife and his goods into the cart, and headed the cattle who drew it for the heart of Africa, not knowing whither they should go. You remember once the ark of God was put on a cart. He and his wife started for the interior, and journeyed 300 miles, a journey of 37 days, straight on. At the end of that time they camped near a company of Hottentots, who sent over to inquire who they were. They made inquiry also as to who the Hottentots were, and found that they were a delegation sent by their people down to the coast to get a missionary, and they had found just the missionary they wanted. "If I had been half an hour earlier," he said, "or they half an hour later, we should not have met." And that after a journey of 300 miles into the heart of Africa! Are not these illustrations of the Spirit of God saying go and go not.

Then I take up that instance about which we speak with such gratitude and astonishment. I take you to a little hill overlooking a vast country, yet sunken in ignorance and spiritual death. It had been proposed to give up that mission because of its unproductiveness. But an old man went upon the hilltop where he could look down, and spent the day in prayer that the Lord would not allow the mission to be given up. That is one side of the story. Then a young man comes and asks to be sent to that field. He has not a theological education, and the committee hesitated about sending him. He had not the qualifications, it would seem, that would fit him for that special work. He said: "God's Spirit has called me to that particular field." He had been a civil engineer on the western prairies. After considerable deliberation they sent this young man to the field. Now how remarkable it is that the whole success of that young man turned upon the fact that he was a civil engineer! There came on a great famine. Thousands were dying. He went to the government and said, "I am a civil engineer. I want the contract to construct a canal." It was given him. He sent out invitations: five thousand men came to work on this canal. Night after night he preached the Gospel to them, and to the relays of men who took their places at the work. And when the famine was ended they began to come from all directions, seeking baptism. You, who are familiar with that wonderful work among the Telugus, know the story, — how the first day they baptized they had two thousand converts, and before the year was out, ten thousand professing faith in Jesus Christ in that field that a little while before was about to be given up.

O brethren, if we are under the sway of God's Spirit, how He places His workers, — puts one here, restrains one from going there! It is His prerogative not only to send whom He will but to send them where He will. And if there is anything wanted in the Church of Christ to-day, in its great missionary affairs, it is a realization of the personal divine guidance of the Holy Ghost into the fields which God sees with His all-embracing and all-surveying eye. Jesus Christ was led of the Spirit.

Then we come to this statement in this same chapter: "And Jesus returned in the power of the Spirit." I pause upon this; I bid you remember that this is the word which our Lord used: "Ye shall receive power after that the Holy Ghost is come upon you." And I go back into Luke's Gospel and read: "Tarry ye in the city of Jerusalem until ye be endued with power from on high." It is the source from which it springs that gives such mighty momentum to this power. The higher the head, the mightier the impetus-power from on high. I believe that, just as certain as wind is the power that drives ships, just as certain as water is the power that moves the ponderous wheels of the great manufactories on the Merrimac and Connecticut Rivers, just as surely as steam is the power that makes the mighty steamship plow the great deep, so explicitly, by divine appointment, the Holy Ghost is the power that moves the Church. But if there is anything that needs to be dwelt upon at this present time, and emphasized, it is this fact; because the Church of Jesus Christ is turning away from its true power, to rest upon paltry expedients to make the Gospel succeed, when God has put the power in the Church itself — power from on high.

What was the one phrase with which Peter described the preaching of the Gospel? "We have preached the Gospel with the Holy Ghost sent down from heaven." He does not mention a single other fact about his preaching than that. And when I say "sent down from heaven" what do I mean? Just as in your city here I see it to-night. I see cars without any apparent motor. But I have only to look under the foundations of the street to see that beneath the street there is an endless chain moving back and forward all day long; and what these cars have to do is simply to grip on to that power and be swept on. I believe it is exactly so with the Holy Ghost. It is an endless wire between heaven and earth, bringing down blessing, carrying up prayer; bringing down the might of God, carrying up our confessions of weakness and inability; bearing down the strength of God, moving evermore. And what we, as believers and workers for Jesus Christ, need to do is to grip on to that power. We have not to beseech the Holy Ghost to do anything, but what is wanted is simply that we should grip to Him by faith. Now, Jesus Christ returned in the power of the Holy Ghost.

Then, the last thing, we find Him going into the synagogue, taking down the prophecy of Isaiah and reading: "The Spirit of the Lord is upon me, because he hath anointed me to preach the Gospel to the poor; he hath sent me to heal the brokenhearted, to preach deliverance to the captives and recovering of sight to the blind, to set at liberty them that are bruised, to preach the acceptable year of the

Lord." "The Spirit of the Lord is upon me, because he hath anointed me," — in other words, He claims the fulfillment of this wonderful prophecy. He was anointed with the Holy Ghost, not for Himself alone, but for us.

Now, if you turn to the one hundred and thirty-third Psalm, you will read these familiar words: "Behold how good and how pleasant it is for brethren to dwell together in unity. It is like the precious ointment upon the head that ran down upon the beard, even Aaron's beard; that went down to the skirts of his garments." And what does the psalmist refer to? You read in Exodus of that wonderfully compounded oil which men were forbidden to make, so sacred it was, and which was forbidden to be applied to any but Aaron and his sons, a symbol of the Holy Ghost, which is not to be bought with money, applied only to those whom God ordains for His work. And we are told how this was applied. When the leper was to be cleansed the oil was put on his right ear, his right thumb, and his right foot. But when Aaron was consecrated this oil was poured upon his head, and ran down upon his beard and his garments and his feet. Herein was a type of Christ. He was anointed not for Himself, but for others; our true Aaron is up there. He is the one that is anointed not for Himself, but for His whole Church; and the Spirit poured upon His head runs down upon the whole body down to the latest generation, down to the last man that needs the gracious influence of the Spirit.

Now, dear friends, this brings me to this practical thought, that all missionary success, at home or abroad, depends upon the Holy Ghost. I say it deliberately: the personal preparation of the Holy Spirit is the greatest need in our ministry in this country and in foreign fields. Here is a book that I think you will say when you glance at it that it looks as though it had been handled. I want to say that I have read that book more than any other book in all my library. If I have read it once I have read it twenty times. If ever I want spiritual quickening I take down that book and read it. What is the history of that book? It is a journal of an early missionary, David Brainerd. He kept it only for his own comfort or remembrance, as we would keep a daily journal. When he died, at thirty years of age, he asked Jonathan Edwards to destroy this journal, because he said it was sacred, and not to be seen by any other eyes but his. Edwards turned over the leaves and said: "The Church cannot spare that. In spite of my half uttered pledge to him, I will take the responsibility to publish it."

It was that book that made Carey a missionary, that sent Henry Martyn to Persia, and that led Murray McCheyne to consecrate himself to the work of foreign missions; that led Dr. Payson to cry out,

' Since I read that book, I have been a new man." Why is it a wonderful book? It is the only book that I know of where you see the two things side by side, the closet and the field. There are the records of how the days were spent in prayer for the power of the Holy Ghost; then the story of what was accomplished as he went out and preached to those barbarous Indians. I know nothing like it since the day of Pentecost. He preaches the Gospel to them, after these days spent with God, and these men literally fall like grass by the mower's scythe. Among all the many days he spent alone in the woods in prayer, of which he gives an account in his diary, there is scarcely an instance of one which was not either attended or soon followed with manifest blessings and outpouring of the Holy Spirit.

Shortly before his death, he said to his brother: " We ministers feel these special gracious influences of the Spirit in our hearts; and it wonderfully assists us to come at the consciences of men, and, as it were, to handle those consciences with hands; whereas, without the influences of the Spirit, whatever reason and oratory we make use of, we do but make use of stumps instead of hands." These were the dying words of Brainerd: " Whatever else you fail of, do not fail of the influences of the Holy Spirit; that is the only way you can handle the consciences of men." Oh, how precious is such an experience as that! How much the Church owes to it! I am sorry the American Tract Society has allowed that book to go out of print; but it has been re-edited and published by Funk & Wagnalls*; and if you want one book worth keeping by a missionary as long as he lives, don't fail to get this Life of David Brainerd.

And so I might go on giving illustrations. I take this, which I read with great interest, from the journal of another eminent missionary of our own time, Rev. Griffith John, of Hangkow, China. In a report of the recent Shanghai Conference he writes, speaking of a certain date of his ministry in a native church: " Feeling my lack of spiritual power, I spent the whole of a Saturday in earnest prayer for a baptism of the Holy Ghost. On the following morning I preached on this subject. At the close of the service I proposed that we should meet for an hour on every day of the ensuing week to pray for the baptism of the Holy Ghost. From fifty to seventy native converts met day by day, confessing their sins, and pleading with tears for the outpouring of the Spirit upon their hearts. And the native church at Hangkow received an impulse from this week, the force of which continues to this day. From that week the Holy Ghost became a living reality in that church. The whole tone and character of the church

---

* See " List of Missionary Books," at end of this Report.

was changed from that week on." Now, why should I dwell longer upon these experiences, that confirm and illustrate the word of God?

But, my friends, let me now bring this matter to a serious close. Professor Beck, of Tübingen, says, to a class of students: "Young men, listen to this word. Theology! Theology! Let me remind you that theology without the Holy Spirit is not only a cold stone, but absolute poison." Why is it that from many very exalted professorial chairs such poison is exhaling to-day, so that many minds are feeling it all over this country? Why is it that this poison is emanating from the most learned theology of our times? Before I answer that question I will ask and answer another: Why is it that in the last decade of this nineteenth century the Church of Jesus Christ exhibits such deplorable weakness,— that our daily papers are crowded with advertisements of what is to be done and carried on in our churches week after week to draw the people in? Have we forgotten that there is a Holy Ghost, that we must insist upon walking upon crutches when we might fly? What is our power in the Church? Let us re-assert it; we know what it is. As to theology, what does the word of God say? "For what man knoweth the things of a man save the spirit of man which is in him? even so the things of God knoweth no man, but the Spirit of God." All the learning of the world will turn theology into poison if theology is not sanctified in its teaching by the Holy Ghost.

When the great Methodist movement had taken place, Lady Huntingdon proposed to endow a training school for ministers. Fletcher, of Madeley, was selected to preside over that school. One who studied under him says: "Fletcher was an admirable teacher. We had our Hebrew and our Greek and our theology. Then he would close the book and say: 'Young men, Hebrew, Greek, theology are very important. We have attended fully to these things for two hours. Now, those of you who want to seek the power of the Holy Ghost, follow me.'" And he would lead out that whole class into another room, where, says this pupil, "We would often stay for three hours wrestling in prayer for the Holy Ghost, after being told that all other learning was powerless without this." That is the secret of that movement. Most of the educated leaders in that movement had been preachers of the Gospel, some of them ten or fifteen years, utterly without power, until, under this great movement, the Spirit of God seized them and they became burning and shining lights. One of them said: "Ten years I had been preaching. I had spent vast time on my sermons, and yet they were powerless as stones thrown among the people. But when by contact with these brethren I learned the secret of the Holy Ghost, such a change came over me that I can only describe the difference between these two periods as the difference between shooting with a bow and shooting with a rifle. In the one case all the force of the arrow depends on the strength of the muscle; but in the other case the power is in the force of the powder that is behind the ball, and it only requires the touch of the finger to liberate it. That is the difference between preaching with the Holy Ghost and without it."

May God give us that which our hearts are moved to ask even now! Let us go back to the experience of that admirable writer whom I quoted in the beginning. He says: "This promise is for us. It is right that we should claim it. It is proper that we should plead it now. It is right that we should look for the fulfillment of it immediately." How difficult to present such a theme! God knows the very great difficulty I have in undertaking it. The Holy Spirit Himself must speak. But if after all that I have said the impression is left in your minds that you desire above all things else to have the power of the Holy Spirit resting upon you, may God lead you to seek that power to-night.

SECOND DAY, FRIDAY, FEBRUARY 27.

Morning Session.

The devotional exercises were led by Miss Nettie Dunn, International Secretary of the Young Women's Christian Association. The Report of the Executive Committee was then presented by Mr. John R. Mott.

REPORT OF THE EXECUTIVE COMMITTEE.

As this is the first Convention of the Student Volunteer Movement for Foreign Missions, it seems best to review its history, and to set forth its present condition.

I. ORIGIN OF THE MOVEMENT.

In July, 1886, a memorable conference of college students was held at Mt. Hermon, Massachusetts. 251 young men from 89 colleges of the United States and Canada had come together, at the invitation of Mr. D. L. Moody, to spend four weeks in Bible study. Nearly two weeks passed before the subject of missions was even mentioned in the sessions of the Conference. But one of the young men from Princeton College had come, after weeks of prayer, with the deep conviction that God would call from that large gathering of college men, a few, at least, who would consecrate themselves to the foreign mission service. At an early day he called together all the young men who were thinking seriously of spending their lives in the foreign field. 21 students answered to this call, although several of them had not definitely decided the question. This little group of consecrated men began to pray that the spirit of missions might pervade the Conference, and that the Lord would separate many men unto this great work. In a few days they were to see their faith rewarded far more than they had dared to claim. On the evening of July 16 a special mass meeting was held, at which Dr. Arthur T. Pierson gave a thrilling address on missions. He supported, by most convincing argument, the proposition that " all should go, and go to all." This was the key-note which set many men to thinking and praying.

A week passed. On Saturday night, July 24, another meeting was held, which may occupy as significant a place in the history of the Christian Church as the Williams Hay Stack Meeting. It is known as the " meeting of the ten nations." It was addressed by sons of missionaries in China, India, Persia, and by seven young men of different nationalities — an Armenian, a Japanese, a Siamese, a German, a Dane, a Norwegian, and an American Indian. The addresses were not more than three minutes in length, and consisted of appeals for more workers. Near the close, each speaker repeated in the language of his country the words, "God is Love." Then came a season of silent and audible prayer, which will never be forgotten by those present. The burning appeals of this meeting came with peculiar force to all.

From this night on to the close of the Conference the missionary interest became more and more intense. One by one the men, alone in the woods and rooms with their Bibles and God, fought out the battle with self, and were led by the Spirit to decide to forsake all, and carry the Gospel "unto the uttermost part of the earth." Dr. Ashmore, who had just returned from China, added fuel to the flame by his ringing appeal to Christians to look upon "missions as a war of conquest, and not as a mere wrecking expedition."

Only eight days elapsed between the "meeting of the ten nations" and the closing session of the Conference. During that time the number of volunteers increased from 21 to exactly 100 who signified that they were "willing and desirous, God permitting, to become foreign missionaries." Several of the remaining 151 delegates became volunteers later, after months of study and prayer.

II. EXTENSION.

On the last day of the Conference the volunteers held a meeting, in which there was a unanimous expression that the missionary spirit, which had manifested itself with such power at Mt. Hermon, should be communicated in some way to thousands of students throughout the country who had not been privileged to come in contact with it at its source. It was their conviction that the reasons which had led the Mt. Hermon hundred to decide would influence hundreds of other college men, if those reasons were once presented to them in a faithful, intelligent, and prayerful manner. Naturally, they thought of the "Cambridge Band" and its wonderful influence among the universities of Great Britain, and decided to adopt a similar plan. Accordingly, a deputation of four students were selected to represent the Mt. Hermon Conference, and to visit during the year as many institutions as possible. Of the four selected, only one was able to undertake the mission, Mr. Robert P. Wilder, of Princeton College. Mr. John N. Forman, a graduate of the same institution, was induced to join Mr. Wilder in his tour.

During the year 167 institutions were visited. They touched many of the leading colleges and seminaries in the United States and

Canada. Sometimes they would visit a college together; again, in order to reach more institutions, they would separate. Wherever they went their straightforward, forcible, scriptural presentation came with convincing power to the minds and hearts of the students. In some colleges as many as sixty volunteers were secured. Not an institution was visited in which they did not quicken the missionary interest. By the close of the year 2,200 young men and women had taken the volunteer pledge.

During the college year 1887–88 the Movement was left without any particular leadership and oversight. Notwithstanding this fact, over 600 new volunteers were added during the year, very largely the result of the personal work of the old volunteers.

In the following year, 1888–89, Mr. Wilder, on his second tour, enrolled 600 volunteers in 93 institutions. At least 25 of these institutions had not been touched previously by the Movement.

Mr. R. E. Speer, also a graduate of Princeton, during the year 1889–90 visited 110 institution, adding 1,100 volunteers to the Movement. He reached many new institutions, especially in the South and Southeast.

Thus far in the year 1890–91 Mr. W. H. Cossum, of Colgate University, has added nearly 300 to the roll of volunteers, and has extended the movement to the Maritime Provinces. Miss Lucy E. Guinness, of London, Eng., has spent nearly three months among the women of our colleges. The outcome of her work was at least 285 volunteers. Other volunteers have added several hundreds to those secured by regular workers. The number of names on the volunteer roll now stands at 6,200, scattered throughout the United States and Canada in 350 institutions.

III.   ORGANIZATION.

About 50 volunteers came together at the Northfield Conference in July, 1888, to pray and plan for the Movement. When the reports were presented, showing the condition of the Movement in all parts of the country, it was found that three dangerous tendencies were beginning to manifest themselves: (1) A tendency in the Movement at some points to lose its unity. All sorts of missionary societies and bands — with different purposes, methods of work, and forms of pledge and constitution — were springing up. It was plain that it would lose much of its power should its unity be destroyed. (2) A tendency to a decline in some colleges. Because not properly guarded and developed, some bands of volunteeers had grown cold. (3) A tendency to conflict with existing agencies appeared in a very few places. All of these tendencies were decidedly out of harmony with the original spirit and purpose of the Volunteer Movement; accordingly, the volunteers at Northfield decided that immediate steps should be taken toward a wise organization.

Another consideration helped to influence them in this decision, and that was a desire to extend the Movement. Not more than one-fifth of the higher educational institutions of America had been touched thus far.

A committee was appointed to organize the Volunteer Movement. That committee, after long and prayerful consideration, decided that the Movement should be confined to students. It was therefore named the Student Volunteer Movement for Foreign Missions. It was also noted that practically all of the volunteers were members of some one of the three great inter-denominational student organizations; namely, the College Young Men's Christian Association, the College Young Women's Christian Association, and the Inter-Seminary Missionary Alliance. This suggested the plan of placing at the head of the Movement a permanent Executive Committee of three, one to be appointed by each of the three organizations, which should have power to develop and facilitate the Movement in harmony with the spirit and constitutions of these three organizations. The plan was first submitted to the College Committee of the International Committee of the Young Men's Christian Association, and was heartily approved. They appointed as their representative Mr. J. R. Mott. The plan was also fully approved by the International Committee of the Young Women's Christian Association, and Miss Nettie Dunn was chosen to represent them. The Executive Committee of the Inter-Seminary Missionary Alliance endorsed the plan, and named Mr. Wilder as their representative. The Canadian Intercollegiate Missionary Alliance, which includes some institutions not connected with the above three student organizations, has also authorized Mr. Wilder to represent them.

The new Executive Committee began its work in January, 1889. They soon perfected a plan of organization which has commended itself to leading men of the different denominations to whom it has been submitted. The plan of organization may be briefly outlined, as follows: —

1. The Executive Committee (described above) has general supervision and direction of the Movement. It has met on an average of once each month.

2. The Committee has three regular secretaries: Traveling, Corresponding, and Editorial.

(a) The work of the Traveling Secretary consists in organizing, educating, developing, quickening, and setting at work the volunteers in the different institutions; and in extending the Movement not only among previously visited institutions, but also among those as yet untouched. The first Traveling Secretary appointed by the Committee was Mr. R. E. Speer, who held the position for one year. Mr. W. H. Cossum holds this office at present. During a part of this year Miss Lucy E. Guinness traveled in the interest of the Movement.

(b) The Corresponding Secretary has charge of all the office work of the Movement. He also acts as Treasurer. The work of the office embraces the enrollment and classification of volunteers, the tabulation of statistics, the distribution of printed matter, and an extensive correspondence with several hundred institutions. Mr. William H. Hannum held this position until shortly before he sailed for India in 1890. Since then Mr. Walter J. Clark has filled this office.

(c) The Editorial Secretary aims to keep the Movement before the churches and the volunteers. He corresponds regularly with the *Missionary Review of the World*, *The Intercollegian*, *The Evangel*, and *The Missionary Echo*. Occasional articles are sent to the denominational papers. Messrs. R. S. Miller, Jr., and E. W. Rand have each held the position. Mr. Max Wood Moorhead now occupies it.

3. There is an Advisory Committee, composed at present of the following : Rev. Geo. Alexander, D.D., Bishop M. S. Baldwin, D.D., Miss Abbie B. Child, Pres. Merrill E. Gates, Rev. A. J. Gordon, D.D., Rev. A. T. Pierson, D.D. The Executive Committee is to confer with them about every important step in the development of the Movement, in order that nothing may be done which shall justify unfavorable criticism.

4. The Executive Committee, through their Traveling Secretary, are unable to touch more than one-fifth of the colleges and theological seminaries during the year. They therefore aim to have a Corresponding Member in every State and Province in which the extent and condition of the Movement demand it. This Corresponding Member carries out their policy ; namely, to conserve and extend the Movement in that State or Province. In States where it is thought to be advisable there is a Corresponding Committee instead of a Corresponding Member. The following States have Corresponding Members : Maine, Southern New England, New Jersey, Virginia, North Carolina, Ohio, Michigan, Wisconsin, and Missouri. In New York and Illinois there is a Corresponding Committee.

5. In each institution the volunteers are united in what is known as the Volunteer Band. In the colleges this is organized as the Missionary Department of the College Association. In theological seminaries the Band is made a part of the regular missionary society. These Bands hold regular meetings for prayer and for systematic study of missions. Moreover, they seek to spread missionary intelligence, to secure new volunteers, to kindle missionary spirit in churches and

young people's societies, and to stimulate intelligent and systematic giving to the cause of missions.

IV. ACHIEVEMENTS.

The Holy Spirit has worked mightily both in and through this Movement during its short history of less than five years. Among the many things which have been accomplished under His guidance and in His strength, we gratefully record the following : —

1. Fully 6,000 young men and women have been led to take the advanced step of consecration expressed in these words: "We are willing and desirous, God permitting, to become foreign missionaries." It is firmly believed that this step has been taken conscientiously and intelligently in the vast majority of cases. Well may Dr. McCosh ask : "Has any such offering of living young men and women been presented in our age, in our country, in any age, or in any country, since the day of Pentecost?"

2. At least 320 of these volunteers have already gone to the foreign field under the various missionary agencies. A noted foreign missionary recently said that not more than two per cent. of those who volunteered in a missionary revival ever sailed. But already over five per cent. of the members of this Movement have sailed ; and fully ten per cent. of the Canadian contingent. A very large majority of the volunteers are still in the various stages of preparation.

3. This Movement has promoted the plan for colleges and theological seminaries to support their own missionaries under their respective Boards. At least 40 colleges and 32 seminaries have adopted the plan either wholly or in part, and in a majority of cases are pushing it with a high degree of success. It is estimated that at least $30,000 have been contributed within the last two years by institutions over and above what they were previously giving.

4. It may be truthfully said that the Volunteer Movement has done more than all other agencies combined to emphasize the idea that each church should support its own missionary. Volunteers have elaborated the plan, and have also printed and circulated a pamphlet clearly setting it forth. Moreover, they have actually introduced it in many churches of different denominations with the most gratifying results. A large number of strong testimonials have been collected. The following, given by the secretaries of the Foreign Mission Board of the Presbyterian Church, U. S. A., is a striking recognition of the importance of this work : —

We have before us a long list of testimonials from pastors who have tried the experiment with most gratifying results ; and we are assured that if this method should become general throughout the churches, it would mark a new era of progress in foreign missions, while, by its reflex influence at home, it would bring one of the greatest blessings that the Church has experienced in a generation. * * * We gladly recognize the influence which has been exerted along these lines by the Student Volunteer Movement in our colleges and theological seminaries. * * * And we recognize, with equal clearness and satisfaction, the large part which this Movement has had in arousing Churches, Young Men's Christian Associations, Christian Endeavor Societies, etc., to a new interest and to a more adequate contribution of means. * * * The interest which they (the volunteers) create and the funds which they raise are a clear gain. * * *

So far as Presbyterian churches are concerned, we most heartily commend the work.

F. F. ELLINWOOD,
ARTHUR MITCHELL,
JNO. GILLESPIE,
Secretaries.

WILLIAM DULLES, Jr., *Treasurer.*

NEW YORK, Nov. 6, 1890.

5. By means of this Movement, missionary intelligence, enthusiasm, and consecration, have been carried into over 200 colleges on this continent in which there was comparatively no interest in missions five years ago. It has made the missionary department of the College Young Men's and Young Women's Christian Associations one of the most advanced and influential departments in their entire scheme of work. At least one-fifth of the officers of these associations are volunteers. Moreover, it should not be forgotten that every volunteer won means more than simply one missionary. He stands for a large constituency who are interested in the work because he goes. Who can measure the importance of thus enlisting the intelligent sympathy and co-operation of thousands who are to remain at home in the great missionary operations of the Church?

6. The missionary interest has been intensified in the theological seminaries. Exhaustive study of the seminary problem has been made, and invaluable statistics have been compiled. These show that the number of prospective missionaries has been greatly increased during the past few years over any previous period. Over eleven per cent. of the under-graduates have volunteered for foreign service. The amount of money contributed has been more than trebled; and a more comprehensive study of missions is being undertaken by seminary men. During the past year, especially, the Movement has endeavored to strengthen the missionary spirit in divinity schools by recommending the formation of five District Alliances, and the inauguration of deputation work. The American Inter-Seminary Missionary Alliance, at its last convention (October, 1890), passed resolutions favoring our recommendations. Many seminary volunteers have been led to urge systematically upon home churches a more intelligent interest in mis-

sions, and far more generous contributions. It is also a striking fact that the men in these seminaries who are to enter the home pastorate are realizing, as never before, their special responsibility to the world field.

7. The success of the Volunteer Movement in the United States and Canada has been so marked that its influence has already been strongly felt in British and Continental universities through the representatives of these institutions who have come from year to year to the intercollegiate meetings at Northfield.

8. Taking as its key-note *the evangelization of the world in this generation*, the Movement has emphasized the apostolic idea, so that thousands of Christians have realized its significance as never before. They not only find it suggested throughout the New Testament, but also hear it from the lips of missionaries of all evangelical denominations to-day. The volunteers ask the question: If they at the front bearing the brunt of the conflict sound the battle-cry, ought not we to re-echo it with equal conviction and enthusiasm?

V. PRESENT STATUS.

During the past six months an extensive correspondence has been instituted with the volunteers for the purpose of receiving information for statistics. A large proportion of the volunteers have responded, and the following figures are based upon the returns, and are considered safe estimates.

1. Distribution of volunteers, according to section where enrolled:

CANADA 335

New Brunswick	10	Nova Scotia	25
Ontario	210	Quebec	90

NEW ENGLAND STATES 570

Connecticut	100	Maine	65
Massachusetts	340	New Hampshire	25
Rhode Island	25	Vermont	15

MIDDLE ATLANTIC STATES 1260

Maryland	50	New Jersey	340
New York	560	Pennsylvania	310

SOUTHERN STATES 695

Georgia	20	Kentucky	150
North Carolina	70	South Carolina	30
Tennessee	140	Texas	15
Virginia	240	West Virginia	30

CENTRAL STATES 1975
    Illinois 600   Indiana 175
    Michigan 340   Ohio 660
              Wisconsin 200

WESTERN STATES 1365
    Iowa 375   Kansas 375
    Minnesota 175   Missouri 275
    Nebraska 150   South Dakota 15

        Total number of volunteers 6,200

2. Distribution of volunteers according to stages of preparation:

(1) In institutions of learning 2600
    Academies | 500   Colleges 1200
    Normal Schools . . 175   Medical Colleges . . . 125
    Theological Seminaries,500   Training Schools . . . 100
(2) Out of institutions (owing to state of health, insufficient
    means, etc.) 700
(3) Graduates (post graduates, special students, etc.) 600
(4) Ready to go 100
(5) Appointed (not including class of 1891) 20
(6) Hindered 250
(7) Unknown (large majority of these lost trace of before the
    Movement was organized) 450
(8) Rejected by Boards 50
(9) Renounced 450
(10) Deceased 60
(11) Sailed 320
(12) Not students when enrolled 600

3. Distribution of volunteers according to age:

    Under 20 years . . . . 14 per cent.
    Over 20 years and under 25 years 46   "
    Over 25 years and under 30 years 20   "
    Over 30 years 11   "

4. Distribution of volunteers according to sex:

    Male, 4,340 . . . . 70 per cent.
    Female, 1,860 30   "

5. Distribution of volunteers according to denomination:

Presbyterian . . . . 27 per cent.
Methodist . . . . 24 "
Baptist . . . . 17 "
Congregational . . . . 17 "
Lutheran . . . . 3 "
Episcopal . . . . 2 "
Friends . . . . 1½ "
Other denominations . . . . 8½ "

6. Distribution of volunteers who have sailed according to fields:

AFRICA 33
East Africa 2   North Africa 2
South Africa 3   West Africa 22
Unlocated 4

ASIA 229
Arabia 1   Burmah 18
China 69   Corea 7
India 49   Japan 46
Persia 9   Siam and Laos 7
Syria 8   Turkey 15

EUROPE 5
Bulgaria 4   Italy 1

NORTH AMERICA 13
Central America 2   Mexico 11

SOUTH AMERICA 12
Brazil 10   Chili 1
United States of Columbia 1

SOUTH SEA ISLANDS 6

MISCELLANEOUS 7

LOCATION NOT DEFINITELY KNOWN 16

TOTAL 321

VI. FINANCIAL STATEMENT.

During the first three years the expenses were borne entirely by a friend of the Movement. Since then $4,852 have been received from individuals, parlor conferences, Young Men's Christian Associations, churches, and from the sale of volunteer pamphlets. Of these amounts, $4,651 have been expended. This includes the expenses of Traveling, Corresponding, and Editorial Secretaries, printing, office furniture, etc.

There are at present $201 in the treasury. Since the inception of this Movement no salaries have been paid. Over $10,000 would have been expended in salaries had the secretaries of the Committee received what is usually paid to men of their ability. $3,000 at the lowest estimate will be needed during the coming year to meet the increasing demands made upon the Committee by the growth of the Movement.

VII. POLICY.

The Executive Committee have marked out the following policy, concerning which they invite the friendly criticism and counsel, and the earnest prayers of the members of this Convention : —

1. This Movement seeks to enroll volunteers in sufficient numbers to meet all the demands made upon it by the different missionary agencies of the day ; and, more than that, sufficient to make possible the evangelization of the world in this generation.

2. The Movement should be judiciously extended to those institutions which have not yet felt its touch. Among them we would especially note the colleges of the South and Southwest, the colleges of Colorado and the Pacific Slope, and the medical schools of our great cities.

3. It is our duty to guard and develop the volunteers as long as they are connected with our institutions. To this end there must be more and better State organizations ; more studying, praying, and working on the part of Volunteer Bands ; closer ties established between the volunteers and their respective church boards. Recognizing the importance and critical position held by the theological seminaries, it is urgent that far more attention be given to establishing and developing the Movement in them. The Executive Committee realize the futility of securing volunteers in colleges unless we succeed in holding them in theological seminaries, because a large number of them must pass through divinity schools prior to sailing. No one can overestimate the importance of influencing the divinity men who are to become the leaders of the Church at home and abroad.

4. It is our aim to do all within our power to assist the missionary societies and boards in securing candidates, in raising money, and in other ways suggested to us. To better accomplish this, it is proposed to come into more intimate and frequent contact with the secretaries of the societies. We shall also try to induce many more capable volunteers to work among the churches during their vacations. Wherever possible,— in colleges, seminaries, churches, young people's societies,— we shall continue to urge the introduction of the plan for supporting their own missionary.

5. Recognizing the wonderful possibilities of the various young people's societies of the day, the Volunteer Movement shall seek to spread the missionary spirit among them. It is believed that these two movements are destined to sustain a very important relation to each other.

6. During the coming year the Committee proposes to employ a Corresponding Secretary who shall give his entire time to the work which centers at the office. This office will, to a limited extent, at least, become a clearing house between the volunteers and the societies. A bureau of information will be established. The best missionary books, tracts, periodicals, maps, and charts will also be supplied to volunteers at cost. It shall be our endeavor to introduce a missionary library into every institution where there are volunteers. Additions will be made to the volunteer series of pamphlets as occasion demands.

7. Invitation has repeatedly come to the Committee from students in Great Britain and Scandinavia, requesting us to send a representative to introduce and organize the Movement among their universities. It is hoped that during the present year we shall be able to enter this most important door. If the students of the Protestant world are linked together by the power of the Spirit in this Movement, it will greatly hasten the establishment of Christ's Kingdom throughout the world.

JOHN R. MOTT, INTERCOLLEGIATE Y. M. C. A.

MISS NETTIE DUNN, INTERCOLLEGIATE Y. W. C. A.

R. P. WILDER, AMERICAN INTER-SEM. MISS. ALLIANCE, AND CANADIAN INTERCOLLEGIATE MISSIONARY ALLIANCE.

Executive Committee.

After the announcement of the committees of the Convention by the moderator, Mr. Robert P. Wilder spoke upon "The Volunteer Pledge," using the arguments for its existence and the continuance of its use which are found in his pamphlet upon that subject, issued in Student Volunteer Series, No. 3. Mr. Wilder then led in the discussion.

Question. What does *renouncing* the pledge mean?

Answer. It cannot be applied to those who are providentially prevented from becoming foreign missionaries. If God does not permit their going they are exempt, for the pledge reads, "We are willing and desirous, God *permitting,*" etc. It should be applied to those who, though having no valid excuse for remaining in America, have renounced all thoughts of becoming foreign missionaries.

What is a valid excuse? This must be settled by each volunteer with God. But if after prayer he be convinced of his unfitness to go, he owes it to himself and to the Student Volunteer Movement for Foreign Missions that this unfitness be demonstrated; otherwise, he will be regarded as one who, "having put his hand to the plough," has looked back. To avoid the appearance of evil, he should apply to the Board of Foreign Missions of some evangelical denomination. The examination of candidates by these Boards is most thorough. One unqualified for the work rarely, if ever, passes muster, since the requirements are most rigid. The candidate need not fear confiding in the secretaries, who can appreciate heart as well as head difficulties. If, after squarely facing the issue, the Board reject him, he is exempt before our Movement, since the Student Volunteer Movement for Foreign Missions co-operates with the missionary societies, and abides by their decision. But such exemption by no means proves that he is exempt before God. Missionary organizations are fallible. One of Africa's best missionaries was rejected by three Boards. Like William Carey, he felt, "Go I must, or guilt will rest on my soul."

As long as a volunteer purposes applying eventually to some Foreign Missionary Board, we keep his name on our list; but if he has not applied to any society, and does not intend to do so, we must regard him as no longer a volunteer. We must erase his name, lest by continuing in our ranks he imperil the steadfastness of others. "What man is fearful and faint hearted? Let him go and return unto his house, lest his brethren's heart faint as well as his heart."

Q. How would you deal with a man who thinks that he is not called to the foreign field?

A. I should tell him that there is nothing in the Bible to indicate that a man needs more of a call to take him to Africa than to Dakota. "The field is the *world.*" There are no boundary lines in our work.

If a man can labor in Texas without a "special call," is it right to oppose his crossing the Rio Grande into Mexico unless he receives a "special call"?

Q. What course would you take with a man whose desire to go abroad is not as great as when he first signed the pledge?

A. First, *pray* for him. Second, set him on fire with the *facts.* One says: "If disciples do not wish to flame with missionary zeal, they must avoid contact and converse with the facts and the heroic souls who are the living factors of missions. It is dangerous business to trifle with the combustible material, unless you are quite sure that there is not even a spark of life or love in your soul."

Q. Could not the pledge be made stronger by changing its wording?

A. (From Mr. Wilder by another question). How change it?

A. By substituting the word "purpose" for the word "desirous."

A. (Mr. Wilder). I think that the word "desirous" should be kept for the following reasons:

1. Because it harmonizes with the central thought of our Movement — the thought expressed in the word "volunteer." We want no drafted troops, but men whose hearts stir them up. There is a true ring about the word "desire." It implies *eagerness.* It means, "To long for the enjoyment or possession of; to feel the want of; to wish; to mourn the loss of."

A drafted soldier may "purpose" to enter the field without having any eagerness to do so. But there is a warmth, a glow, an element of spontaneity about the word "desire." "Purpose" is purely a matter of the will. "Desire" is a matter of will and heart.

Definition of the noun desire: "The natural longing that is excited by the enjoyment or thought of any good, and impels to action or effort for its continuance or possession."

2. The home contingent of hindered volunteers can truthfully keep the pledge as it now reads. They are still willing and *desirous* to go to the foreign field. Can they say we *purpose* going if their path is absolutely blocked?

These hindered volunteers can be of great service to our Movement as missionary pastors and workers at home. It is essential that we keep their names on our list of volunteers. We need their sympathy and help.

The present pledge is applicable to both classes of volunteers. We cannot have one pledge for the hindered and another for those who are going abroad; the existence of two pledges would obviously invalidate the unity of the Movement.

3. .Substituting the word "purpose," even though the pledge seem **more** rigid in statement, it would not be more rigid in spirit. The

pledge as it now reads means only one thing; that is, a determination to go, God willing. What else can it mean? If it be misunderstood by the signer, the fault lies with him, or the one who uses the pledge.

4. The word "desire" is approved by many outsiders whom "purpose" might alienate. It is necessary for our field Secretary to gain an entrance to institutions of learning. Often the mere mention of a *pledge* has led teachers to shake their heads. I remember a ladies' seminary where the principal would not allow our pledge to be presented. In a college there was a strong objection to the pledge because of its binding character (little thought had I then that any one would regard the pledge as too weak). In a leading theological seminary I was notified by the faculty that they did not wish me to pass the pledge. If we make the wording more rigid in appearance, still greater opposition would be met, and the doors of some institutions would be shut in our faces.

5. I do not believe that the suggested change would enable the pledge to hold any more of our wavering volunteers than the present pledge is holding. If men want to renounce their expressed determination to become foreign missionaries the words "God permitting" will furnish them an avenue for escape. The word "desirous" does not present as large a loop-hole as "God permitting."

Mr. Wilder then closed the discussion with the following arguments against *any* alteration of the pledge: —

1. *Historical argument.* The pledge in its present form is signed by 6,000 volunteers.

2. *The present pledge is satisfactory.* Whatever defection there is is very small. A noted foreign missionary said that not more than two per cent. of those who volunteered in a missionary revival ever sailed. But *five* per cent. of the members of our Movement in the United States have already sailed, and ten per cent. of the Canadian volunteers. Most of the defection has been due to the fact that the Student Volunteer Movement was not thoroughly organized during the first two years and a half of its existence. During those years the same efforts were not made to conserve the interest of volunteers as are now being made.

3. Changing the pledge would necessitate losing our hold upon the signers of the present pledge. Let us suppose that "purpose" is substituted for "desirous." If the word "purpose" means the same thing as "desirous," what is the reason for a change in the wording? If the two words are not synonymous, using "purpose" for "desirous" means that the new pledge has no claims upon the 6,000 who signed the old pledge.

Who shall sign the pledge?

1. All theological students who desire to sign it, since they are taking a course of study expected to prepare them for service at home or abroad.

2. In colleges the *active* members of the Young Women's Christian Association and the Young Men's Christian Association may sign. The various departments of Association work furnish the training needed by candidates for foreign service. If a student be faithful in studying the Bible and missions, in personal and neighborhood work, you need not hesitate to let him volunteer. But do not allow those who are not Association members to sign until you are convinced of their fitness to take this step.

3. In educational institutions where there are no Young Men's or Young Women's Christian Associations, also in churches, do not permit any to sign until you are satisfied that they possess the requisite qualifications for foreign service.

Mr. Walter J. Clark, Corresponding Secretary of the Student Volunteer Movement for Foreign Missions, introduced the discussion of the topic —

The Classification of Volunteers.

From the inception of the Movement there has been occasion for classification of volunteers. Only a few weeks after the Movement began, letters began coming to the leaders of the Movement stating that the persons who had signed for various reasons felt that they must renounce their pledge. Because of the unorganized condition of the Movement during the first two years and a half, and the great pressure of work that fell upon the Traveling Secretary, it was impossible to keep a thorough record of these communications. In the past two years an effort has been made to classify the correspondence and to follow the requests received. The results have been presented to you this morning in the report of the Executive Committee; and that we may thoroughly understand what these twelve classes indicate, it has seemed best that I should explain them in a few words.

It was customary until recently to make only two classes of volunteers — those who intend to go, and those who have renounced. But it became evident from the large correspondence that came to the office that there were many detained at home who had a strong purpose to go to the foreign field, and whose hearts were in the work. These we could not say had renounced, and their co-operation was very essential to us as a Movement, and we could not cut them off. This classification has been prepared that we may have a view of the present condition of the Volunteer Movement.

The first class embraces all who at present are pursuing their regular courses of study. We find this number to be about 2,600, distributed among the following institutions in about the number given here: in academies, 500; in normal schools, 175; in colleges and universities, 1,200; medical colleges, 125; theological seminaries, 500; training schools of various kinds, 100.

Those who are connected with our normal schools, are expected in some States to teach for two years after they have received their education. And others who are supporting themselves must be absent, at least for a time, to secure the means for their education. And so at present there are out of school, of those who intend to finish their education, but for various reasons are compelled to absent themselves, at least 700.

The next class is composed of graduates. Here we classify those who have finished their course of study but are uncertain as to their professional course, and those who are taking special professional courses as post graduates. The class of graduates amounts at present to 600. The number of those who are ready to go, but have not yet received their appointment, is about 100.

The next class contains only 20. It consists of those who have been appointed a year or more, and does not include those who are in theological or medical schools and who have received appointments and will sail in the coming summer.

Passing over the class of "hindered," we come to another class, "unknown" — those of whom we have lost all trace. The records were not kept for over two years, and as students are somewhat migratory, it has been difficult to find all of the earlier volunteers. And so we have about 450 names in this class. About 50 have been rejected by Boards on account of ill health and for other reasons. We classify as "renounced" every individual who has signed the pledge but has willfully given up his intention to become a foreign missionary. In some cases religious convictions have been surrendered. This class embraces about 450. Those whom God has taken to Himself for His work above number at least 60: we have 56 names. Those who have reached the foreign field have been repeatedly mentioned. They number at least 320. When our Traveling Secretaries have addressed audiences of students, there have often been persons in the audience who were not students, and so there has been an enrollment of at least 600 of this class.

I return to the class omitted — "hindered volunteers." First, who are the volunteers? Those who intend to go to the foreign field, God permitting. Hindered volunteers are those who have had their way blocked by providential circumstances. These must serve as a reserve corps of the Volunteer Movement. They cannot come to the front, but still in the rear they can provide the means and the prayer that will bear on this work. The circumstances which hinder volunteers are often of a private character. The difficulty of dealing in correspondence with persons to whom I am an entire stranger — the difficulty of gathering from their letters just what they mean, unless they are very explicit as to their hinderances, has made this class a little indefinite. Yet I believe there are scores of them who are in such poor health that they cannot go. There are others who have the support of parents and dependent brothers and sisters, and who for the present cannot go.

Now, what is their relation to the Volunteer Movement. They are first a part of it. We cannot cut them off: we cut off the renounced, though we keep their names for our own good, as well as hoping that some day they may change their minds. The hindered volunteers are a part of the Movement, and we must keep them as such. Their relation to the Movement is a vital one; *because* they are to *advance* the Movement in their way and in their place.

Let me indicate four things they can do to help the Movement. 1. They can go when the Lord opens the door. I know many a volunteer who has written to me saying, "the Lord has blocked the way, it is impossible for me to go;" and yet, in some instances, the Lord has in a few weeks removed the obstruction, and made possible the departure of the volunteer by so severe a trial as the death of a friend. 2. They can *send* others. It has been pointed out to you this morning the influence which one who has set his face to the foreign field can wield in getting others to go. 3. He can *interest* others in the work. The amount of ignorance in our churches, among the young people and older people, is *enormous*. 4. He can offer *prayer* constantly for those who have sailed and those who are preparing.

Mr. Richard C. Morse, of New York City: —

I was asked to say something upon this subject, and it occurs to me to state first, concerning the hindered volunteer, that there are some of these hindered volunteers, as Mr. Clark has said, who go. Mr. Forman was a hindered volunteer for a year, — hindered in the best interests of the foreign mission work. Mr. Wilder is a hindered volunteer. There are hindered volunteers that either have gone or are very sure to go, and whose detention has been due to the very best interests of the foreign mission work itself. Mr. Wishard was a hindered volunteer. Thirteen years ago he came to me ready to go to South America, to form with some of his classmates a band of missionaries there. But he felt that in the college department of the Young Men's Christian Association he could serve his Master upon the foreign field. And I was in familiar intercourse with him when he became represented on that field by at least a score of men, and before he went to labor in the land which he loves so well.

Now, the hindered volunteer can do just as much as the unhindered while they are together here, and we want to conserve that element. I believe that in the last 50 years the hindered volunteers have been a potential element in the sustentation and carrying on of the foreign mission movement as it stands to-day. Thousands of the men rescued in the name of Christ on the foreign field owe that rescue as much to the prayers and efforts of hindered volunteers in this country during the last 50 years as to some of the men who have gone on the field. The hindered volunteer has an immense work that he can do in keeping the conscience of the Church right on this subject at home, for that is a most important thing, a most necessary, essential, fundamental thing in connection with this Movement.

Robert E. Speer, of Princeton Theological Seminary, then addressed the Convention upon the topic of —

THE VOLUNTEER LIFE IN THE INDIVIDUAL INSTITUTIONS.

I think we all believe in the *reality* of this volunteer life, both from the nature of the work and from observation of the volunteers. I presume there is one question that arises in our minds as we begin to think about this subject, and that is, as to the relation between the volunteer life, as we call it, and the Christian life of the institution. It seems to me that the relation is just this: that the volunteer life should be the Christian life; that the first work of the volunteer in each institution is not with regard to foreign missions, is not to arouse interest in foreign missions in the Church outside, but is earnestly to claim each student in his institution for Jesus Christ. And so the volunteer life, when we speak of it as a whole, is not so much a life lived with regard to the foreign field as with regard to the community in which it finds itself placed. The volunteer life in each institution should be relatively what that volunteer life should be when it is put on the foreign field.

In addition to living the real Christian life before his fellows, the volunteer should strive, so far as he has any time apart from general Christian work, to make his life tell on the great work in all the world.

Now, just a word about the *expression* of this volunteer life. It seems to me that of course it will be twofold: First, in the life of every individual volunteer. He should be above everything else the best Christian in his institution. He should be the best personal worker, the best Bible student; as far as possible, the best student in every way to be found in that place. But, in addition to this, each individual life should burn also with a zeal that cannot be quenched, and with an intelligent zeal for spreading the Gospel in all the world. Second, to this end the individual lives will gather themselves constantly into the life of Volunteer Bands.

First, then, with regard to the position of such a Band. In its relation to the Student Volunteer Movement, it is simply the expression of that Movement in any one institution. Whatever the Movement is for all the colleges of the land, the Band must be for the institution in which it is placed. The Band should be an extension of the missionary activities of the Christian Associations, where such Associations exist. It should not be anything independent from them; they all of them have their missionary committees, or ought to have them. If they have not, the Bands ought to introduce them. Each Band should be a large missionary committee for its institution.

In regard to the *work* of the Band :

1. It seems to me natural that they will have meetings to nourish the volunteer life and to keep in view the object for which that life was brought into existence. Something will certainly have to be done in these meetings, and I suppose most of us have our own ideas of what things are best to be done. Of course we are going to learn all about the world that we can. We will study missionary subjects, taking up the fields, biographies, and general questions in missions. The Bible is the special book, above all other missionary books, that we are to study. We will endeavor to find out all about the Missionary Boards, their methods, their work, their conception of the missionary problem. We will take up the missionary magazines and find out what each one is teaching from month to month. In addition to all this, we will make these meetings places where we shall become so acquainted with the Bible that it shall be to us an exceedingly familiar book long before we ever set our feet on a foreign missionary field. So much for the work of the Band in the meeting.

Beyond that, secondly, it must be the work of each Band to acquaint each volunteer with the best missionary literature available to that Band ; and much more literature is available than we have ever imagined. A third work of the Band is to keep each volunteer the kind of volunteer he ought to be, and as soon as his feet go out of the institution, not to let him wander away from his expressed purpose until he has been put under the guiding influence of the Missionary Board. And, lastly, Volunteer Bands should be training schools of prayer.

2. The second work of the Volunteer Band is outside of itself, among the other students of the institution ; and it too should be fourfold. (1.) To hold meetings of such a character that students in general shall be led to take a deep interest in the foreign missionary work.

And these meetings should be made of all meetings the most interesting ones that are held in that institution; and they should be so frequent that each meeting shall come before the memory of the last shall have passed altogether away. (2.) It should be the object of the Band to lead each institution that is capable of doing it to support a missionary in the foreign field. And where it is absolutely impossible for an institution to do that of itself, let it combine with a church, a Sabbath School, a Young People's Society of Christian Endeavor, or with some other educational institution. We have our leagues among the colleges to do other things. Why may we not have them also to support our representatives in the fields abroad? (3.) Its third work among students should be to interest every student in the foreign work. We ought not to let a single student pass out of the walls of our institutions without having thoroughly familiarized him with the work of foreign missions and with the work of the Board under whose influence he will come, and with the needs of the field, so that he will be an intelligent giver and an intercessor in prayer when he gets out among the churches. And, lastly, the effort should be made constantly to secure from among the students more volunteers.

3. The third work of the Band should be among the Sabbath Schools and Christian Endeavor Societies. In a Methodist institution it should be to spread the knowledge of the work of the Methodist Board among all the Methodist Churches and Epworth Leagues. But it should go outside of the mission work of the Methodist Church and inform itself about other fields. And let it, of course, as far as it is possible, as has been suggested this morning, ally each church with the foreign field by its own living link in that field.

4. Lastly, the work of the Volunteer Band in each institution will be the development of its relations to other institutions, to the Student Volunteer Movement, and to the Boards. Let it get Board secretaries into the institution if possible; come in contact with them; learn about the Boards from their representatives. Go to the city where the Board offices are: let them get acquainted with you, and consult with them.

So much then for the work. May I add just a word about the *importance* of it? If we get the importance of it in our minds, the methods of the work will take care of themselves. It is important to the individual volunteer. Go where you will in this land to-day, in all our institutions where there are not Volunteer Bands, and you will find that the life of the individual volunteer, so far as it is a missionary life, is slowly dying away. He does not have interest enough, after the first breath of inspiration has gone, in most cases, to keep informing himself about the foreign field, as he must if his interest is to keep intelligent and to grow. It is important, secondly, for the institution's sake.

*The most spiritual institutions in our country to-day are those that
have been most touched by the missionary spirit.* It is of the greatest
importance to the institution to which we as volunteers belong that we
should make the volunteer life an active life for the institution's sake.
Then it is important for the Church's sake. The Church must draw on
these volunteers for help in the foreign field. Should their interest die
away the Church will have to do the work over again.

And then, lastly, it is important for this world's sake. If we are
going to spread the Gospel within the reach of every part of the world
in this generation, we must not only, in the first place, rouse men's
minds and hearts with the desire to go, but, having done that, we must
gather them into this life in each institution and keep them there until
the time when their faces are parted from us. And if they do not go
into the missionary field, they will have received such an impress that
they cannot carry on any other work without making it resemble the
missionary life they lived in seminary or college.

It seems to me we can get *inspiration* enough for this life in the
watchword we have taken, and in the fact that if we do not perpetuate
the Band in each institution, it will probably not be perpetuated.
The fact that when we go out from college we may leave a Band in our
place, or another volunteer to stand where we stood, is inspiration
enough to make the life that we are living now the volunteer life that
it ought to be.

But then, of course, we get our deepest inspiration from that child's
school, where I trust we will all go and enter our names for the tuition
that the Great Teacher has to give as we sit down at His feet to learn
how to pray. And there we shall catch more of that needed faith in
Him, whom having not seen we have learned to love so well, who is
the Lord of this Volunteer Movement as much as He is the Lord of
each volunteer's life.

Mr. William H. Cossum, Travelling Secretary of the Student Volunteer Movement for Foreign Missions, presented the topic —

IMMEDIATE SAILING: ITS ADVANTAGES, AND HOW SECURED.

Some one said, as he stood on the wharf seeing a party of missionaries set sail, that ships were made to carry missionaries in. It was an
inspired utterance. And it is only as we keep these ships busy that
the Student Volunteer Movement reaches its true objective point and
has its true reactionary influence on the Church. 6,200 names are not
what we are after. Our object is to evangelize the world in this generation; and it is not until the missionaries pledged are on board ships
aiming towards fields that this Movement reaches it true objective
point.

Touching the advantages of early sailing, there will be:

First, an advantage to the volunteer himself. The sooner you get into contact with your field and become adjusted to your environment, the sooner you can begin your life work. You have a climate to become accustomed to, possibly a different language to acquire, and these ought to be gotten out of the way as soon as possible. And then again your own heart will be satisfied best by coming to the field. Remember you have chosen this work yourself, and your own heart, if true to that consecration, will be best satisfied by your getting to the field as soon as possible. And so, do not defer your sailing, but go.

Then it will save you another heart struggle. The man who says, " I want to get a little experience in this country, and take up some difficult phase of work here," that man will find himself tied to that work, and he will have to go through a new struggle. He will say, " Here is work enough for me ; " and that is the penny which, held before his vision, hides the sun. The man who gets tied up to the local field will have to go through a strong struggle to tear himself loose. Don't tie yourselves to work here. I know, as a matter of fact, that there are men who have expected to be volunteers, who are now laboring on fields in this country and are settled down there permanently. Be consistent to your pledge, and go to the foreign field immediately.

The evangelization of the world in this generation is our key-note. The honor of the Student Volunteer Movement demands that we reach our fields at the earliest date possible. Here are critics, friendly and unfriendly, who are watching this Movement. Men in our colleges want to know whether we mean business or not. And it is only when they see the volunteers sailing when they finish their course that they feel we are living true to our watchword. So, for the sake of the honor of the Movement itself, we want to reach the fields as soon as possible.

Again, such a course is necessary in order to increase the acquisitions to the Volunteer Movement from the best men in our colleges. Conservative men do not want to sign a pledge which they may be in danger of renouncing. Here are 6,200 volunteers enrolled, and 320 on the field. They do not take into consideration all the facts that keep these other men here; and hence show hesitancy with reference to enrolling themselves as volunteers. When they begin to see the number of those on the field increasing each year, they will have more confidence in the Movement, and we will have acquisitions to our Movement from the strong conservative men in our colleges.

Then again, the missionary department in the work of the Associations will be strengthened by the departure of volunteers in large numbers. The reactionary influence exerted by men on the field will quicken them. It will strengthen the appeals of the representatives of the Student Volunteer Movement to the churches. If we can say we have a large number of men on the field, we will have a more practical basis of appeal to the churches for the necessary funds to send them.

Going to the foreign field is bringing bread to starving men and light to the man who is stumbling and liable to fall into the ditch. If these people need help at all they need it immediately. Dear fellow volunteers, we must go into this field as fast as we can. The starving man must have bread at once; the man who is sinking beneath the waves needs a helping hand now, or he will go down. They need you over there; they need me. Don't stay in this country theorizing, when a hundred thousand heathens a day are dying without hope because we are not there teaching the Gospel to them. Get to them as soon as you can, dear friends.

How shall it be secured? I say first and most important of all, the immediate sailing of volunteers shall be secured by having our heart so tied to those fields that when the time comes for you to finish your course, nothing but absolute duty very clearly defined will keep you. Absolute duty is the only thing that ought to keep us here. And the only way we can have our hearts tied to these fields is to make ourselves thoroughly intelligent with reference to the concrete needs of these fields. Study the missionary field you have chosen. Find out the habits of life and the individual needs of these people; and then, if you are really a Christlike man, you will want to depart as soon as you can. Above all things else, be prayerful, morning, noon, and night. Pray that God may use your life with reference to this work, and the result will be that you will speedily reach the field of your choice.

A delegate said: —

Something has been said about working one's passage over. I have been there. I was converted in India, and I saw no way to be sent over to this country for an education. I went down to the harbor and asked at six different steamers, and finally found a good opportunity of working my passage over by painting the inside of a big vessel. And I say to the strong men here that it was a delightful time to me. I had some blisters on my fingers, but I always painted, " All for Jesus," one way, and " All for Christ," the other way. If there are young men here that wish to go out, let them believe that God will take care of them.

Afternoon Session.

A brief song song service was conducted by Mr. Arthur J. Smith. The representatives of the foreign missionary societies were invited to take seats on the platform; after which the Convention took up the subject, " The volunteer between graduation and going."

The Rev. J. N. Murdock, D.D., of the American Baptist Missionary Union, addressed the Convention on the first topic: —

The Requirements of Missionary Societies.

Mr. Chairman, brethren and sisters of the Convention, I cannot express the sense of gratification I feel in being permitted to look into your faces, to drink in your spirit, and to listen to the earnest, sober, and wise words that I heard from you this morning. There was no need of my coming to you to speak of the requirements of Missionary Boards, or of any other question pertaining to the details of missionary work, for you have been making these things a study for years. I rejoice in the results which have been achieved, and I should be glad to contribute anything in my power to your enlightenment and the quickening of your zeal.

We want men: we want every person who is eligible from your great body of student volunteers. You need not expect that all of them will go to the missionary field. But if 2,000 of them go, and 4,000, pervaded by the true missionary spirit, spread missionary intelligence and keep the conscience of the Church sensitive on the subject of the divine claims of foreign missions, that would solve the whole question. There are 7,000 pastors of churches connected with the society to which I belong. If I could get 4,000 of those men to do their duty in reference to means, I would fold my hands and go home, so far as any sense of absolute and pressing necessity resting upon me might be concerned: the work would be done. What we want to-day more than missionary candidates is missionary pastors,— pastors of churches that will simply do their duty, that will lead their churches in the way they ought to go and are waiting to be led, some of them longing to be led.

But I am not to speak of this; I am to speak of the requirements — that is, the conditions of your acceptance, as I understand it — by the Missionary Board. Now, there is no extra-critical sense in the nerves of Missionary Boards. We are not allowed to be too particular. We scarcely have a chance of making selections for the places that we want to fill. One of the things that I have hoped might result from your seminary alliances, and from this Convention, is that you may present to us a sufficient number of missionary candidates to allow us to select the best. We want the best. I speak for my own society,— but I doubt not what I say is true of other societies,— that we have sent many men to the foreign mission field, good men, Christian men, men that are worthy of confidence, and yet they are not such men as we would have sent if we could have sent better. We want a chance to make a selection; and we are submissive to the Providence who keeps every man from the mission field who can be better employed among the home churches, so that they cleave to Christ and do not neglect His work.

Well then, what must we have in our missionary candidates? One of the first things is good health. We want the sound body. We want the man of sound nerves, of reasonable muscles, of good stomach, the man who can make himself contented and easy, and rest when the possibility of rest shall come. We want men of good health, and so we institute medical examinations. There will always be one or two men in an examining committee who will lay great stress upon the health of a candidate. And there will be another man who, from his financial carefulness, will second the man who is anxious about the question of health. And so we are obliged to have a medical examination. When in three months time a man comes home by reason of failure in health, we must be able to go back to the record and see if we have not been at fault.

Then I need not say that we want men of ability. We do not want a man who cannot succeed anywhere in this country. A gentleman wrote me once recommending his pastor as a candidate for foreign missions. He had understood that it was not necessary for a missionary to preach as ministers preach in this country; that they only wanted a good, careful, prudent man, who would not do anything very foolish and never anything very wise. He thought his pastor was just the man that ought to go to the heathen; he was so much in advance of the heathen. I tell you, Mr. Chairman, there are not so many of us that are in advance of the heathen. The intellect of the Hindoo, of the Chinaman, of the Japanese, will put you to your mettle when you come in contact with them.

We also want men of good sound common sense — not simply mental ability, but we want the roundaboutness of common sense. We want a man who will look at things with an even eye, a man who will not be suddenly moved by unpropitious junctures of circumstances, a man whose expectations of success, whose demands upon the people for whom he labors, will not be too extravagant. We want a man who can take a common sense view of the problems that are presented to him and of the work that is committed to his hands.

We must have men of good repute, so we are obliged to look up the record of every man who comes to us asking for an appointment.

We are very glad sometimes to adopt the rule of Oliver Wendell Holmes, who, when he was asked when he would have the moral culture of a child begin, replied, " One hundred years before he was born." We are glad to have men come to us and say: " I was the child of godly parents. My father and my mother were Christians before me, and they taught me the way of salvation through Christ, and they instructed me in the duties as well as in the doctrines of the Holy Scriptures."

We want spiritually minded men. We want men who live day by day in communion with God, who cleave to Christ, and in whom Christ abides. We want men who are sound in the faith. We do not want to send anybody to the heathen to learn anything that they can teach him. There was a man who went to India from Boston, and though he could not fully believe the Bible, he took the Shastas without any sort of compunction. We have got one returning from Japan who went out to make a sort of exchange with the Japanese. He found that Unitarianism was simply esoteric Buddhism, and having made that discovery he is on his way back. We want men who believe something, men who believe they are going to save souls from ruin and from death. And if we are not to do this, then, in the name of all that is reasonable, let us just suspend this work.

We want men of missionary convictions; men who feel that God has laid this work upon them. We want men with a missionary purpose, who are called by the Holy Ghost. The only point in which I have had any fear about this student Movement is that we shall forget that God only can call a minister, God only can make a missionary. The apostles, when one fell out of his place, sought to supply it. God paid no attention to that. He may pay just as little attention to you who have taken the pledge. He may see only here and there among these thousands the man whom he has chosen. Let us remember always that only the Holy Ghost can select a minister, and when He selects one He will do something.

When John E. Clough came before the missionary committee in Boston, he was somewhat angular in appearance, not an elegant, learned, or cultivated man in the ordinary sense, and there was some doubt about sending him. When the late Dr. Stowe, who always observed the proprieties, said to him, " What if we should think it not best for you to go ? " " That would make no difference with my opinion," was the reply. " What if this committee should think it best not to send you ? " " I should be obliged to go in some other way." There was nothing arrogant about it, — it was very politely said; but everybody there saw that that man had a conviction. He said, " I have lived twelve years in a United States surveying expedition, and

I have never slept on a bed or under a roof during all those years." And as soon as he got out among the Telugus he wanted his tent. He did not stop in his station for people to go to him, but he went out and began to preach to them, and immediately there began to be conversions. He soon had his native preachers so trained that they could tell their friends and neighbors the way of salvation through Christ; and throughout all the villages in all the region, from one extent of the country to the other, those native preachers went forth proclaiming the lessons they had learned from their teacher. And in 1878, 10,000 of these people were united with the Church of Christ; and they stand to-day. They have suffered persecution, they have undergone hardships, they have endured trial — and yet they stand, and during the last few months thousands more have come.

The Boards require and expect from men, no matter how learned they are or how able, subordination to rule; for let it be understood that there are some things that must be settled in this country which cannot be disturbed on the other side, — as to how much money you shall have, as to the form and method of your work, — and no man will ever be able to lead his people wisely who has not learned to be in subjection himself. Our responsibility is divided. Let us bear ours, and may you take your burdens in the spirit of a missionary in Burmah, whom I was obliged to advise when we had not given him half of what he had asked for to do an important work. I expected a sharp letter from his wife, — God be praised for the women. The answer was: "You have done all you could; I must do all I can; and the Lord must do all the rest."

Question. Do you not think that one of the qualifications to go abroad which would influence greatly an acceptance is the work that a man has already done at home?

Answer. Yes; I had something to say on that, and I am glad you gave me an opportunity to say it. It is one of the questions we always ask of a candidate for the ministry, whether he has been engaged in active religious work at home, in the Sunday School, in the church, in the community; especially, if he is a young man who has associated with clerks in a store or with students in college: "Did you labor for the personal conversion of the young men with whom you associated?" We very generally found that the answer was in the affirmative.

Q. What relation has a college course to a man's fitness for a missionary?

A. We are always glad to know that a man has enjoyed a full college course and a full seminary course, and we would be glad if we could add to that a year or two of Christian evangelistic work at home. We never expect to see a man too well educated for a missionary.

And yet, when the Lord calls men evidently of another stamp, puts a missionary purpose into their hearts, endows them with ability, and gives them good common sense, — men who are willing to take a subordinate place in the mission, — we send them out, and the Lord has sometimes brought those very men up to the first place.

The Rev. F. A. Steven, of the China Inland Mission, spoke as follows : —

Much that Dr. Murdock has already said would be equally applicable to the topic that is allotted to me ; namely, " What is required in candidates for the China Inland Mission ? "

We may remind ourselves in the first instance — we cannot remind ourselves too often — that unmistakable evidence of the new birth is the first essential for a missionary. No amount of culture can possibly take the place of this. Zeal for God's glory in the preaching of the Gospel among the heathen is the next essential. That a man should go out to represent a missionary society, or to represent a church or denomination, and not put God first, not live wholly for God among the heathen, is a deplorable thing indeed. The heathen are sunken in idolatry, and unless we represent a pure, simple, joyous, powerful Christianity among them, we shall never be able to move them from their heathenism.

A fair acquaintance with God's word, and a real deep love for it, is a requisite that cannot possibly be dispensed with. I say a fair acquaintance with God's word, because a man is always learning, and if he have a deep love for the word of God will go on perfecting himself in the knowledge of it when he is in the field. Let us remember that a man's training by no means ceases when he leaves these shores. In the China Inland Mission a man's training begins then, or rather a very important part of his training and fitness for his work begins after he leaves these shores. We have, I thank God for it, established two training homes in connection with the mission, one for ladies and one for gentlemen, and at the present time there are I suppose somewhere about thirty young men at the training home, and about the same number of ladies, studying the Chinese language and the Bible under competent teachers. This is a very, very great advantage in the carrying on of the work.

As Dr. Murdock has already said, in regard to the other Boards, so I would emphasize in regard to the China Inland Mission — soundness in the faith is most essential. We do not want any to go to China to teach heresy. There is plenty of heathenism, plenty of wandering from God, in China already, without adding to the confusion of the people by new heresies. Let me read from the " Principles and Practice " of the mission : " Candidates are expected to satisfy the Directors and Home Council as to their soundness in the faith on all fundamental truths by handing in, together with the schedule of application, a written statement of their views as to the inspiration of the Scriptures, the Trinity, the fall of man and his state by nature, the atonement, the eternal salvation of the redeemed, and the everlasting punishment of the lost." If a man is shaky upon that last point we don't want him. They must be catholic in their views, and able to have fellowship at work and at the Lord's table with all believers holding these fundamental truths, even if widely differing in their judgment as to the points of church government.

A willingness to trust God for supply, without human guarantee, is an essential to membership in the China Inland Mission. I read again from the "Principles and Practice": "The mission is supported entirely by the freewill offerings of the Lord's people. The needs of the work are laid before God in prayer, no personal solicitations or collections being authorized. No more is expended than is thus received, neither borrowing or going into debt being consistent with the principle of entire dependence upon God. The Directors therefore cannot and do not give any promise or guarantee of support to the members of the mission. They seek faithfully to distribute what is available, but each missionary is expected to recognize that his dependence for the supply of his need must be on God, who called him, and for whom he must labor, and not for any human organization. Dr. Langford, who is expected here, was in China when the first band of fifteen missionaries, accompanied by Mr. Hudson Taylor, arrived in China in the summer of 1866. At that time the whole number of the missionaries of the new China Inland Mission was about 20; to-day we number between 430 and 440.

God has been faithful to His promises. Not one iota of all His pledge of love to His children has ever failed. I have been in connection with the mission about eight years, and in journeying right across China from side to side and over into Burmah, and for three years and a half I have never lacked any good thing. To the praise of God be it spoken, His right hand has supplied after His own bountiful fashion.

I must say here that in the China Inland Mission we wear the native dress and live in native houses, which, however, we can accommodate to our requirements by internal changes. We do not make external changes in the interior provinces of China, in order to avoid prejudice in the people. Wearing the native dress and living upon the food available in the districts, we are able to live comfortably and well upon $300 per annum, including traveling expenses. I have never found it either necessary or advantageous to use so much as the figure I have mentioned.

I want now just to say that candidates must count the cost. They are expected to be willing to live lives of privation, of toil, of loneliness, of danger; to be looked down upon by their countrymen; to be despised by the Chinese; to live in the interior, far from the comforts and advantages of European society and protection. They will need to trust God as able to meet their need in sickness as well as in health, as it will usually be impossible to have recourse to the aid of European physicians. But, if faithful servants, they will find in Christ and His word a joy and strength that will far outweigh everything that they have sacrificed for Him.

A fair English education is desirable for all who go to China, and without that we should advise a time of further training in this country as a test of the ability and perseverance that would be necessary for the acquirement of the Chinese language. Yet we do not ask that all should be highly educated. If a man were to say: "My house that I am to build is to be such as none ever was before. Not a man shall touch trowel or carry mortar on that house but who has been bred as an architect and passed his examination," we should say that the man would be a long, long time before he got his house built. In the China Inland Mission we recognize that God calls men of different qualifications for different fields of labor. I rejoice that most of the Boards also recognize this. I believe that the time is coming when men of capable business habits and ability will do a still larger share of the work of foreign missions than heretofore. Send us the best, send us the most highly educated; but oh! do not forget to send us the competent, clear-headed, common sense business men, who give up all for Christ and come to preach the Gospel to the heathen.

A word about medical education, and I have done. Some say "Is it not good to take a medical course?" Yes, by all means, unless you have the burden of the heathen resting upon you; and if, on the other hand, you have some special, definite message from the Lord that you ought to study medicine. If not, get to the work as quickly as you can, and believe that God can call men, already qualified, from the medical colleges and the medical profession in this country.

The Rev. J. O. Peck, D.D., of the Missionary Society of the Methodist Episcopal Church, spoke on —

THE MODE OF APPLICATION TO THE VARIOUS MISSIONARY SOCIETIES.

Mr. Chairman, to put a missionary secretary, who is accustomed every time he speaks to have an hour or an hour and a half, into five or ten minutes, is like cramping an Olympus into a nutshell. You saw how Dr. Murdock struggled with it; it will be worse with me.

I do not know what the modes of application are in other societies, and therefore I confine myself to our own society, and say, that if any one of you, or any one from any part of the land who wants to go as a missionary under the auspices of this society, would write to the missionary society and offer yourself, stating whatever facts you may choose to state concerning yourself, the Secretary would reply to you, sending you a blank form, which you are to fill out concerning your age — we don't want you too old and we don't want you too young. A missionary may occasionally at twenty-one be successful, but he is usually a stripling. He must know vastly more than I did when I was in Amherst College at twenty-one or he will not know enough to be a successful missionary. We would rather have him a little older than that. We would ask him to give his age, his birthplace, and his new birthplace, the conditions of his health, — whether there were facts that would militate against our sending him to bilious climates. We would want to know where he graduated in college, — in short, his educational accomplishments; and then, after he has filled that blank out, we send two or three more to different parties; for instance, to the president of the college or one to the professors of the college or of the theological seminary, and another to somebody else whom we can find out knows him thoroughly well. We inquire in those blanks, which he does not see but which we examine, all about his disposition, his studies, his powers of application, his health, his qualifications for acquiring languages, and his social qualities. In short, we try to get a thorough measure of the man and know all about him from independent sources. And then we require him to go before a physician, whom we shall designate if we please, and be examined with reference to mission work in India, for instance. He is to be examined with reference to the climate into which we propose to send him, in order that we may have the best certification of medical science that he is qualified for work in that field so far as can be ascertained.

This is the mode of application and our treatment of it. We write a good, loving, brotherly, hearty letter, avoiding everything that is unnecessary, that may be possibly a discouragement; for, I assure you, the older I grow, the more I believe that the man who unnecessarily puts a burden upon a human soul and discourages it, is a traitor to humanity. There are burdens enough already upon all men. And, as Dr. Murdock said, they are careful of their treatment of young men and young ladies who are applicants; so missionary secretaries, I believe, always are full of charity and of a disposition to encourage and help forward every one whom God has called and into whose hearts He has put a desire for missionary work. That answers, I think, all that need be said about the mode of application. I think, in all societies men apply to the missionary secretaries at the headquarters of their denominational societies, and directions are given which result in bringing them into such relations with the terms and qualifications and accomplishments as are required. And though the forms vary in different societies, the facts I think are generally the same.

Now, I want to take the rest of the time that belongs to me to say something that does not belong so much to this subject as to something more important; for if a man is called of God to be a missionary, the mode of application will not trouble him. He will get there if it is in his heart to go; and I believe in the men who get there, for they are the men who never renounce their pledges and who are determined to get to this foreign work. And I do join with my distinguished brother, Dr. Murdock, in rendering thanks to these officers of this society who have permitted us the honor of being present here in this Convention, coming here not to instruct you, but to bring our older blood into contact with your blood, to be filled with this great inspiration which I believe has come down from God upon the colleges and universities and schools of our land, moving this great Student Movement for the salvation of the world during this generation. I do not say it will be done. Perhaps I am not as hopeful as some of you; perhaps I know more about the difficulties. But no matter: it is possible for it to be done, in my conviction, and it is a magnificent testimony, both that God is on the throne with purpose to save this world, and that men are being moved by the Spirit of the living God, in response to His own impulse, to answer, " Here am I; send me."

This great Movement that has sprung up in the last four years is the result of prayer to God from all along the cottages and humble places of our land, as well as in missionary circles. Men and women who have the burden of the Lord upon their souls have been praying Him to hasten the coming of the kingdom of Christ throughout the world. And I believe your Movement is one of the factors in the execution of that great, sublime purpose of God that the kingdoms of this earth shall be the kingdoms of our Lord and His Christ. The secretaries of the Missionary Boards to-day feel it a joy to come in touch with you, to feel this great inspiration; and we will go home with a livelier and keener sensibility and profounder conviction. I see such an earnest Christian spirit in your meetings that I am convinced that it is the Spirit of God that is carrying you on.

Now I suggest to you, as a solution of matters that were in the air here this morning, that you make your consecration to this work when you sign the pledge, and teach others so to make it. Make that consecration in such a spirit as the old Jew made his offering on the altar. When he brought his lamb in his arms and held it, that was the Jew's lamb; it was his and he had a right to it. When he laid it down by the altar with his hands on it, it was still his lamb, for he had claiming hands on it. But when he lifted his hands and left it on God's altar, he had nothing more to do with it. Make your consecration to God like that, and when you are laid on God's altar there will be no renunciation, save as Divine Providence shall interpret the impossibility through death or sickness or other providential considerations. In that spirit, called of God and utterly surrendered to God, you will do a work that shall be felt to the ends of the earth. And the reflexive influence of this work from you in distant lands, as you write with that spirit, and as you come home at proper times with that spirit, shall thrill the churches at home. And perhaps one of the greatest needs of the Missionary Boards to-day — which is money — will be met when men under that spirit shall speak from distant lands to the home churches, or shall return from distant lands to plead as only such men can plead. God bless you!

The Rev. Alexander Sutherland, D.D., of the Methodist Church of Canada, addressed the Convention on the same topic: —

A few minutes will suffice for what I wish to say just at this stage. Let me touch upon these two points.

First, who should apply? That has been partly dealt with. In the first place, only men and women that are in sound, vigorous health; and that for a very practical reason. As a rule, the foreign field takes you into a climate different from the one in which you are living, and the constitution that is enfeebled, the strength that is partly exhausted already, is very apt to go down, not only under the influence of the climate, but under the mental and spiritual strain that seems to be upon so many who go to the foreign field.

Then again, only those should make application who are so constrained by the love of Christ along this line of foreign missionary work that they see and feel that there is no other way open for them. We get a good many applications of various kinds, and a brief experience in the matter will enable one in receiving the application to read between the lines; and very often we find a good deal more between the lines than in the lines themselves. It is very easy to tell, when we get an application, whether the person making it is moved by the constraining love of Christ and a deep conviction of duty, or whether they are merely moved, as sometimes persons are moved, by a disposition to try an experiment, or moved perhaps by a little sentimental idea about the gentle heathen on the coral islands, and the cocoanuts, and all that sort of thing. And it is very important at such times to have men at the head of affairs who can deal promptly and decisively with that class of applications.

When we have these two things we have perhaps two of the essentials. The question has come up more than once with regard to this matter of educational qualification. As has been said to-day by one of the speakers, we are very thankful for all the advantages of the widest scholarship. But after all, let me say here, that is a secondary consideration. Some scholarship there must be, some educational acquirements must be possessed; and there must be a pretty thorough knowledge of the word of God and ability to teach its truths. But there has been two ways of training men with reference to missionary work — one to train them *for* the ministry, the other to train them *in* it. I think by the good providence of God we are getting about to the right point to-day, when we are seeking to combine both methods, and that we have the training *for* as well as the training *in*.

Now, then, with men and women of this stamp making application, what is the best mode of application? That might seem at first sight a very needless question to ask, and yet a good deal depends upon it; and I have known in the course of my experience applications rejected, and I have known applications accepted, where the turning point after all was the mode of application. Sometimes, for example, you will get an application, and you will feel the moment you read it, "This man's heart is not in it;" there will be some allusion to prospective income, or when he can come back to the country from which he goes, and a dozen questions of this kind, and you feel almost instantly that the salvation of souls is not the great moving power with that man — I will not say with that woman, because we never get such applications from women. Now, to whom is he going to make application? First of all, let me emphasize, to your Divine Master. Do not apply anywhere else until you have applied there and received an answer, and then the rest of the way will be clear enough.

Perhaps I can best illustrate by an incident. Twenty years ago or more a letter was published by a missionary who resided in British Columbia, describing the terrible destitution of the condition of the Indian tribes, and appealing to the young men at home, saying, "Is there any young man who will come and do something for the Indians on this coast?" That letter came under the eye of a young man in Ontario, a man of comparatively limited education, but of great spiritual earnestness and zeal. He first of all went to the Lord with the matter, and spread it before Him and said: "Lord, here I am ready, if I can do anything. Only open up the way for me to go." Some days after that he met an old friend of the family, and this old friend said to him: "What is the matter with you? You are looking rather downcast." And after a time he got it out of him: "I want to go to preach to the Indians in British Columbia." "Why don't you go?" "I have not the money to take me there." "That need not stop you. I will let you have the money. If you can ever pay it back, all right; if not, it is for the Lord's work anyway." He took the money and went. He did not apply to any Board, or say a word to anybody but the Lord and this one friend. He went out there, and the result has simply been that in the course of years he has become one of the most successful missionaries employed by the society; for it was not long before the society employed him.

A year ago or more I received two letters within the course of two or three weeks. In one of them a young man gave me his name, residence, and so on, and said he was a student at Toronto University in the department of civil engineering. While there this wonderful wave of missionary enthusiasm in connection with the college Movement reached him. It came with great power to his own mind; but he waited and watched and prayed until, in the calmness and quietness of afterthought, he was clearly convinced that it was a providential call. He immediately abandoned his professional studies, and went to a medical college in Chicago to qualify as a medical missionary. He offered himself first of all to the Church of his early association and choice, in which he had been converted, but intimated that if God opened the way he was going anyway. A week or two later I received another letter from a young man, written from the city of Kingston. The writer said: "I am a graduate in arts of Queens University, and also a graduate in medicine. My friend is a graduate in arts, and is now pursuing his theological course." He opened up his heart as to how they had felt for years this call to the foreign field, and now, they said: "We think we are about as far equipped as studies can prepare us. We offer ourselves first to the Church of our choice. If you can send us, we will go; if not, we will offer ourselves to the Lord in some other direction." In every case these young men said: "We are ready to go to any part of the world the Church desires to send us to. We would suggest, however, the hope that the Church would see its way clear to send us to one of the neglected provinces of China." These were model applications. Go they must, but their first offer is made to their own Church and Board: "If you can send us, we will be glad; if not, perhaps somebody else will." What is a volunteer good for if he is not ready to go wherever he is required? And so they were ready to go anywhere, but suggested the hope that they might be permitted to go to this grand field.

The Rev. H. N. Cobb, D.D., of the Board of Missions of the Reformed Church in America, then followed on the same topic: —

I am very much pleased, Mr. Chairman, to be asked to address you. I can only add my hearty amen to all that has been said in regard to the great pleasure and gratitude that I feel in the privilege of being in such a gathering as this. I want simply to make a single remark in reference to the hindrances which may come up. I was fearful that some here who have an unnecessarily low sense of their abilities might be somewhat discouraged in regard to the requirements for service in the foreign field.

It was stated that a man who cannot make an impression or secure a ready hearing in this country ought not to think of going abroad to preach the Gospel to the heathen. All that has been said about wanting the best men, about the work needing the best men that can be obtained, is absolutely true. But yet we believe that the Lord has a place for every man whose heart is moved, and whom the Spirit leads to offer himself for that service. I want to testify, as a missionary Secretary, that some of the most successful missionaries we have are men who are not successful to a very large extent in interesting audiences in this country. I have one in my mind at this moment, who is perhaps, with one exception, the most successful missionary we have in China, who is not heard with interest when he addresses audiences in this country. And I have another man in mind who has been one of the most successful developers and managers of one of our most successful educational institutions, of whom, when he spoke at a missionary convention in our church, one of the members of the Board heard some one in the audience behind him say, " What have the heathen done that that man should be sent to them." I only want to emphasize that when the Lord calls a man to go far hence unto the Gentiles, it is not so much a question of natural ability ; He knows what He is about when He says to a man, " Go here " or " Go there." And the design of this application spoken of is simply that those of the church upon whom the responsibility rests may be able to ascertain, so far as it is possible for man to ascertain, whether these men and women who present themselves are really God-moved or self-moved. And if we ascertain to our satisfaction that they are God-moved, then, if it is a possible thing, it is our duty to facilitate their way into the field.

The Rev. A. McLean, Secretary of the Foreign Christian Missionary Society, added the following words on the same subject : —

I agree with all that has been said about the best method of applying. But there is one thing that our Board does in addition to all that has been said this afternoon, and that is, we like to see the candidate ; we like to feel his pulse, to test his spirit, to see what he looks like ; and we like to |have him stay around the mission rooms for two or three days, that we may directly and personally learn as much as we can about him. We have found that a very good and profitable thing to do. Sometimes we can tell from a letter whether a man is worth inviting or not. If a man is inquiring simply for the money he wants to get out of the missionary work, we do not want him at all. If it is evident from his letter that he is a man of no scholarship or ability, we do not want him. But if we are satisfied from his recommendations that he is the right kind of man, he is invited.

We want the best. We cannot always get the best; there are not enough of the best to go around. We take a good average man if we can get him; a man with a good heart, a man with an average good mind — if we can get a man of that kind we are glad of it, and we feel very certain that a man of that sort will do great good in the mission field. I remember, when I was a child, seeing old Dr. Geddie, missionary to the New Hebrides. When he was examined as a candidate for the ministry, the examining Board said if he were going to the mission field they would allow him to pass, but if he were going to stay at home they would not. He was accepted, and went into the mission field and did a great work there. And when he died they wrote this simple epitaph over his grave: " When he came to us there were no Christians; when he left us there were no heathen." I think no grander epitaph was ever placed on any man's tomb than that of this man who came within a handsbreadth of being rejected when he sought entrance into the ministry of Jesus Christ.

Brethren, we want the best if we can get them, men worthy to stand before kings, men of great attainments; but we do not want to keep the bars that high in all cases. The average man who is willing to go, the man of consecration and good sense and good health, the man of tact and patience — that man, if he offers, we are glad to accept and send out into this great field, feeling certain that a man of that sort will be abundantly blessed of the Lord.

The Rev. George Scholl, D. D., Secretary of the Board of Foreign Missions of the Evangelical Lutheran Church, followed on the same topic : —

It seems to me, my friends, that it is the whole aim and scope of the Gospel to teach the privilege and possibility and duty of every follower of the Lord Jesus Christ to stand on the same high plane of Christian manhood on which He stood. Many of the qualifications that the brethren this afternoon have said are required for a foreign missionary are no less required for a teacher in the Sunday School in Cleveland, Ohio, who has half a dozen boys or girls to instruct. It seems to me that the time has come when we all are to preach the Gospel ; that not a few chosen ones here and there are to rise to great eminence in their qualifications and in the dedication of themselves to the Lord Jesus

Christ, but that the men who by their money are to send these young men to their work need to consecrate themselves also.

We have ten offers to every one that we are able to send. And it seems to me that these young men could inaugurate no greater movement, after they have consecrated themselves to the Lord Jesus Christ, than to go out among the churches, and go to men and women of wealth and say to them : " Here I am. I am ready to go. What can you do toward sending me ? " I wish we had more men like one we sent to India a year ago. He appeared before the Board and said, " I want to go to India." They said, " We have no money." He said, " I am going." " We cannot send you." " Give me the privilege," he said, " to go to the children of the Sunday Schools, and talk to them about it." They said, " You may try if you wish to." He went, and in a year he had money enough to support more than half a dozen missionaries. The children responded.

I believe in high mental qualifications. I know that in India the very keenest intellects are required to meet the subtle minds of the Hindoos, and especially of the Brahmins. But there are other places where a keen intellect is not the pre-eminent qualifications of a successful worker. Seventeen years ago a young man applied for work on the west coast of Africa. I was not directly connected with the Board at that time, but the brethren said something like this : it was not likely that he could get a church in this country, and he was about as good a subject for African fevers as any one else they might send. They felt that they were in desperate straits. It was a deadly climate, and they could not afford to send a first-class man. He is there yet, and there is not a man in our church talked, written, and prayed for as that man, and he is continually being lifted up on the prayers of the whole Church. More than one young man has said to me, " I would esteem it the greatest privilege of my life if I could be a laborer under him on the west coast of Africa."

The Lord knows the men He selects : let us try and put ourselves entirely under the Divine guidance — Secretaries, Boards, candidates, all of us together put ourselves under the Divine guidance. And then, perhaps, we are compelled to say, as the venerable Dr. Clarke of the American Board said to me : " Perhaps, after all we have done, the only way to decide on the fitness of a young man is to send him on trial." The Lord shows the way, and the Lord brings about wonderful results sometimes from what to us would seem a very little outgo.

Prof. H. H. Harris, of the Southern Baptist Convention, closed the discussion with the following remarks: —

In the first place, we have found, and I am sure it will always be true, that if God gives us the men and women, His people will supply the means to sustain them. . . Let us not wait for the money in order to appoint the men; but the best way in the world to stir up the churches and get the money is to appoint the men and women and send them out. It has been presented here to-day, that one who comes to a Board for appointment should be determined to go whether the Board will appoint him or not. I believe it. Furthermore, I believe he ought to feel so called from a higher source that he must go. And yet, I do know that the Board ought to sit in judgment on his qualifications, and ought to reject some applicants. I will give you a case. A young man came before the Board. He said: "I wish to go to Brazil. It has been on my heart; it has been laid on my conscience by the Spirit of the Lord. If you will send me I will be glad; if not, I am going anyhow. God has called me to that work." We sent him. In less than two years he was back again, and is now at home, a very earnest, active pastor. Now, I believe that God did not call him; I believe he was mistaken about it.

I will give you another case. Two men came before the Board very highly recommended, — men of fine qualifications. They were rejected. They are to-day among the most influential men in behalf of foreign missions in all that region of country. There are men — I beg to impress the thought — who are called of God to stay at home. There are men upon whom the burden of souls in foreign lands is laid, who are to be made interested in the work and to be informed on the work, and yet their duty is to stay at home and stir up the Church itself.

From four to five o'clock simultaneous meetings were held, at which the peculiar features of the various fields were discussed. As a rule these different meetings were attended by volunteers who have some particular field in view. The "Africa" meeting was conducted by Mr. I. N. Merrifield, of Morgan Park, Ill. The Rev. Geo. A. Wilder, Mr. C. J. Laffin, and Rev. and Mrs. E. B. Sage — all returned missionaries — spoke upon work in Africa.

The "China" meeting was conducted by Mr. W. H. Cossum, Traveling Secretary of Student Volunteer Movement for Foreign Missions. Revs. Geo. L. Mason, Jno. L. Nevius, D.D., Rev. and Mrs. F. A. Steven, Mrs. D. Z. Sheffield, and others, spoke upon work in China.

The "Japan" meeting was conducted by Mr. J. Campbell White, College Young Men's Christian Association Secretary. The Revs. Kajinosuke Ibuka and W. R. Lambeth, M.D., returned missionaries, discussed missionary problems in Japan, and answered questions put to them by volunteers.

The "Papal Lands" meeting was conducted by Rev. Alex. N. O'Brien. Revs. J. M. Allis and Geo. W. Chamberlain, D.D., spoke upon work in Papal Lands.

The "Turkish Empire" meeting was conducted by Mr. Robert Eliot Speer, of Princeton, N. J., who was aided by Rev. C. F. Gates and Mrs. Etta D. Marden.*

The "India" meeting was conducted by Mr. Robert P. Wilder, of New York City, who opened the hour by reading a passage from the the Book of Jonah. Mr. Wilder said: —

We wish to call your attention to those few verses from the first book in the Bible offering an opportunity for repentance to the heathen: "Arise, go to Nineveh, that great city, and cry against it." He (Jonah) rose up to flee from the command. I have often regretted the first foreign missionary taking that course, for his action has often since become contagious. "He rose to flee, and, finding a ship going to Tarshish, he went into it to flee from the presence of the Lord." You will notice the reason — Jonah hesitated to go to Nineveh lest it might repent. Many among us hesitate to enter the foreign service lest the work at home lose their support. There was a mighty tempest in the sea, and they cast forth the wares that were in the ship into the sea to lighten it of them; but Jonah was gone down into the sides of the ship, and he lay there fast asleep,— the only man who, in such a trial, could go fast asleep. And yet to-day in India scores of men and women are calling upon their God; and shall it be said that we are asleep and do not send the aid that is within our power? We must not do so: we must respond. "And the word of the Lord came unto Jonah the second time, saying, Arise, go unto Nineveh, that great city, and preach unto it the preaching that I bid thee." Just notice it was only one sentence. When God gives work for us to do, we should go and do that work. If God gives us work to do in India, if he tells us to go to India and do His work, if He tells us to do that work, to do the work there required, if He says to us "Go into India and preach the preaching I bid thee," then we should obey His command.

The remainder of the story is familiar to us all. Jonah went to Nineveh and cried out to the city, "Yet forty days and Nineveh shall be overthrown." The people repented and the judgment was stayed.

---

* We regret that lack of space forbids the insertion of full reports of all the Simultaneous Meetings, as they formed an important and instructive feature of the Convention.— *Editors.*

Rev. Henry Forman addressed the audience upon —

THE EDUCATIONAL PHASE OF MISSIONARY WORK.

I am asked to speak five minutes on the subject mentioned. It is a subject upon which a great deal can be said. First among the people of India are the Hindoos and Mohammedans: they comprise the vast majority; while from all branches of these we must take the native Christians, — that is, we must educate them to become Christians. And why must we do this? Now, there are Hindoos and Mohammedans both which will never become Christians unless we do educate them. Is it not fitting they should be educated, and by us? It is a problem for solution whether we shall educate them or they shall be educated by the government. The people of India are to be educated. The English government has pledged itself to that, and is securing for them larger facilities than are to be obtained in any other way; and, if educated by the government, they must be educated in neutral schools, and that means "not for us, but against us." It may not be theoretically so, yet it is practically so. Neutrality in their education means infidelity or non-Christianity; and, if a man is Buddhist, Hindoo, or Mahommedan, then his mouth may be opened, but, if he be an earnest lover of Christianity, his mouth is shut. Again, taking the anti-Christian schools, unless we want those young men growing up with various creeds, — unless we want them to be infidels even, — we must go on with our school work.

Education in our schools is carried on in all the different grades. There are not only high schools, but we carry men up to the A.B. and to the A.M. degrees; and these degrees are worth just as much as they are in our country or in the colleges and universities of Europe. Then, again, there are many schools from which boys go on through the common grades and prepare for the colleges; and that curriculum of study means a ten years' course. In Allahabad there are 350 boys thus preparing in the schools, in Lahore 850, and in other cities of India a proportionate number in these high schools.

Then we have the lower vernacular schools, in which no English at all is taught. In these there are 600 boys in Lahore alone. We use every means to carry this work forward. All denominations are engaged in this commendable work. The English Baptists and the Presbyterians are very zealous in carrying this good work forward. Now there is a great call for teachers for this work; it may be made most interesting. Robert Nevins has just sent a letter urging for teachers, offering to give them a house and 115 rupees, almost $60; and the school or mission may be made safer, as the salary is increased by an income from the school. Now we need these teachers. We need some men of high attainments able to carry the young men up to every degree — we have a call for such teachers. I do not know if teachers will be sent out at once. We need to bring these young men under our influence. The teachers can get more influence over them than the preachers, if preaching alone. They can influence them wholly.

And now, just a word to our teachers in the work among the Hindoos only. There are the schools for the women in the zenanas, where only girls and women are taught. Now we need young women very much in these. The appeal for these is greater than I can state it to you — multiply it by one hundred and you will realize something of its great need.

Mrs. Capron then spoke as follows: —

I am sure that any lady desiring a larger sphere than she has followed in this country will find it in India and in the responsibility attached to the instruction of the women of India. I believe the women of India are sympathetic and intelligent. I believe, when they are once alive to another life, to the life of the Christians, they will cast away all their old superstitions. To this end all our education tends — the education of the young girls in the schools, in the houses, talking with their mothers, their aunts and sisters; all these gathered together, and the Lord Jesus looking down upon them and upon our work to bless it. We are just waiting until all shall be ready, and then one and another, and another still, will lead the life of the Christian. From Cape Cormorin, in 1856, the work began, and it still progresses. In India all the ladies work among the women and the girls, and the work is most inspiring. What a wonderful sphere of labor this is! Another thing, I used often to say, "We love these women of India, giving our lives for them." Nothing moves them so much as to see us going from this country to aid them, Jesus helping us. It was very interesting to me on one occasion when I heard a Hindoo woman say to her daughter, — this woman you call a heathen, but I do not like that name, — in reference to another missionary, "The talk is different, but the meaning is the same." And that responsive heart of that Hindoo woman recognized the fact of the bond of love between us, and knew that we "meant the same."

Question. Has woman's work broken down the caste in India?

Answer. (Mrs. Capron). Women's work will break it down just so far and fast as the love for Christianity comes into the work. Yes; I think so. I have often been amused at the way that one of our missionaries — one of our Bible women — described the visit she paid to a house: she sat on one side of the room on one mat, and the other woman on the other side of the room on another mat; but after a while the two sat on the one mat, which means a great deal.

Q. Do you find the women eager to learn?

A. (Mrs. Capron). I think the young girls have been very eager to learn, and consequently the mothers and aunts, finding the young folks have learned these things, they have talked together and felt they could not be left in the distance; and, once having begun with us, they have never yet said to us, " We have heard enough." They read the Bible. One thousand women in Madras were learning to read; and I never knew one to lay down the Bible and say, " Oh, yes; we are educated." Yes; they are eager to learn.

Q. I would like to learn how lady physicians are received.

A. (Mrs. Capron). There is a wonderful sphere in India for lady physicians. I do not know how you can reach so great a number of women as in that way. This being shut up all night in the house and having numbers of women about you brings you in the closest contact with them. I have sat whole nights and talked with them of nothing but the wonderful things of the Lord. We always reach the heart through suffering, which suggests His suffering, which was greater than physical agony.

Q. Was there as much prejudice and conceit among the women of India as among the men?

A. (Mrs. Capron). I should say quite as much, if we take into consideration all things. I think, there is a strong superstition, I think it hardly worth the name of prejudice; but this is passing away, as other generations are now coming on; and, when a young man about to be married asks for a Bible to present to his bride because his mother had had one and it made her so good and gentle, I should call that doing away with prejudice.

Chairman : —

Let me state a short instance upon that point. I think, if Mrs. Capron had not been a woman, she might have said that women are more prejudiced than men. They are in general far more faithful to their religion than men are. Just one instance has come to my mind, which I will narrate. One of our missionaries had a baptismal service, and a native wanted to be baptized. The native said his wife was not ready and would not be baptized then, but that he would. He said his wife was outside and would not come in. The missionary looked for the wife and found her outside, looking in the window. At first she would not come in; finally she consented to do so. She held a baby in her arms, which she said she was going to keep on her side, and which she would not allow to be baptized. He wanted her to come in and sit while the services were going on, which she finally did. Then he asked her if she would allow him to baptize the baby; and at last she consented to this. Then he said to her, "Won't you hold the baby while I baptize it, that it may not cry." She finally agreed to this. And then he went on with the other exercises: he baptized the father and the older children. Then he at last asked her if she would not allow him to baptize her, and she cried out, "Yes; I must be baptized, too; I cannot help it."

Mrs. Jennie Fuller, of Akola, India, made the following address:—

A few years ago we had a refuge for girls. We undertook to have one for boys also on the same plan. With God to help us, we went on and established a shop containing carpenter and shoemaking departments. All the influential Brahmins opposed it, on the ground that the different castes of boys would prevent their working together, and that it would not succeed. But we went on; and after a while we had two high-caste boys both shoemaking. God has wonderfully prospered us. In the two years we have been carrying this on we have gathered twenty-four boys, and nine of that number are engaged in making shoes. We did add a tailor, but that was not a success. There was one boy's mat, and we had to cut that mat in two, as no two Hindoo boys would sit on the same mat, but after a while all sat there together in peace.

The shoemaking department has become self-supporting. It has earned wages, and does a good repairing business; and we have a good custom among the English people.

The carpentering work has been slower, as they find it hard to learn the use of the plane and to handle tools well enough to ensure success as yet. I hope it may be self-supporting.

We had one lay brother with us from Dakota who knew four trades. He also teaches blacksmithing. That, together with the additional trades he knows, leads him to hope to establish a good business outside,— an independent business,— and form a sort of industrial center, so that, when the boys who have learned these trades marry, they may be able to support themselves, by working at these trades, entirely through their own resources.

Question. Is the industrial phase on the whole a success?

Answer. I believe the industrial work on the whole has not yet proved a success; but the American Board is making a strenuous effort in that direction, and has already established an industrial plant at Sirur, and proposes to have similar plants in Northern India. Last week Cawnpore followed by having industrial work inaugurated there.

Dr. Graham : —

I never studied medicine, but when I went to my last field of labor, which was some thirty miles from Cawnpore, the natives came to me and asked me to give them medicine ; and one can always do that, to a certain extent, provided he is supplied with a few simple medicines which will enable him to carry on this necessary practice. If you have a bottle of quinine, some sulphur, a few bilious pills, and some other very simple remedies, you can get a great reputation — such a reputation as any doctor in America would be very proud of. I began practicing medicine on men needing very simple remedies, and the few cases were successfully treated, and the persons were cured. The result was that, inside of one month, I had men coming to me with every manner of disease. All these wanted treatment. I had to tell them I had received no training as a physician. That made no difference. I was expected to give treatment just the same. There was one case that I shall never forget. A man came to me and said, " You have treated so-and-so, and I want you to give me some medicine." I said to him: " Now, if I should tell you that I could give you medicine and cure you, and that I know how to do so, I would not be telling you the truth. I never studied medicine, and I cannot give you this medicine that you want." But he still persisted that I could; but I did not, and I left him. But he would not and did not go home ; and when night drew on he was still there, imploring me for medicine. At last he said: " Give me medicine or kill me. I want medicine from you."

Most of the natives of India have more confidence in physicians from Christian countries, especially missionaries, than anybody else. They will take it from such with more confidence, because they think there is more merit in the person giving it. This has been my experience. A year and a half ago a medical missionary was sent there. Of course, not speaking the language, he was unable to have any dealings with the natives, and so I was with him in his work. In a short time he had so many people coming to him that from morning till night he was busied with them.

I remember the first surgical operation he performed. It was upon a Mohammedan. This Mohammedan had a tumor in his side and wanted it removed. In India, especially in our part of the country, there is a great aversion to the use of the knife. This man at last consented to an operation. I sat by him ; and I did pray most earnestly that it might prove a success, for I knew if the physician failed it would injure his work permanently, and that all future work would receive a damper in India among the natives. As he went under the anesthetic he began to rave and cry out. His brother said, " That is enough;

we will stop." But a friend who was with them urged him to go on. He did; and the operation was successful. I never saw a more grateful man than he was. He never met either of us afterwards without showering thanks upon us.

I remember the second operation that was performed. It was for a Brahmin, and was also successful. A very nice little note was sent, with a fee for the services. The fee was not very large, but it was very fair to be received from a native. But I shall never forget the words of that letter. He said, "Accept this as an expression of gratitude, and I will make up the rest in prayers." It is in this way that the missionary goes everywhere into the families and homes of the natives; otherwise it would be impossible to enter the homes. Good men and good women with a knowledge of medicine can find an entrance into the homes of India as no others can. The natives will avail themselves of his medical knowledge, which they feel certain a medical missionary possesses.

I have just lately heard from Dr. Wanless and his wife, who were the first volunteers I ever saw. When I heard of the volunteer Movement in America, for some time I felt grave doubts about it. I thought too much was expected of such a movement; and, in a certain sense I was not prepared to comprehend it until we received three of them to our own number. I saw at once that they were moved by the Spirit of God. And what we need in India is a great outpouring of that Spirit. The field is ready for the harvest: it only rests with the reapers to do their share towards the great work. We need God's Spirit to bless it.

In the station where Dr. Wanless and his wife has been he has had 4,642 patients, and during the last year he has had over 10,000 visits from these persons. If he had had the strength he could have multiplied this number. Any man receiving his benefit will come to him again for help. I believe there is no medical missionary north of Dr. Wanless for 150 miles, to the east for 450, none on the south until you reach the territory crossing the Ghauts. There is plenty of room there for medical work.

I will state that while the government dispensaries will give them medicine freely, yet the natives are afraid of them, and can hardly be got to go to them; but they will gladly go to a missionary, because he does this good work for affection, and the government servants take compensation for this business from the government. So the government work does not touch ours.

Mr. J. P. Jones spoke as follows : —

We have gone very extensively in Madras into medical work, not neglecting the educational part, which we believe of great importance. We believe, however, that the evangelical work should precede, and the educational should follow not far off. We have gone more into evangelism than into the other; and we find, as we go from village to village and from town to town, that we reach a great number of people. We have now an agency which does this work. Our work is more entirely in superintendence. We have 445 or 448 agents working with us or under our superintendence. We start off a missionary who will go from twenty to forty miles in a day, taking with him eight or ten of our best native preachers, and they will preach in from ten to thirty villages in a day, meeting from twenty to forty thousand people in a day sometimes. Sometimes they will, perhaps, spend from eight to ten days right in the villages among the people in their houses or homes. There will not be any immediate conversions; but we see that the seed is sown, and it will spring up in time. We find now as never before a readiness to listen. Their minds are quickened: they now compare religions and notice the distinctions. Formerly they did not do that. Now we find that the people sometimes oppose us. I have seen a man standing on the opposite side of the street from where I had gathered a crowd, and he has tried to oppose my preaching; and he has begun to call out in the native tongue a name for Krishna, so that I had to give up our meeting and go away. We have changed our tactics, and in this evangelical work we now do differently. We have now ceased that contradictory method; we do not abuse heathenism, we do not attack Hindooism. I find all over that land so many distracting agencies at work — civilization, education, that is, Western education — all these at work in the minds of the people. We try to present religion in another way; and there is less opposition where we do not attack their faith, and we find it lessening here. There seems to be a right mind to receive a good deal of the truth if properly presented.

In the city of Madras I have four parties in four different places each Monday evening. If you could meet with me in my large room you would see some twenty-five men, mostly young men, who are teachers in our high school, catechists, and preachers. We dwell on the subject given out at the beginning of the month. I ask this or that man what he thinks about this subject, and each gives his idea; and so we have an interchange of thought. We have prayer and singing, and then we part. The following evening we meet and begin with singing. Then another party meets in the beautiful schoolhouse which Mrs. Capron built in Madras; and another party, and still another, meets in the boys' schools at the south gate of the city. And they begin to sing their hymns; the people commence to gather. Five minutes are devoted to singing; then five minutes to speaking; then five minutes to the beautiful lyrics. And so it continues: five or six minutes to preaching, and the same period of time to singing; and the addresses are full of life and vigor. And so we proceed in this way to reach the hearts of the people, by this vigorous method. There are other schools for the means of reaching the boys and girls through the Bible women. In all these departments we are doing grand work in building a solid foundation for the Lord in that place.

The Sunday School work in India presents one of the grandest themes for evangelistic work. I would speak of this in addition to what our brother said yesterday of preaching to 100,000 children in India in the Sunday Schools. In India there are 75,000,000 children between five and fifteen years of age, and one of the most beautiful things about this is that we can have just as many Sunday Schools as we can get teachers to teach them. We have so many in the little towns where I go and work that we have these Sunday Schools through the week. We can get room to hold them all, for we can find plenty of trees under which to sit down. There is a great door open to us all over India. It was something a few years ago that we did not think possible. We can gather the children into the fold: it is the children we must strive to impress particularly. There is a little incident I recall to mind, and which impressed me deeply. An old man said one day, when his friends were chiding him for talking to me, and were asking him, "Are you going to be a Christian?"— the old man replied sadly, "They do not want old people like me; they want the children and the young people."

This is a vast field for Sunday School work. Teachers can teach in English. On Christmas Day and other Christian festivals we make much of the occasion, and gather all the children we can. We have hundreds in our yard sitting around. The Bible reading and Sunday School supplement the educational work; and this is one of the most important things we have to consider. And I pray every day of my life for the children of India.

Evening Session.

In the devotional exercises, the Rev. D. C. Rankin, Secretary of Foreign Missions of the Presbyterian Church South, offered prayer, and the Rev. A. J. Gordon, D. D., made the following remarks:—

Dear brethren, I confess that I withdraw from this Convention with sincere reluctance. I have been exceedingly profited and stirred by what I have been permitted to hear to-day. What I have to say will be in the form of two or three practical exhortations.

What is our greatest need? First of all, we need more missionary pastors. If all pastors were missionary pastors we should have all the missionary money that we need. I almost wished I could have heard words this afternoon, not simply for the great, the strong, the highly endowed, but a few words to those whose powers and attainments were of a humbler sort. It is not simply the man, but the spirit and purpose of the man, that determines what the ministry of Jesus Christ shall accomplish. I believe that a small minister with a great Gospel can accomplish more than a great minister with a small Gospel. Let every pastor, whatever his sphere, his attainments, his surroundings, make it his first business to use his church for a missionary church, and I believe God will bless that church. Pastor Harms, with his ten thousand gathered into that one church, and he not a great man, is just a living illustration for all time of what God will do for a pastor and a a people when they make missions their first business.

I say, secondly, we need more missionary churches. Yea, I say that we need missionary churches for the purpose of perpetuating those churches and preventing them from dying out. A church that ceases to be a missionary church will very soon become a missing church. I live in a city of extinct volcanoes, as somebody has said, — of churches that have burned out. The names and organizations are there, but for years the power has been gone. And if you ask why, you find out that simply because these churches became self-centered and occupied themselves with attending to their own affairs, building up their spiritual life, and forgetting that it was their great mission to give the Gospel to the world, — so ceasing to be evangelistic they have ceased to be evangelical.

The life of the church depends upon its being a missionary church. I believe to-day that if those eminent theologians who lived upon the coast of Africa, and who wrote so grandly upon theological themes, — men, like Augustine, and Cyprian, and Tertullian, — had made it their business to carry the Gospel into Central Africa with all the zeal and earnestness they gave to settling theological problems, Africa to-day, instead of being the Dark Continent, might have been the Light Continent, and instead of containing the open sore of the world, might have had planted in it the tree of life, whose leaves are for the healing of the nations. I believe that the Gospel died out in Africa from the fact that these men gave themselves to theological speculation instead of to the great purpose for which they were appointed of evangelizing the world.

And now, just a word to those whose hearts burn within them to preach the Gospel in the regions beyond. Let us understand what our commission is. Pardon me if I say I do not believe our commission is to bring the world to Christ, but to bring Christ to the world. What is the difference, you say? You will find that to lift the world is a great lift; but if you get hold of Jesus Christ, that is a different matter. You have Him with you always; and when you carry Him to the world, instead of carrying Him, He carries you. "Take my yoke upon you," said Christ, and some one has said, "it shall become as wings to a bird, and as sails to a ship." God will take care that the world is brought to Christ, if we will carry Christ to the world.

Supposing I touch just a moment upon another point, about which there may be some controversy. I say, it is our business to preach the Gospel in all the world, among all nations. "Ah, that is superficial!" you say. But is it? Are not we perfectly agreed that there is going to be a great outpouring of God's Spirit upon all flesh? "And it shall come to pass afterward that I will pour out my Spirit upon all flesh." God maintains vessels to contain His Spirit and distribute it. What did Jesus Christ say about the Holy Spirit? "Whom the world cannot receive, because it seeth him not, neither knoweth him. But ye know him, because he dwelleth with you and shall be in you." God wants us to do just what Jesus commanded us to do — to preach the Gospel in all nations for a witness. And when the great outpouring comes there will be all over the world these vessels that will take it up and distribute it among those yet unsaved. Literally, He will pour out His Spirit. O, the blessedness of doing this work for Christ, and in that work being thus intimately linked with Him who was the first great missionary! When Dr. Pierson and I were in Scotland I came upon something one day that startled me. It was that little white stone, in Melrose Castle, on which was written the simple inscription, "The Heart of Bruce." And instantly it came to me what that meant. You know the heart of Bruce was taken out by his request. He said: "When I am dead, take out my heart. Let my successor, when he goes into battle, carry this heart fastened with a chain about his neck, that you may understand when you are fighting that Bruce is still with you." And so his successor carried the heart of the great warrior into battle; and one day when they were beginning to break ranks and scatter he took out the heart of Bruce and swung it into the ranks of the enemy and said, "Go forth, heart of Bruce; we will follow thee or die." And they routed the enemy. So Jesus Christ has thrown His heart into the world, and we go after it. Is there any sublimer or higher honor than to be a missionary of Jesus Christ?

And now let us think, just in a word, what our joy is in that great commission. Let us remember, first of all, that God has not simply a select body that shall be preachers and another body to be hearers, and a select body to be missionaries and another body to be the objects of the labor of these missionaries; but he has made all to be kings and priests, and all of us to be missionaries. Jesus says to every sinner, "Come," and he says to every Christian, "Go," without distinction. I believe in the universal offer of the Gospel; therefore he says to every sinner, "Come." And I believe in the universal priesthood of every Christian. "Come, see the place where the Lord lay." "Go quickly and tell His disciples that He is risen from the dead." We cannot go until we come, and after we have come, if we have the Spirit of Christ, we cannot help going. Think of our resources, our endowment! What is it? "All power in heaven and in earth." What is our field? The world: "Go ye into all the world." And what is our testimony? All the Gospel: "Teaching them to observe all things whatsoever I have commanded." And what is our consecrated inheritance of time? "Lo, I am with you every day" — "all the days," according to the Revised Version; not simply speaking of time in an abstract way, but all the days, — the cloudy days, the bright days, — "I am with you all the days, unto the end of the world." And may God help us to be out and out for Him, and help us to remember that it is not in the greatness of our numbers but in the greatness of our consecration.

In a burst of passion and eloquence, in which there was condensed wonderful wisdom, John Wesley said on one occasion, "Give me one hundred men — I ask for no more — who know nothing but Jesus Christ, who hate nothing but sin, and are determined to know nothing among men but Jesus Christ and him crucified, and with that one hundred men, who know nothing else than preaching Christ, I will set the world on fire." May God give us so much of the Spirit that we ourselves shall be worthy to be counted into that triumphant hundred, and may God pour out his Spirit marvelously upon these young men; and may he so fill you with the Holy Ghost that when you go forth to your fields you shall know what it is to labor in the power of the Spirit, so that your toil will be triumph and your very defeats victory.

I was looking over this great company this afternoon, wondering what would be the history of these young men and women. There is one thing, dear friends, that I have to say — that it does not matter what our history is if we are consecrated to the Lord Jesus Christ. That is one of the joys of missionary service, that our reward does not depend upon success. The Master does not say, "Well done, good and successful servant," but "Well done, good and faithful servant." There is a beautiful face, so much so that if you have once seen it you will never forget it, that of the young man who is called the pioneer missionary of the Congo, Adam McCall. He went forth in the vigor of young manhood to preach the Gospel on the Congo, and died, and when dying said, what ought never to be forgotton: "Lord Jesus, I consecrated my life to preach the Gospel to these poor Africans, but if it has pleased Thee to take me instead of the service which I proposed and promised to render, what is that to me? Thy will be done." May God help us so to be in the will of God that nothing can defeat us, daunt us, or discourage us.

The Chairman read a telegram of greeting from the New Jersey State Convention of the Young Men's Christian Association, after which Mr. Robert E. Speer made the first address of the evening on the topic —

The Evangelization of the World in the Present Generation — a Possibility.

One of the singular things is the power that can be centered in a catch-word. There have been great political crises turned by some clever phrase that gathered up into itself the passions of human hearts and swept along with it the deep tides of human action. There has been more than one time in history when some few words aptly phrased did great things for or against God. And it is only an illustration of the better side of this truth that in the day in which we are living this watchword, about which we are to think and speak to-night, has gathered up into it the devotion of a great many hearts who follow the banner of Jesus Christ — *The Evangelization of the World in this Generation.*

I am to speak this evening upon the possibility of this evangelization, and it seems to me of the very greatest importance that at the outset you and I especially, my fellow students, should know what we mean when we speak of the evangelization of the world. We do not mean the *conversion* of the world. However much or little it may be in God's purpose to win this world unto Himself; however many souls He may be gathering out of each foreign field to Himself; and however much it may be our effort to win individual souls to Jesus Christ, — we do not take as the watchword of this Movement the conversion of the world in this generation. If that phrase means anything at all, it means the conversion of all the individuals in the world, and with conversion in itself you and I have absolutely nothing to do. So I think you may take it at the outset that when we speak of the possibility of the evangelization of the world in this generation, we are not to be misunderstood as implying the conversion of the world.

Nor, in the second place, do I think that any of the student volunteers mean the *Christianization* of the world. Many times we are told, in this day, that the end of missionary work is to carry the civilization of our land into every heathen land; and I am sure that we believe that that is the result of missionary work, and that it can be obtained in no other way than by missionary work. But the Christianization of the world and the civilization of the world are not the ambitions of the Student Volunteer Movement, and no intelligent volunteer seeks to claim that the watchword of this Movement means either the Christianization or the civilization of the world in this generation. We do mean, however, that every intelligent, thoughtful, sincere volunteer believes in and prays for the evangelization of the world before we die, and by that simple phrase is meant simply this: the presenting of the Gospel in such a manner to every soul in this world that the responsibility for what is done with it shall no longer rest upon the Christian Church, or on any individual Christian, but shall rest on each man's head for himself.

Now, sometimes we are told that this takes away a great deal of the dignity from the missionary purpose. But if this is the purpose which our Lord Jesus set in his Book for the missionary work of the Church in the world, I think we may well afford to have any dignity taken away that does not attach to the conception of missionary work that Christ had. And yet it is not a very narrow thing when we take into consideration the millions in the dark forests of Africa, the millions more on the plains and in the mountains of Asia, and the millions more in the other darknesses of this world, who have never yet seen the face of any one who knew the Lord Jesus.

May we make just this observation as we pass. Will you notice what an advantage this conception of our work gives us as we face those who make the objection that there is work enough to do at home? Under this conception of the work of the Church, this land, Great Britain, and some other Christian lands have been practically evangelized already; and as long as our work is evangelization merely, these lands, however great their need may be in our eyes, have, comparatively speaking, generally lost their claims upon us. Let me say yet once more that, however much this conception of missionary work may be bound up with the convictions you may have as to the time of our Lord's return, and however impossible it may be to gather together into one those parties that believe different things about the time of Christ's coming, there is no excuse whatever for transferring the disadvantages of the incompatibility of those two views to these conceptions of missionary work. The man who believes in the evangelization of the world does not necessarily lose sympathy with all efforts for establishing colleges, or for making the work permanent. It is largely a matter of emphasis. The man who wishes to evangelize the world will certainly do that other kind of work too, because he wants to make his evangelization permanent; and the man who does that other kind of work will certainly do evangelistic work, because it is the only way by which he can do that other work. So you need not jump to the conclusion that there is opposition between the purpose of this work and that of those who have more permanent and institutional views of missionary effort.

One thing more before we face the question of possibility. Our position on the question of possibility will be largely determined by our views of its desirability. If we do not think we want the world evangelized, we will not have to search far before we find it impossible to evangelize it. But if to-night, face to face with our glorified Master, we catch His Spirit, hear His word, and are willing to do His will, and will open our hearts a little to catch that other cry that comes across the seas to-night from every heathen land, I do not think we can refrain from brushing away a great many objections to the possibility of the evangelization of the world in this generation that may now confront our view.

In the first place, then, the evangelization of the world in this generation is a possibility, so far as the *world* is concerned. There is nothing in this wide world apart from the Church and the Head of the Church that renders it in the slightest manner an impossible thing to evangelize the world in this generation.

A hundred years ago it might not have been so; but what a contrast between that day and now! Many, many lands then not open to the gospel; and now — with perhaps one or two exceptions, and the doors of those probably pretty soon to be thrown open to the Christian Church — not a land in which we may not go and preach the glad tidings of Jesus Christ. One hundred years ago the Bible was accessible, so far so the human languages in which it was printed were concerned, to only one-fifth of the human race; now it is printed in over three hundred tongues, and spoken by over nine-tenths of the population of the whole world. A hundred years ago not a missionary vessel steamed in any waters. In the vast majority of heathen lands a Christian man's face was never seen. But to-day the Christian Church stands, so far as the open door is concerned in the world, at the Kadesh Barnea of the ages. The promised land is in full view before her, and the Lord of Hosts is giving the command to every man to go up straight before him and take possession.

There is no difficulty with regard to the foreign field, so far as the acceptance and understanding of the Gospel on the part of the heathen are concerned. If one thing has been demonstrated more clearly than anything else it is, that the fact which Mark records, that the common people heard Jesus gladly, is true to-day; because, in the heathen lands no less than in this land, all men are competent to understand, and poor and degraded men are specially ready to accept, the Gospel of Jesus Christ. I know we are sometimes told that a Gospel from which we have taken all things that are miraculous, but which after that wonderful subtraction still has God in it, is the best Gospel we can take to the heathen world. But this is not the Gospel that has won the greatest triumphs this world has ever seen; nor is it the Gospel that is to evangelize the world before your eyes and mine close in death.

There is no impossibility suggested by the Church's ignorance of the world's need. There never was a time when the need in all the world was so clear, so impressive, and so well known to the Christian Church. Nor is there any impossibility, so far as this world is concerned, in the supposed unreadiness or unwillingness of the heathen to accept the Gospel. We have already heard more than one instance cited in this Convention of men in the foreign field who seemed to have been already touched by the Holy Spirit to accept that Gospel when it came. He, whose Church was to embrace people out of every nation and kindred and people and tongue, hath not left Himself without some in every place who will respond to the Gospel of the King when it is brought by the ambassadors of the King's Son. So that, in the first place, there is nothing in the world to render impossible the evangelization of the world in this generation. It may be that sometimes we think the heathen faiths stand like impassable barriers before us. I suppose the missionaries here to-night would say that all the heathen faiths of which they know anything at all are crumbling away. Whatever the influences may be that are undermining them, still the great power of the King is shaping events for the coming of those who shall do greater things than even Jesus Himself did, in the years that are very shortly to come.

2. In the second place, the evangelization of the world in this generation is possible so far as the *Church* is concerned. In the first place, the Church has the agencies. There was a list made out just a little while ago in which it was shown there were something like a hundred missionary societies in this country. We might increase it by a large number of missionary societies in other lands. There never was a time when missionary methods were so well developed as now, when so much priceless experience, bought often with blood, had been gathered, and so much knowledge of missionary lands amassed as to-day and when all the machinery — if any machinery were necessary — seemed so ready to the hands of Christian men.

In the second place, the Church has the agents ready. There are 10,000,000 Protestant Christians in this land. Ought not 10,000,000 Protestant Christians to be able to preach the Gospel inside of 30 years — the length of an ordinary generation — to a population a hundred times that number? We had out of every 77 ministers, until the last few years, only one going into the foreign field; out of every 5,000 Christian men only one entering the foreign work, and only one in 2,500 Christian women.

Coming on the train from Pittsburg the other day was a young doctor who was not a Christian. He asked us where we were going. We said we were coming up to Cleveland to a missionary convention. "How are you able to give so much attention to the work abroad? how is it that the Church wastes so much energy on the work abroad," he asked, "when there is so much to be done in this land of ours?" I asked him what he would consider a fair proportion of workers to keep in this land and a fair proportion to send abroad. He said, " I suppose two-thirds here and one-third abroad would be treating ourselves fairly." If we sent one-third of our workers abroad and kept the other two-thirds at home, we would more than ten-fold multiply the ordained missionaries in the heathen fields from all the Christian nations in the world, and would send 400,000 lay workers out into the foreign world, if we did what an unbelieving doctor said would be only a fair proportion to do with reference to this work. Would it not be possible, if 400,000 missionaries went out in the next twenty-five years, each one of them having out of the thousand million unevangelized people in this world only 2,500 to reach, who could be reached by speaking to only one a day for about eight years, to evangelize this world thoroughly before we die? I know it means a mightier consecration than the world has ever yet seen; but the consecration can come when we are willing.

The Church, so far as educated men are concerned, has more than enough to evangelize the world before we die. Just the other evening reference was made to the 2,000,000 young men who will graduate from the higher institutions of learning, in this land, in this generation. If one out of every hundred of them should go 20,000 would be sent into the foreign field. 20,000 men would be one to every 50,000 people in the heathen world. In a generation, one missionary from this land, if supplied with the necessary means and with native helpers, could, without difficulty, have the gospel preached, and preached effectually, to every one of those 50,000 souls.

In the third place, the Church of Jesus Christ has the means. I put it very low when I say that the wealth in the hands of Christian people in this land is not less than $12,000,000,000. To that sum every year, over and above all money spent for luxuries or given for benevolent purposes, or used in any other way, the Christian Church adds $500,000,000. Now, mark you, out of this $12,000,000,000, and this added increase of $500,000,000 a year, we give about $5,000,000, perhaps a little over, to home and foreign missions put together.

$5,000,000 is one twenty-fifth of one per cent. of the wealth of the Christian Church in this land, and only one per cent. of the money that is clear gain every year in the coffers of Christian people in this land. He asked for one-tenth of our wealth, — for the tenth, at least, of our income every year, — and we give Him only one per cent. of the amount of money we save over and above all expenses of every other kind. And this is for the Lord Himself, who owns every penny of the silver and the gold that you and I may ever hope to touch.

Will you notice what we could give if we would? Suppose we gave one-fiftieth of our savings every year, it would more than suffice to send out 10,000 missionaries. Suppose we gave a tithe merely of the money that we add each year to our wealth, it would suffice to send out into the foreign field 50,000 more missionaries. If the Protestant Christians of the world would give a penny a day each, it would amount to over $100,000,000 every year; and if they gave eight cents a day, it would more than suffice to send out those 400,000 missionaries, which even a skeptical man says the Church ought to thrust forth immediately into the dark places of this world.

Sometimes we say we are far beyond the position of our fathers. We have not yet approximated to the place our fathers held. We give just one-half as many mills on the dollar to-day as they gave in 1840. We may give more money, but in the sight of Him who looks, and sees not only the gift but the motive and the proportion of it, it is only one-half as much according to our ability as we gave fifty years ago. We contrast it with other things, and say we are giving bountifully. Do you know that if we added up all the money we have given for the evangelization of the world since the beginning of this century, it would not amount to more than $75,000,000, — less, by far, than the drink bill of this nation for thirty days. And, facing all these things too, we have to remember lastly, as touching the means in our power, that the Church of God in this land has money enough buried in rings, jewelry, and useless ornaments, in gold and luxuries that we might easily dispense with, to thrust forth missionaries sufficient to cover every field in this world more completely than even the most sanguine missionary has ever dared to pray for; to print the Bible in such abundance that it might be flung broadcast over the world; and, within fifteen years, to flash the Gospel light around the world.

I speak of only one thing more as touching the ability of the Church, and that is its power of prayer. Never, in all the history of the world, has the Church crossed the threshold of its privileges in prayer. Never, up to this very day, have we been spiritually and wisely selfish enough to lay hold on that might of God which He offers to us if we would only be faithful enough to draw on Him.

I pause to say that if this were a human issue there would be no doubt of its possibility. When we remember that each year Europe maintains in standing armies three hundred and thirty-three times as many men and spends nine hundred times as much money as the cause of foreign missions obtains, we are sure that if this work of evangelization were a military or worldly movement, men and money would be poured out in bountiful abundance to accomplish it speedily. Wars and financial crises demand and secure unlimited sacrifices. The last great war between England and France cost $4,000,000,000. The costs of our civil war were immensely more than enough to evangelize the world, so far as money is concerned in the problem. The recent Baring failure illustrated how quickly millions of pounds could be raised to save a banking house. Is not the question of the world's evangelization of far more transcendent importance? Shall we value men's sovereigns more than their souls? If this were a task set before some human government, the question of its feasibility would not be raised.

It is said that the census of London is taken in one day. The statement of the theme this evening allows over 10,000 days to evangelize the world. I remind you of the remark of the English soldier, who replied, when a proclamation was put in his hands with the question, "How long would it take you with all the forces of England at your disposal to give this proclamation to every soul in the world?" "I think we could manage it in about eighteen months." *Eighteen months!* And he was the subject of a human sovereign, thinking of a human issue.

3. But this is not a human issue. God is in it. I have said that there is nothing in the world or the Church, except its disobedience, to render the evangelization of the world in this generation an impossibility ; and now, in the third place, it is possible so far as *God* is concerned. Nay more, it finds its pledge and inspiration in Him. We often talk as though God was not interested in this question. We enumerate our human forces and look over the field to be possessed, and, just as we are hopeful or despondent, say it can or cannot be done. But this leaves out the mightiest force of all. You recall the question said to have been asked Luther by his wife in one of his despairing moods, — a question, I believe, alleged to have been addressed to Frederick Douglass also, by Sojourner Truth, — "Is God dead?" I repeat it to those of you who doubt and hesitate to-night : "Is God dead?" If we cannot rely on Him I am willing to surrender the whole question. But who has arranged the condition of affairs

that I have described? Is not the hand of God plain in them? From the beginning He had us in mind upon whom the ends are come. The long years of progress, at times painfully slow, are culminating now. The walls of exclusion are broken down. Light stations break the gloom of nearly every land. The fortress of the enemy has not long security in the future years. The field is arranged for the final conflict—perhaps a long one, but is it less final therefore? The General unrolls His plan of campaign. Will you take a grasp of His conquering hand and go forth to the mighty struggle? Oh, my fellow students! the power of God in this work has never yet been tested. Once tap those measureless sources, and what we speak of *as a possibility* to-night will be before our eyes a glorious reality.

It will be objected, doubtless, that all this is childish and visionary. It is. I rejoice in the charge; for "Where there is no vision the people perish," and "except ye be converted and become as little children, ye shall not enter into the kingdom of heaven."

What then remains, if all this is true? This: that it is high time to awake out of sleep, and, banding ourselves with new and deeper devotion, to swing out on the currents of God's purpose, to accomplish our mission in the world. Are you ready then, fellow students, to throw your lives in with this watch-cry: "Christ to the world before we die"? Can you endure the thought of anything else in the presence of the thorn-crowned One, who died not for our sins only but for the sins of the whole world?

Apart from all else that may be said, may these great testimonies abide in our hearts from this evening: the dying words of Simeon Calhoun, "It is my deep conviction, and I say it again and again, that if the Church of Christ were what she ought to be, twenty years would not pass away till the story of the Cross would be uttered in the ears of every living creature"; the assertion of Lord Shaftsbury, that in the latter part of these eighteen centuries, the Church of Christ has had men enough and money enough to have evangelized the world fifty times over; and the words of One greater than they all, aye, greater than all kings and princes, seated to-night above all principality and power, and dominion, and every name that is named, who in the days of His flesh, after His interview with the woman of Sychar, looked out over the plain upon His returning disciples and the townspeople who accompanied them, — sheep scattered abroad, a flock without a shepherd, — and said to them as they drew near, as He says to you and me to-night: "Say not ye, there are yet four months, and then cometh harvest? behold, I say unto you, lift up your eyes and look upon the fields; for they are white already to the harvest. And he that reapeth receiveth wages, and gathereth fruit unto life eternal: that both he that soweth and he that reapeth may rejoice together."

Rev. A. T. Pierson, D.D., then addressed the Convention on —

The Evangelization of the World in the Present Generation, — How Made a Fact.

This is a council of war. In the tent of the Commander we are gathered, and the Commander-in-chief is here. Here are his subordinates, the heads of departments, the under captains, and here are the volunteers in the army. And the question for consideration is, How can the marching orders of this invisible Captain be carried out promptly and energetically? And nothing but this council of war would have brought me here to-night. This is to my mind a very august occasion.

Our great Commander-in-chief has supplied the material basis, if I may so call it, for the progress of our work. As you have already heard, we do not need to ask or answer certain preliminary questions — the question, for instance, of access to the heathen world no longer perplexes us; for from the time that the sun shall rise on the Morning Empire of the Rising Sun, all through his marvelous circuit of the heavens, until he shall close the day on Pacific shores on our own land, his beams will scarcely dart upon a single stronghold of Satan, or a single hamlet, into the midst of which the Church is not free to go to-day if she will. Nor need we ask the question as to the means of approach to these distant people. I can start to-night from the city of Cleveland, and within six weeks be exactly at the antipodes of where I now stand. Lightning and steam have yoked themselves to the chariot of the Church of God, and the chariot of God's Church can speed where she will.

In the presence of the facilities, instrumentalities, and implements which God has given us, the question, Can we bring the Gospel into contact with these people? need not even be asked. The Marquis of Worcester, who wrote a book on the sixteenth century, called it the century of inventions; and Dryden wrote a poem on the year 1666, which he called *Annus Mirabilis* — the wonderful year. And yet, in this nineteenth century, there have been packed into a single decade, events more magnificently grand than were crowded into the whole of the sixteenth century; and there have been single years in this century — like 1853, 1858, 1878 — that embraced events so magnificent that they might have filled a decade of the most prosperous years of the world's history, if not indeed a century of such prosperity. Science is the handmaid to piety in these days. She offers us every facility that even the imagination of man could have suggested to accomplish this warfare of the ages. It may be that twenty-five years hence we shall be navigating the air as now the waters. No forecast can possibly exhaust the possibilities of even a decade of human history at this supreme hour of human progress.

Now, there is a natural basis for the world's evangelization. That natural basis is the human side of the whole world, in contrast to the supernatural. It has already been so powerfully presented that I need only to advert to it. The natural basis consists in three things — men, money, and methods. We must have workmen; we must have means to send them and support them in the field; and we must have proper, adequate business methods by which to bring the force and the field into permanent and feasible connection.

Now, I have just one word to say to you, in addition to all the garnering of mighty facts which have been before you, as to men. It is a very easy thing to demonstrate that instead of six or seven thousand missionaries in the field to-day from Christian countries, we might easily have 400,000 missionaries from Christian lands, and yet have a hundred members at home for every member of a Protestant church that went to foreign fields. And as to means, I am ashamed to say that without touching one of our necessities, without touching the staple of our life, without interfering with proper raiment or housing, we can give $600,000,000 within six months to carry on the evangelization of the world. Suppose we begin simply with our luxuries. It has been estimated that in Protestant Christian nations there is at least $100 worth of luxuries on the average to each church member. That makes the astounding sum of $4,000,000,000 in luxuries alone. Suppose we give one tithe of these luxuries to God, and kept the nine-tenths for ourselves, we should be giving to God $400,000,000. Then pass from luxuries to comforts and conveniences: we could certainly give one-twentieth part of those to the Lord, and they reach again the sum of at least $4,000,000,000, and would make $200,000,000 more — $600,000,000 — without having come down at all to the necessities of life, or those things which we call necessities, which, as has been said, ought to give way to the extremities of the poor.

In my recent visits in Great Britain and this country I have been greatly delighted and gratified, as well as somewhat startled, at the multitude of gifts that have been put into my hands for missions, especially on the part of the wealthy. The very last of these gifts I now hold in my hand. A young lady, who is an heiress in her own right, who has passed through great sorrow and suffering of late, hearing me preach in the Reformed Church at New York, and having heard my remarks on the text, " If there be first a willing mind, it is accepted according to that a man hath and not according to that he hath not," came to me at the end of the service and presented me with this magnificent marquise ring, set with seven diamonds, which could not be duplicated for seven hundred dollars. She said: " I will never again wear that ring. Take it and use it for the proclamation of the Gospel among the destitute." And I said to myself, what treasures would pour into the coffers of the Christian Church if we began simply with our luxuries!

My friends, I am going to use no polished or smooth words tonight. I am a little afraid that the seeds of a great apostasy are in the Church of God to-day, that in the midst of this century and its closing decade it should even be questioned whether we could evangelize the world in our generation, when the luxuries alone that crowd our homes, that cover our persons, that are hung upon our walls and stuffed into our library cases, the gold and silver, the jewelry and the ornamentation, the costly furniture in our homes, would of themselves suffice to make the Gospel speed its way around the earth inside of a decade of years. It is a pretty solemn question whether we ourselves are saved if we allow this state of things to go on much longer. I used to think I was in earnest about missions. I made up my mind that I had been trifling with the whole subject, and I could not get over the conviction that I was trifling with it until I came with my wife and my seven children and said to God and to his Church, " If we can be of more service in foreign lands than here in spreading the Gospel, we will go and take our places in the foreign field."

My friends, begin at your garret and go down to your cellar, and make an estimate of the useless things that are lying in the drawers of your bureaus, in the cabinets of your curios, on your walls, and on your library shelves, and wherever the secret treasures of your house are lodged, and consider how far towards the evangelization of the world in this generation the simple sacrifice of your superfluities might go. Then go down through your conveniences and comforts until you come to the necessities of life, and consider what a marvelous awakening there would be in the Church, and in the world too, if we came to the point of dividing the last crust of bread for the sake of giving bread to starving men, and consented to go without two coats where there was another man that had none. That is the only way to deal with the question of missions, and any other way of dealing with it is in a sense hypocrisy, or at least disingenuous and insincere treatment of our God and of lost souls.

Now, a word about methods. I mean by methods the bringing into contact all the force and every part of the field. There are a thousand millions of human beings that have never heard of Christ. I say that we ought to distribute whatever be the available force in every part of the destitute field; that the whole policy of diffusion is the policy of the Scriptures, and the policy of concentration is the policy of a worldly-wise Church. We ought to scatter the seed of the kingdom over the whole field — better thinly sow the whole field than thickly sow a portion of it. And, until we come to the Lord, and take up whatever we have of men, of money, and of means, and regard the whole field to be sown with the seed and to be filled with the workmen, we shall never do this work according to business methods.

It seems to me that the Church of God is trifling with the whole subject of missions. Why should not we show a spirit of enterprise in the Church such as the world shows in all business schemes? What is the matter with the Church, that in this nineteenth century she has scarcely one of those great master agencies which men use to carry their inventions to the ends of the earth? Why should we not have a great church exploration society, and go forward and pioneer the way into destitute fields, on the basis of inter-denominational comity and courtesy, and put into every field some working force, so that no absolutely destitute place should remain in the world? Why should not we have a pioneer information bureau, to guide missionaries into new districts and teach them the laws of health and climatology, and, in advance, familiarize them with the habits and customs of the natives? also, assist them in acquiring the rudiments of the languages of the people among whom they are to dwell? Why should we not have a great transportation society to carry missionaries to other fields without cost, and keep up channels of communication between them and their sustaining churches? Why should we not have new church relations? Why should not the Church come to every 300 members and elect one of those members to go abroad to the foreign field, on the principle of drafting recruits, and have it understood that the person selected should either go or furnish a substitute? Why should not the Church agree and covenant that it is as much a matter of necessity to give to the support of missionaries as to come to the Lord's table or to the prayer-meeting, or to make a decently punctual attendance at church? Why should not we have great world agencies to carry on this work for God? What is the matter with the Church, that she has not learned even from the men of this generation the wisdom that guides them in matters of this world? What is the reason that you will find the sewing-machine and the parlor organ, the kerosene lamp and the circlet of glass beads, in districts where as yet the Gospel of Jesus Christ has never been carried by its heralds?

I say to you solemnly to-night, conscious of the fact that I may never again speak on the subject of missions, that Dr. Duff was right when he said, thirty years ago, " The Church is playing at missions." There is nothing serious in the way we have been treating this grandest subject ever brought before the consciousness of converted men and women.

When Francis Xavier stood and looked from the island on which he died, upon the colossal empire of China, he cried out, "O rock, rock! when wilt thou open to my Master?" If Francis Xavier could come back to-day and look on a world wide open before that Master, and on a Church lying in sluggish idleness in her hammock of ease, one end fastened to mammon and the other end nominally to the Cross, and see that Church supinely looking on the destitution of a thousand millions of the human race, that she might reach in twenty-five years if she had the energy of mind and the consecration of heart to do it, he would turn from the colossal empire of China and face the Church and say, "O thou rock, thou rock! when wilt thou open to my Master?"

My friends, I want, before I leave, to say a word to you on the supernatural basis of missions. I am only sorry that I have not the evening to give to that most magnificent department of this most magnificent theme. I want to say to you, that with the 40,000,000 Protestant church members in the Church of God, with the $12,000,000,000 in her treasury, with all the capacity for carrying on the work in business methods, according to the very best and wisest and most sagacious suggestion, I have not the slightest idea that we shall see the world evangelized in this generation, nor that it will be evangelized in ten, twenty, or a hundred generations to |come unless the supernatural element enters into it as it has never entered into it since apostolic days. And for that, may I reverently say, I am living just now, and hope to live for a few years to come, that by voice and tongue I may, in this and other lands, impress upon the Church that it is not by might nor by power, nor by wealth nor by numbers, not by the patronage of human governments, not even by the best business methods, is this world of ours to be evangelized, but by the coming of the Holy Spirit upon the Church of God.

Three things enter into the supernatural basis. The first is the command of God. Two passages of Scripture commend themselves to my thought and yours — one in Ecclesiastes, the other in 1 Samuel: "Where the word of a king is, there is power." And if you will examine the Hebrew you will find that the force of the word "power" is authority. When Christ says, "Go ye into all the world and preach the Gospel to every creature," that means there is authority to do it; and authority from God means ability to do it, for He never commands what it is impossible for His disciples to do. Therefore, the existence of the command is the answer to the question of possibility, and is the answer to the question of practicability.

In the second place, the supernatural element depends on the presence of Jesus Christ. I want to take time enough, even in this hurried address, to call your attention to a distinction I have never seen emphasized outside of the humble writings of my own pen; and I marvel it is not more emphasized: Christ never speaks of the promise of His presence as identical with the promise of the Father. He always distinguishes the two. He says: "All power is given unto me in heaven and in earth. Go ye therefore and teach all nations, . . . and lo, I am with you always, even unto the end of the world." And then He says, "Behold I send the promise of my Father upon you!" The presence of Jesus Christ is His presence, first, on the throne as governor over the nation, and especially over His Church; and, second, it is Christ's presence on the battle field, to conduct the campaign, to lead in the engagement, and inspire by the banner of His earnest of victory, and insure final success.

The promise of the Father is the enduement of the Holy Ghost — not a presence on the battle field to guard and guide and govern, to protect and defend and insure success; but a power from above, to make me witness a confirmatory witness with the witness of the Holy Ghost, and to make the witness of the Holy Ghost a confirmatory witness to the witness which I render to my Lord; to break down inferior obstacles that remain after the walls have been broken down; to open the gates of conscience, of conviction, of emotion, of resolution, after external gates have been forced by the armies of Christ and they have entered within stormed walls. Two quite different things. But, until the Church understands these two things, she will never carry the Gospel to the bounds of the earth, or do it effectively.

We must understand that our blessed Master is at once there and here — there to persuade, there to hold out His golden scepter to the suppliant, there to turn the other end of His golden scepter round, and with the iron extremity to break in pieces those that conspire against His little missionary army; and here also, on the battle field, to show me where to go, to break down walls of adamant, to break through gates of steel, to prostrate obstacles, to provide facilities and appliances, instruments and implements. And then, after all that is done,— while it is being done,— the Holy Ghost, in answer to the devout and believing prayers of God's people, comes down upon the Church, as He came in regeneration, as He came in sanctification, now anew in enduement for service. Then, having the witness of the Spirit with my spirit and in my spirit, I am enabled to speak words that shake the consciences of men, words that uplift communities to the higher level that is impossible for learning, culture, intellect, or natural eloquence. It makes possible all these triumphs in the absence of learning, culture, natural eloquence, and the human facilities of approach.

I am very thankful that Dr. Gordon emphasized to-night that magnificent thought, which, so far as I know, he was the first man in this generation to bring before the public; namely, that one reason why the Lord Jesus Christ emphasized the presence of His believing children in all parts of the earth, is that He may have anointed witnesses and scattered vessels to convey His grace — "He is a chosen vessel unto me, to bear my name among the Gentiles." I have been a somewhat extensive reader of missionary history and biography: I have yet to find the first instance of a revival of religion in the absence of any believing child or children of God to be the vehicles of divine communication. Somebody has been where any religious work is done in the conversion of men; some colporteur has scattered Bibles and tracts; some humble evangelist — it may be simply a native servant in some missionary family — has become the reservoir, first to receive and then to distribute the grace of God.

What did Christ say at the great feast of tabernacles, when they were pouring the water from the pool of Siloam upon the morning sacrifice? "If any man thirst let him come unto me and drink. He that believeth on me, as the Scripture hath said, out of his belly shall flow rivers of living water. (But this he spake of the Spirit, which they that believe on him should receive.)" And if you will go with Christ to the woman at the well as she drew the water, you will find the same lesson: "But whosoever drinketh of the water that I shall give him shall never thirst; but the water that I shall give him shall be in him a well of water springing up into everlasting life." Now, will you answer me this question, and remember what responsibility that conception of God's work lays on you and me: if the Holy Spirit is given only where believers are residing, if a community can receive the Spirit of God as a converting Spirit only when the witnesses are there upon whom the Holy Ghost has come in regenerating and sanctifying power, will you tell me how any portion of this world is to be visited with the converting grace of God until you have scattered the witnesses to Christ in these localities? I have never had a thought come home to me as that thought has come. It is tremendous in its outreach, tremendous in the sense of responsibility it impresses, tremendous in the encouragement and the uplift of its suggestiveness. And this is the reason why I plead with you to do your part in scattering the force, however small the force may be, into all parts of the world, however wide the world may be, however thin the supply of workmen may be in the destitute regions beyond, so that in every part of the earth the workmen are scattered. For I solemnly believe, and I say it with the emphasis of a dying man, that if the Church to-day should resolve that the year 1891 should not go by until she had sent at least one representative of Christ and His Gospel into every destitute district on the surface of the earth, so that there should be no district a hundred miles square that should not be represented by one witness for Christ, before the year 1891 passed by there would be an outpouring of the Holy Ghost to which even Pentecost would be simply the first drops of a coming latter rain.

But so long as the evangelization of the world is neglected, every interest at home suffers. Look at our churches! deluged with ritualism, with rationalism, with Romanism. Look at our churches! the world in them so that you cannot tell where the world begins and the Church ends; so that the only way to distinguish the members of the Church from the sons of Belial is oftentimes the examination of the church roll. It means a serious thing when, even in our seminaries of learning, men in these days are denying the plenary inspiration of the word of God, overthrowing this trust on miracles as well as prophecy, and shaking hands with rationalists.

I say to you the hope of the Church of God is missions. It is not simply how we shall save the world, but how we shall save ourselves. The Church that forgets the world will speedily be forsaken of the Holy Ghost; and the Church that embraces the world in her love and in her labor is the Church that, in losing herself for her Master's sake, shall gain herself, her Master, and the world.

THIRD DAY, SATURDAY, FEBRUARY 28.

Morning Session.

The devotional exercises were conducted by Miss Corabel Tarr, International Secretary of the Young Women's Christian Association.

The Convention then took up the topic, " Phases of Foreign Missionary Work."

George D. Dowkontt, M. D., of the International Medical Missionary Society, addressed the Convention on —

THE MEDICAL PHASE OF FOREIGN WORK.

The Lord Jesus Christ was a medical missionary. His twelve disciples were all medical missionaries. The seventy afterwards chosen were all medical missionaries, all appointed to heal the sick and preach the gospel. And in the 10th chapter of the Gospel according to Luke, in which you read of the seventy being sent out, you get the parable of the good Samaritan, who, having no miraculous power, used the power that he had in lifting from the ditch the man that the priest and Levite had passed by. And the Saviour's commendation was of him and is to us, " Go thou and do likewise." Medical missionaries try to carry out that command. They go to the people with the fruits of Christianity, and thereby seek to plant the roots. The Saviour said, " By their fruits ye shall know them." And when John the Baptist sent, inquiring as to whether Christ was the one to come, He said, " Go and show John what things ye see, how the lame walk, and the blind see, and the deaf hear." And when he wanted a credential He said, " If ye believe me not for my words, believe me for my works' sake." So much for our authority ; so much for the command for this work.

The greatest joy that can be given to a Christian man or woman on this earth is to go up and down it as the Master did, relieving suffering — physical, mental, and spiritual ; and the greatest suffering into which, I think, you can put a man or a woman is to send him into the midst of suffering without the ability to relieve it. In regard to the need for this medical missionary effort, we find that among these thousand millions of heathen, we have actively employed at the present time about 250 medical missionaries, male and female, fully qualified. That gives one medical missionary to 4,000,000 people on the average. 4,000,000 people with one medical missionary to attend to their physical needs !

I have no time to go into the horrible details of the suffering of these people through lack of the help they need, through the ignorance and superstition and cruelty with which they are treated in time of sickness. But I ask you to read for yourselves. Many of you probably have been reading the Medical Missionary Record, in which we try to put as much as we can of information upon this line. We beg of you to look into this question. In China, not long ago, there came a young man to one of our medical missionaries with a great, gaping hole in his arm; and, upon inquiry as to how that was caused, it was ascertained that a Chinese physician had said to that young man, whose father was dying: "There is only one thing which can save your father. If you will submit to have a piece cut out of your arm, it may save your father's life." He submitted to the operation, but the patient died notwithstanding.

Three points as to the value of medical missionaries:

1. Success in Gospel effort. When physical relief has been brought to people suffering from disease, confidence is won; and you can readily see how oftentimes an opening wedge is thus driven for the Gospel to enter in.

2. Self-support. I cannot dilate upon this question, but give you one or two points only. Dr. Summers landed on the West Coast of Africa in February, 1885. He died in May of 1888. From the day he landed upon African soil until the day he died he did not take a dollar from any society for his support. He won the hearts of the people, and obtained not only funds for his own support, but also for his work. Dr. Ellen Mitchell, for the last three years in Burmah, pays out of her earnings her personal expenses and the salary of an assistant. Dr. Simms, who is laboring on the Congo, receives as his salary from the Board $500 a year. He receives $600 from the Congo government, and pays $600 in for the $500 he gets out. Last year I received a letter saying that the Chinese government wanted two men to come out to places where there is no missionary, that it may have the advantage of their medical knowledge. The Chinese government is willing to give $1,000 a year to two missionaries, with the privilege of doing all the Gospel work they wish.

3. Self-preservation. This is not a small point. Mr. and Mrs. Farnsworth were in Turkey. They had four children. One took sick and died. A second one died. A third died. The fourth was about to die, when they took a long journey to a doctor, only to hear the words, "too late," and turn back, and after they had been two days on the journey the child died, and our missionaries had to carry that dead child back to lie by the side of the other three.

One other point only — four reasons for medical missions: 1. Christ commands. 2. Sympathy demands. 3. Wisdom dictates. 4. Experience has proved the value of this agency.

Question. I wish to ask how much scholastic training a man ought to have before he takes a medical course?

Answer. It is not needful, I think, that he should have a college education. If he had education enough to enter college it would be sufficient.

Q. Would you advise taking a full four years' course in medicine, or a shorter course?

A. I would say, never go out unless you have a full medical course. And unless you have a degree, do not allow people to call you a doctor, and do not dare to assume the title. You ought to have a full medical course if you are going to be a doctor; but you may have a shorter course, such as we have provided.

Rev. Henry Forman, of India, then spoke, as follows, on —

The Educational Phase of Foreign Work.

I speak of one thing in the great work. The evangelistic is more attractive, and a greater work. Medical work is as attractive. Woman's work is more attractive, and a greater work.

I speak first of the reason for educational work among Mohammedans and Hindoos. It is put this way by those who do not believe in it: " You are educating thousands and thousands of young men and boys, of whom scarcely ten will become Christians, in all probability. Why this great expenditure of money and time?" The answer is this: Thousands and thousands are going to be educated. Shall we educate them, or shall an infidel government institution? not an infidel government, but an infidel institution. The government institution of India is neutral avowedly, really non-Christian; but the effect is that young men are coming out of the government schools by the thousands who have not only no religion, but scarcely any distinct ideas even of morality. Even now they are trying to prepare a moral text-book for the schools. My father has been on the committee for the Punjaub for years, and every time they bring up a book it is rejected because it has too much Christianity in it. They cannot make a moral text-book without Christianity in it.

Shall we then leave the schools to these teachers who cannot even give them morality for fear of introducing Christianity? No, we must go on with the work, for the young men are being educated and will be educated; and the question is, Shall we educate them and give them a knowledge of Christ, or shall we let them go on in this other course? There is no question as to which is the wise course.

Another point: the character of these schools. We begin with little boys and keep them until they are prepared for college, — teaching them English until they are able to study in English. Then we have some colleges that carry them on up to the A.B. and the A.M. courses.

The extent of this work: I speak only of Northwestern India; I want to talk of what I definitely know. There are schools, several in Calcutta, with thousands of pupils, — I mean, mission schools; of course there are government schools all through the country. There are mission schools in all the other districts of Bengal: Allahabad with 450 pupils; Lucknow, 500; also Lahore, 650; Rawal Pindi, 850; and many others I will not mention. But this is not all. We have our thousands of boys in the purely vernacular schools. It is a very widespreading system, and if it were not a wise one it would not have been so widely adopted.

What about the difficulties in the way of this work? In the first place, these boys do not come for love of the Bible; they come because it is just a little cheaper than the government school. Then again, they come because their fathers came and formed a liking for the mission schools. But they do not come for the sake of religion. They want education so that they can get good salaries. If they are impressed by our Bible teaching and are converted, it is not always a permanent influence, because we cannot always baptize these boys. To baptize a boy under fourteen is a criminal offence; and it is a serious thing to baptize them over fourteen, because they must be separated from their homes. Still, we do that. Not always: we have to look always to the character of the boy. Will he stand under the pressure from the outside? Will he waver and fall back? Can he stand, at the age of fifteen or sixteen, against his parents, his family, and every one, when they bring every means against him — argument, persuasion, affection, and then try to tempt him into immorality and sin in order to break his Christian character? Still, we do baptize some of these boys.

Then a little more of this dark side. From our schools go forth occasionally a few of those who oppose Christianity, who have learned their Bible, but use their knowledge to oppose. There are very few of these. From the government schools they go out by hundreds and thousands; so that is not an argument against our schools. Sometimes, after we have worked long with a boy, he will fall back. I taught a boy for years. He was dissatisfied, uncomfortable, because he knew he was in a false religion; at the same time he was full of doubts, and well informed on all sorts of objections to Christianity — such as Voltaire's, Tom Paine's, and Ingersoll's. He hesitated long, and finally he said, " When I seem to come to the point the devil seems to take possession of me." He hesitated until he fell back and became an absolute hater of Christianity.

There is Ramsay College in Almora, of the London Missionary Society. Lately they baptized one man. It stirred up great hatred toward old John Ramsay, — who has been honored for years, and who has done more than any other Englishman for that native state, — because he was anxious for the conversion of young men. A great mob of young men and boys came and gathered all the Bibles they had, and scattered the leaves as they went, and made a bonfire of them before John Ramsay's house. Do not imagine it is all simple and easy sailing; but it is just these things that bring it out. You know how in Madras College a few years ago the conversion of one man led to a great furore. But there is encouragement too for this work. Who can want a better field than three or four hundred bright, intelligent boys, to teach them day by day, and to influence them? It is a splendid field.

Mr. R. R. McBurney, Chairman of the Missionary Committee of the Young Men's Christian Association, then addressed the Convention on —

The Work of the Young Men's Christian Association in Foreign Lands.

Mr. Chairman and Christian friends, I take it for granted that the members of the Missionary Conference and of the Volunteer Movement recognize, as the Young Men's Christian Association do, that their first allegiance is to Jesus Christ as a personal Saviour, and that next their allegiance is to the Church of Jesus Christ which they join, and that allegiance to the Church carries with it allegiance to the Boards of the respective churches with which they are connected. The Young Men's Christian Association did not seek the field of usefulness which has been opened to it in foreign mission lands. And let me say, in relation to this Student Volunteer Movement, this Movement has a very direct connection with the Young Men's Christian Association, more direct perhaps than some of the younger members of the Volunteer Movement are aware of. You have been hearing during these days a little of the history of the organization. One thing I have not heard in connection with it; namely, that a secretary of the International Committee of the Young Men's Christian Association, Mr. Wishard, asked Mr. Moody for an opportunity for some college students to meet him at his home in Northfield for the purpose of Bible study. They gathered together those young men who met at Mt. Hermon, and at that gathering commenced this Volunteer Missionary Movement. So that this

Movement has of course a very warm place in the heart of Christian men, and an exceedingly warm place in the heart of the members of the Young Men's Christian Association of the United States and the Dominion of Canada.

I said a moment ago that the Young Men's Christian Association had not sought this foreign mission work. In our home work we do not begin Young Men's Christian Associations in towns without the concurrence of the pastors of the evangelical churches in those towns. We never think for a moment of seeking to force the organization of an Association in a town. We believe that if the need exists in a town, the pastors and Christian people of that town will recognize it much more quickly than those who live at a distance. The International Committee of the Young Men's Christian Association pursues the same course, and is pledged to continue that course, in relation to the organization of Young Men's Christian Associations in foreign mission lands.

A few years ago, in 1885, a request came from some of the missionaries in Japan for aid in the erection of a building for the Young Men's Christian Association in that place. They asked for $5,000. The United States contributed $2,500, Canada, $1,500, Australia, $1,000. The building was erected in Osaka, Japan. The testimony of the missionaries was that the building was a great aid to the Christian community scattered in the different parts of the place.

Of course, I have not time to go into the development of the work in the two countries to which it has gone. In 1887 the American missionaries wrote to friends in America that there was a large opportunity for teachers in the colleges of Japan; that those who went there as teachers would be able to support themselves from the salaries they received, and at the same time carry on a Christian work as they might have opportunity. The first band sailed for Japan on the 4th of February, 1888. Among those that went out in that band was John Trumbull Swift, a graduate of Yale College and of the Columbia College Law School. He had been Assistant Secretary in the 23d Street Branch of the Young Men's Christian Association, and also Secretary of the Young Men's Christian Association of Orange, New Jersey. He had a thorough knowledge of Association work and methods, and was heartily enlisted in it. While teaching, he became of course interested in his pupils. He gathered some of them together for Bible study, and the question arose in his mind, in view of the fact that Christianity is not taught in the Imperial University, or allowed to be taught there, Why not organize a Young Men's Christian Association, in connection with the students of the Imperial University? The missionaries said to him, "How can you organize a Young Men's Christian Association in the Imperial University when there are no Christians there?" Mr. Swift is a quiet, judicious man, of a very inquiring mind, but a thorough gentleman in his manner. He quietly investigated, and finally secured the names of fifty young men who were nominally Christians. I infer that they were experimental Christians, but they were secret Christians. He gathered them together. Thirty of them came to a meeting to which they were invited, and it was said that no one man of that thirty knew that there was another Christian young man in that institution save himself. It gave each man courage to know that in that institution there were numbers who, like himself, though cowardly, believed in their heart of hearts in Jesus Christ as the personal Saviour of their souls. The result was the organization of an Association there. Mr. Swift, at the request of the missionaries in that country and the International Committee, was set aside to give attention exclusively to the work of the organization of Associations.

The object of the Young Men's Christian Association is not to send a number of secretaries to each country, but rather to send one or two, with the hope and expectation that young men will be trained in those countries to do the work of the country. Mr. Swift has already been instrumental in securing the co-operation of two young men who have been under training with him, and are going to devote themselves to that work. Let me say that half of $60,000 was raised in this country for the purpose of erecting a building for the Young Men's Christian Association right in the vicinity of the Imperial University, and a like amount for the young men of the city of Tokyo. It should be borne in mind that Tokyo is the largest university city, and has the largest number of students probably of any city in the world; between 60,000 and 80,000 students are there each year. And they are of the most influential class, — the controlling class in that country, as they are in every country.

The missionaries of India, in the vicinity of Madras, sent a unanimous request to the International Committee to send out a trained secretary to Madras. Mr. McConaughy went, and is accomplishing an excellent work.

Now, before I stop I think it will be well for me to read for your instruction the attitude of the Young Men's Christian Association to this work. The following resolution was adopted in 1889: "*Resolved*, That the National Committee be empowered to establish such Associations and place such secretaries in the foreign mission field as in its judgment may be proper, and receive such contributions for its work as Associations and individuals may contribute to it."

I would like to read the balance, but I want to say something that is exceedingly important. We have a man ready to go to Brazil. The missionaries in the missionary societies interested in that country had a conference this morning. They expressed a desire that a young man should be sent there. The young man is here in this Convention — a trained secretary.

The only difficulty we experience in connection with our contemplated work in Brazil, work in India, and in Japan, is the difficulty of procuring money. Men are abundant. We are receiving urgent appeals from other cities in India to send men as secretaries to aid in this work. Now, it seems to me that if the volunteers that are here, and are intensely interested in the progress of foreign missions, will go around and seek to awaken interest, so that money may be given in the respective churches, you who are devoting your services to this work can have an influence upon these churches which the secretaries cannot probably have, and which other men cannot exert.

Rev. Mr. Lambeth : —

I would like to say that I saw Mr. Swift only a few weeks ago, and he said at that time that he desired five men as soon as possible, who should go upon the field during the middle or by the last of the summer, so as to secure places for them in the government schools, which will bring them one hundred yen a month, about $75 United States currency. Will the young men be forthcoming ?

Rev. Mr. Kyle, of Brazil, then addressed the Convention on —

EDITORIAL WORK IN THE FOREIGN FIELD.

This is pre-eminently an age of newspapers, and our own land a land of newspapers. More papers are published in the United States than in all the rest of the world besides. It is nothing more than natural that American missionaries, in addition to their other work, should turn their attention to the publishing of newspapers, that through them they may propagate the truths of our religion and make the Gospel go into places where they themselves cannot go. A newspaper can go into every post-office, into the homes of those who openly would refuse to recognize us, who would not attend our services, or perhaps even talk with us on the street. So that this editorial work is one of the important works of the missionaries to-day in any of our fields, — especially is this so in South America. The Brazilians and the Spanish speaking people of South America are a newspaper reading people.

In Rio Janeiro, a city twice the size of Cleveland, there are nine daily newspapers. Now, in this newspaper work we want to reach three classes of people. We want to reach our native church members. We want to instruct them in the doctrines of our holy religion. We want to edify them — build them up in the faith. And then we want to reach another class — those who are beyond the reach of the missionaries, who live so far away that they can at most receive only an occasional visit. And then we want to reach the educated men of the country through the newspapers. It can go into their homes; it can go into their reading-rooms, into their libraries, where the truths of the Gospel may be set before them. And if in our schools we can have grammar and arithmetic and geography, why might we not in our newspapers, teach them things which, while not essential truths of Christianity, will give them information upon general subjects, upon what is going on in the world, news of how God is working in this world, bringing it nearer and nearer to the Gospel of Christ? History can be taught, news can be gathered from all over the world which will interest and attract the people, and bring them to read articles, tracts, books, and the Bible, that they may know what is essential, and learn of Him who is the way, the truth, and the life.

But in this editorial work we not only have the newspapers, but tracts and Bibles of all kinds and sizes must be prepared. The people of the United States have their tremendous English literature behind them. There is no literature in the world so full of good religious books as the English literature; and those of us who have been out into those lands where there is almost an absolute dearth of religious books, feel and see this need as only those can see it who have been there to feel it. The list of evangelical books in the Portuguese language is not more than twenty-five or thirty. Think of twenty-five or thirty religious books in the English language! This is a tremendous work which must be carried on, that we may educate our young men to disseminate the truths of the Christian religion.

Now, those who go into this editorial work must have some taste for it and preparation for it. We all know that those make the most successful editors who have given themselves to the work of editing newspapers and who study the needs of the people, and prepare themselves for it by actual experience. It would do no harm if every missionary — every young man who expects to go to the mission field — should spend two or three weeks in some printing office and see what type looks like, see what printer's ink is, and handle a proof-sheet. The man who goes into the foreign field never knows what day he may need any part of this information and experience. And it seems to me that in the future, if the evangelization of the world is to be brought about in this generation, a great part of it must be accomplished through the printed page, through which we may preach and we may evangelize.

Rev. John L. Nevius, D.D., American Chairman of the recent
Shanghai Conference, then addressed the Convention on —

THE EVANGELISTIC PHASE OF FOREIGN WORK.

I am expected to speak of evangelization as one of the phases of
missionary work. Now, my idea of evangelization is that it in itself is
a generic and not a specific term, and that it includes all the phases of
missionary work. It seems to me that we must change our terminology
with reference to this great work of missions. The important idea to
begin with is, What is the Scriptural idea of evangelization? If I
mistake not, the idea that prevails at home is that the principal function of the missionary, as he goes abroad to the ends of the earth, is to
preach, in the modern, specific, technical sense of that term; while, in
addition to this as the principal function, there is the educational, the
editorial, and other departments of missionary work.

But, dear brethren and sisters, if you examine a Greek concordance
of the New Testament, you will find about six words in the original
that are all translated " preach " in the English version, and hardly one
of the six has the modern technical sense that we connect with the
word " preach." The two Greek words principally used mean to proclaim as a herald or transmit good news. And the best way of com-
municating this information is the best kind of preaching. It has been
said here that Jesus Christ and the Apostles were all medical missionaries. I will add that Jesus Christ and his Apostles were all educational missionaries, they were all industrial missionaries, and they were
all editorial missionaries. What a wonderful editorial missionary the
Apostle Paul was! I use the word " editorial," not with reference to
periodical literature, but to tract literature and book literature. These
are all different phases of the one great work of evangelization.

I suppose that by the evangelistic phase is meant the work that is
carried on in chapels, on the street, and in itineration. Let me here
give you an idea of the different state of things in the great Eastern
lands, especially in China, from what we have here. Our idea of the
evangelist is of one who gives a stirring address, bringing those before
him to a definite result or determination of will. That presupposes a
great deal of intelligence and instruction beforehand. What would an
evangelist do here unless all his people had a familiar and an intimate
acquaintance with the Gospel? Absolutely nothing; there is no
ground of appeal. We go to China. We have a language that is
steeped with idolatrous association, — we almost have to convert the
language before we can use it to discourse to an audience on the
Christian faith. It presupposes, too, persons who are accustomed to
this way of being influenced, who from childhood have listened to

public discourse, with its introductions and conclusions; those who are accustomed to churches, to lectures, and great lecture halls. There is no such thing in China; there is not a lecture hall in China. I suppose that a regular, formal discourse has hardly ever been delivered in China, I was going to say for the last 2,000 years, but they are very exceptional; and a lecture hall does not exist among them of which I know; it is something to which they are entirely unaccustomed. Their method is the individual, catechetical, conversational; and the method of the great sage of China was the Socratic method.

But I must come back to my theme, and that is evangelization. I suppose I cannot do better than to refer to my own experience. My time has been spent in several channels. In editorial work I believe I carried out my own theory. But I have had a great deal to do with long itinerations in the interior of China. In the province of Shantung, with twenty-five or thirty millions of inhabitants, I suppose I spent half of the last fifteen years.

The first phase of that particular kind of work is immense crowds. Everybody, moved by an intense curiosity, turns out to see. Even the women forget the proprieties of social life to come with the children in their arms, and there they stand, with the gaping crowd, looking at the strange apparition of the "foreign devil" who has entered into their village. We use this opportunity to the best of our ability. That comes nearer to our idea of preaching to crowds than anything we ever meet. The next time there is less of a crowd. The school teacher has told them that this new doctrine we preach is exclusive, that it is intolerant; that the God we worship we proclaim as one God, the only God, who demands the single and whole worship of all human beings. They are afraid.

After we go around two or three times in these villages where we had nearly the whole population out, not one comes near us. I have gone over that same ground year after year, and year after year, and the great burden was that I could find no one to whom I could talk of Christ. That is the second stage. It shows progress. It shows that all the people in that field have come to know that there is one God, and that Jesus Christ is the one Saviour He has sent. It shows that the truth is working among the masses.

Then we come to the third stage, when here and there a person comes out and stands up for Christ. That means a good deal. The last stage is when around these little centers little churches are started. And now the work is all evangelistic. The evangelistic work is training these native Christians, teaching them to be evangelists, and developing them in this great work.

And now I want to present just one thought before closing, and that is that the great qualification for evangelization is for us to feel that we can do absolutely nothing — that it is God's work. We heard last night of the spiritual forces which are the great forces that move the world. We must be made to feel that unless God interposes we can do absolutely nothing. After five years' preaching on that field to thousands and millions of people, and sometimes feeling that here is one and there half a dozen just ready to become Christians, at the end of five years I had not a single convert. Numbers, intellectual force, anything, everything, that we as men can bring to bear on this subject, will be utterly fruitless unless God in mercy pour out His Spirit.

I believe that was the lesson that it took the Apostle ten years to learn before he was fully prepared for his life's work and the special call to him at Antioch, " Separate me Barnabas and Paul." And you will remember, when as a young man he attempted to debate the question with the Lord Jesus in the temple at Jerusalem, Jesus said to him, " Depart." Paul believed there were special reasons why he, the persecutor, should testify to Christ in that great center of influence; but the Saviour said, " Depart: for I will send thee far hence unto the Gentiles." It was several years before he was sent, but when he was sent he had learned that lesson, — that he could do nothing. And when he reported the results of his work over the Roman Empire, notice how in every case he spoke, not of what Paul had done, but of what God had done through him. Brethren, learn that lesson early; learn it, if you can, before you leave the United States; but be assured you must learn it before God will use you to carry on His own work.

The closing exercises of the morning session were conducted by Mrs. S. B. Capron, of Moody's Bible Institute of Chicago, who introduced the topic —

PRAYER AND MISSIONS.

I am to speak on the blessedness and power of prayer in missionary life. When another and I were talking together in 1856 about an outfit, we wrote on the top of a foolscap sheet of paper, " Prayer — ask of God." It is a very wonderful experience, my dear young brothers and sisters, when you write at the top of a page, " Ask of God," and under it what you ask and the date, and then write His marvelous fulfillment beneath it, — " Received," — and the day. Now there can be no better way of treating this interesting and valuable subject for this twenty-five minutes than to confine ourselves to the value and power of prayer in missionary work.

I believe there is nothing in our missionary life like the consciousness that the Church of God carries us on its heart in prayer. How many times I have been hurried from one day to another, and have then gone to my place of prayer, and I recall at this moment a small rattan chair, which seems to me like the throne itself, as I remember how many times I have knelt there and said: "O, Lord Jesus, I have no time to pray for myself, nor this afternoon's work. Oh, inspire at this moment some dear heart in America, who may know me by name only, to offer a prayer for the need of this hour!" And I believe that that has been done over and over again. For, as I have gone from one place to another, how I have been thrilled at a stranger's face and a stranger's voice coming to me saying, "I have never seen you before, but how often I have prayed for you and read what you have written."

Dear young brothers and sisters, these are the great facts of the missionary life. And let me remind you of it when you are about to set out on your work. Begin now, begin at once, and let it be known here and there among all your dear ones that you need their prayers now, for preparation; for it does seem to me that the time has come when we need men and women filled with the Holy Ghost and with power to do the individual work that now needs to be done. After all these great plans have been brought almost to their fulfillment, now it remains to go one by one and win souls for Christ.

And now, one word from God's word, because we cannot take a subject like this without a word from Him. You will remember what He said to Moses, who led Israel out of Egypt, as you in your foreign missionary work will lead many out of Egypt: "Behold there is a place by me." And when, as the Psalmist says, "the God of glory thundereth," and the nations stand afar and tremble, we hear God say, "You have a place by me," and then add, "Thou shalt stand upon a rock;" and when we stand upon a rock we can be lonely and bear it. And then the Lord said of Moses, "With him will I speak mouth to mouth, even apparently, and not in dark speeches; and the similitude of the Lord shall he behold." Now that is verified; it is "even apparently" when you least expect it. It is the power of prayer, it is the power of the Holy Spirit, so that you may sometimes say: "O Comforter divine, I know not what to ask for. I am still, and thou shalt pray for me." And now, let us all sweetly, tenderly, and with blessed expectation, sing one verse, and then I trust that all over this room will come the spirit of prayer.

Now, if there is some dear missionary brother or sister who has a sweet and precious testimony to give to this power of prayer, of being borne up by the prayers of those at home, or some wonderful and blessed answer to prayer in loneliness, let us hear it. You will remember that Paul said, "That I may know Him, and the power of His resurrection, and the fellowship of His sufferings." That ofttimes seems to come to us as we feel the droppings of glory down into our hearts brightening and sweeting our missionary lives. I think the foreign missionary realizes one element of that fellowship, and that is loneliness — loneliness unutterable and indescribable. Will some one now give us a word?

Mrs. J. N. Cushing, of Burmah : —

Once at our mission in Burmah only one woman and myself were left to conduct the work of the mission. There were books and accounts to be kept, teachers and Bible women to be led, proof-sheets to be read. Mr. Cushing was in England, very ill. Just then there came a word to me from New York, from a lady, saying, " We fear you are in distress and trouble, and at twelve o'clock in the day we are praying for you." Twelve o'clock in the day at New York City was eleven o'clock at night with us. At eleven o'clock at night down came a blessing — all the peace and joy and strength and comfort and courage that I wanted for the next day came to me. Day after day for eleven months I felt the power of that prayer.

Mr. C. F. Gates : —

I became a Christian on the day of prayer for colleges. I went out as a missionary to Turkey in answer to prayer. I was just graduated from the seminary, and a call came to me from the American Board to go to Mardin. It was not a question of desire, for I did not want to go, but of duty; it seemed to me that God was calling me, and what could I do but go? That same month I picked up the Missionary Herald and read a request for prayer like this : that a young man might go out to the mission field from a sense of duty.

On the mission field there came a time when we were building our schools. Saturday was coming, the workmen must be paid, and there was nothing to pay them with. I knelt in prayer and asked aid. Friday there came a letter from France. It said : " Our daughter has died, and on her death-bed she said, ' I want you to send ten pounds to Mr. Gates for his work.' I put with it fifteen." When we remembered that the letter had been sent a month before, we said, " God has performed His promise, ' Before they call I shall answer." On another occasion we were traveling. Storms had beset us. Three swollen rivers lay before us, and we knew not how to cross. Just then a man joined our caravan, and carried us across in ways we could not have devised for ourselves. One or two of us said, " God sent that man for this time and this emergency."

One word to those who expect to go out as missionaries. Do not go unless you can stand alone with God. The loneliness of mission life is awful. It is only as you can lay hold of God's right hand and depend upon Him to hear and answer prayer that you can have any success.

Dr. G. W. Chamberlain, of Brazil : —

At one time in Brazil, when my colleague Howell was broken down and was at home and the work was doubled up, one Sabbath, leaving the church weary, and anticipating ugly questions that had to be decided about nine o'clock for school week, I lifted up my heart to the Lord and said, " If help does not come quick it will come late." There came into my mind a man whom I had not corresponded with in fifteen years ; a man who had gone to Brazil from ambition for wealth, but whom the Lord had used to teach and had made a popular teacher. He had been away from Brazil for fifteen years. I knew he was practicing medicine in Missouri or Kansas, and that the Lord had broken his heart by taking his wife, and that he had become a Christian. I had not enough faith to write him a letter, but I thought I would waste a postal on him. I said, " Are you in condition to hear a call to come and help in educational work in Brazil ? " It was the first Monday in November. We always observe the first Monday of the month in prayer for the missions. I took that postal in my pocket to the prayer-meeting and said : " This pasteboard is going to a man in the United States. If the Lord wants him we want him. If He does not, we do not. Let us have prayer before this goes to the post-office." An answer came in a month : " Perhaps you do not know that my wife is dead, and I have eight children too small to be left alone. But my heart is in Brazil ; and now since the Lord took away my idol, my heart is His. If it is His call I am going. I am in good practice of medicine, have my children all about me ; but if it is His call I am going." I then wrote him a long letter. Three months later came his answer : " My shingle is down. I am going to leave my children with my sister for a year. If that year proves that I am the man for the place, I am there for life." That placed me in a quandary. I knew if I corresponded about it, it would take a year. I took a shorter cut : I went to a Brazilian I knew. He said, " That is the kind of man we want." I said, " I need his salary, and I can't wait for the necessary correspondence." " How much will it be ? " he said. I told him. " I will pay it for a year," he replied. And the man is there.

A few moments were spent in brief prayers to God for a revelation of the power of prayer in mission work, and then Mrs. Capron closed as follows : —

The time has come for our meeting to close. We can always pray, but we cannot always pray together. Let me in closing give you a Hindoo woman's definition of prayer, which has more than once made me rise from my knees and walk the floor to ask if I were ready for it. She was not a Christian. Some one in her hearing was saying, " What do they mean by prayer?" And she replied, "Come here next Sunday afternoon, and when she prays it makes a living brightness in the earth." Those of us who know what it is to feel the thrill of consciousness that we are being heard, and that there is a glory and a blessedness just before us, can understand the meaning of this beautiful description of prayer that moves the heart of God.

The session closed with singing, and the benediction by Dr. Murdock.

Afternoon Session.

The devotional exercises were conducted by Mr. F. S. Goodman, General Secretary of the Cleveland Young Men's Christian Association.

The discussion on the general topic, "How can the volunteer help the cause before going?" was then introduced by William Walter Smith, of the General Theological Seminary of New York City, who spoke on the following topic: —

INCREASING CONTRIBUTIONS TO THE SOCIETIES.

You have heard about our 6,000 volunteers, and we heard Dr. Pierson's address last evening, telling us how the purse strings of our individual Christians in our churches have been tightly closed. We hear the old cry from Board after Board, "Retrench"; man after man coming forward ready to go, and no money to send them. I think I can safely say to-day that there is not a single Missionary Board that has enough money. I want to tell you as briefly as I can how we volunteers are trying to meet the money problem.

There are three ways of doing it. In the first place, to get individual colleges and seminaries to support their missionaries in the foreign field. In 1887 Princeton was asked to send two men. The students said they could not do it; they were too poor. We tried it. We thought we could not raise $700, but we raised $1,300. Princeton Seminary took it up, and raised $700 that year. Union Seminary did the same. The plan adopted was this: The men in the different classes agreed to give a certain sum, monthly, weekly, or quarterly, towards the support of a missionary in the foreign field. The pledge read: "I promise to give so many dollars, or cents, each month, week, or quarter, during a period of five years from date, towards the support of a missionary in the foreign field, that sum to be over and above my present offering to foreign missions." In accordance with that plan, the men pledged for five years in the colleges, in the seminary for four years, so that each class coming in will overlap one year.

The Board agreed to take that man if his support was pledged for five years. The men are sent out under their own church Boards. Up to the present time, in the United States and Canada alone, the number of colleges supporting their missionaries in whole or in part is about 40; the number of seminaries is 32; making 72 institutions supporting their missionaries in the foreign field. They raise by this means over $30,000.

The second method is to get individual churches to send out their missionaries. This work was not developed among the volunteers until the summer of 1888. Several of the volunteers agreed during the summer vacation to try to get churches to support their missionaries in the foreign field, the money given to be over and above their usual offerings to the cause of foreign missions, and to pass through the regular Boards. To-day over 100 churches are, in whole or in part, supporting their missionaries in the foreign field, raising over $50,000. We have found no case where this plan has not directly benefited the other collections of the church. One volunteer on the point of sailing to the foreign field has already had offers from six individual churches asking the privilege of supporting him in the foreign field. I believe, if we have the enthusiasm and the zeal for foreign work we can get the money without any trouble whatever.

It is estimated that 135 persons giving ten cents a week would support a missionary. A church which could not raise enough to support a missionary entirely could combine with other churches. If the money raised in one church is not sufficient for the support of a representative in the foreign field, and it is impossible to combine with other churches, the money raised could be sent to the Board to be used as they direct. I could name a little chapel with only 35 members, poor people, who are raising over $85 a year for foreign missions by this plan. We find a great many churches where the pastors have not allowed us to put in our plan to support the missionaries. In those cases we try to get them to increase their monthly contributions.

The third method is to induce individuals to support their missionaries. A lady of our acquaintance is working twenty-four hours a day. She works twelve hours a day here, and she has a missionary in India working twelve hours a day for her. Those of us who are not able to go to the foreign field can perhaps support a representative there. If we cannot go, we must send.

Miss Hattie Dyer, State Secretary of the Young Women's Christian Association of Pennsylvania, spoke briefly on the next topic, emphasizing prayer for missions.

Mr. E. B. Haskell, of Oberlin Theological Seminary, spoke as follows on the next subject: —

SECURING RECRUITS AS VOLUNTEERS FOR FOREIGN SERVICE.

On the 15th of April, 1861, President Lincoln sent out a call for 75,000 volunteers. On the 19th, U. S. Grant was drilling a company in Illinois. Foolish Grant! by the 19th he might have reached the front. Where is he? In a few days he has a regiment, and goes with a thousand men at his back.

A mine has caved in upon fifty men. A youth discovers it. What is his wisest plan — to stay and dig away alone, or to run through the hamlet, calling at the doors and telling the people of the calamity, and bringing a hundred workers to help him?

Is there any reason why we should try to get other volunteers? Why, the world is death struck! While we sit here deliberating how to help them those millions are dying at the rate of two every second. If the 400,000 spoken of here last night should offer themselves to-morrow to go to the foreign field, and the Church should offer the money to send them, before they could learn the language at least 12,000,000 would have died. Every month a million die in China. Three times every year those hopeless graves receive a population equal to that of the State of Ohio. Why try and get volunteers? It has been told you that we can do a great deal more for the foreign cause before we go than we can ever do afterwards. When I hear appeals from Japan, it seems as though I must go to Japan. When I read the report of the Shanghai conference calling for 1,000 men for China, China claims me. When I read Dr. Chamberlain's address calling for 5,000 volunteers for India, it seems as if I must go to India. When I hear the appeals from darkest Africa, it seems as if every man ought to go there.

We cannot divide ourselves into a thousand men and women; but by getting volunteers before we go we multiply ourselves over and over again. By getting volunteers before we go we may do the same brilliant thing which Andrew did. It is recorded in the first chapter of John: "He first findeth his own brother Simon and said to him, we have found the Messiah, which is, being interpreted, the Christ. And he brought him to Jesus. And when Jesus beheld him he said, Thou art Simon the son of Jona: thou shalt be called Cephas, which is by interpretation, a stone." That was a brilliant thing for Andrew to do; he brought a man to Christ who was forty times the man he was himself. You may do that yourself. You may seize upon some person, and get him consecrated to the foreign work, who will accomplish a hundred times the work you will do yourself in the foreign field. It was a very ordinary sermon, by a man who did not begin to compare with him in ability, that touched the heart of Adoniram Judson and persuaded him to go to India.

Again, if we secure volunteers before we go, and die on the way, our work goes on. If this young miner of whom I have spoken is struck by lightning after he has aroused the community, it makes little difference; the work goes on. In the past we did not have that organization and apostolic succession which we get by this method of securing volunteers before we go. And what a great privilege it is!

Just a word as to how to get volunteers. By personal work is the most important way, just as you would go to work to get men to be Christians. I would pray over it; I would reach them in just the same way I would try to get people to be Christians. Be courteous, be candid, be careful in your statements, weigh their objections, above all, never get angry at their stupid or frivolous excuses, or anything of the kind. Be Christlike, be earnest, and stick to it, and try to get volunteers. So, to close with the same kind of illustration as that with which I begun, if I see a hospital on fire, I may well spend part of my breath, while rushing to the rescue, in sounding the alarm and rousing the community. And so, as we go to the foreign field, let us sound the alarm and get others to go with us.

Mr. Robert P. Wilder then spoke as follows on the two topics —

DISSEMINATING INFORMATION AMONG THE CHURCHES; AND, ACCUMULATING INFORMATION.

Though two-thirds of our race know nothing about Christ, the mass of the American Christians know little and care less about these lost ones. To the great majority the subject of foreign missions is a signal for disgust; and I have often been cautioned by pastors, when speaking in churches, not to announce my theme as missions, but to use the words, "Student Volunteer Movement." The word "missionary" usually seems to be a signal for a *miserere*.

No theme can be of more intrinsic interest. Comparative philology, as a science, owes its perfection, if not its existence, to the service of foreign missions. The subject of missions is world-wide in its scope. It marks the reach of the Church's commission and the climax of the Church's coming triumphs. Yet, to the average American Christian, it is uninteresting. It is because they do not know the facts. Ignorance and indifference are twin brothers. Not long since, when speaking to an audience, I asked how many before me had ever read a dozen missionary books. Not a hand went up. How many had read half a dozen? None. How many had read four? Three. I asked how many had read three? Four or five hands went up. When I asked how many had read two missionary books, counting in the Bible as one, not more than fifteen hands went up. I felt strongly tempted to ask them how many had read one missionary book, counting in the Bible as one.

The addresses which are made to these churches are not always of the very best character. There are two ways in which we can disseminate information among the churches: first, through Ear-gate — through the spoken word; second, through Eye-gate — through the written page. There are two or three kinds of missionary addresses: the first the kind that palls upon the audience, the other that penetrates the audience; the first that leads the people to pity the speaker, the other that leads them to pity the heathen. In speaking upon the subject of missions, there are two ways of making our addresses interesting. First, to have the address merely amuse the audience. I know of a theological student who spoke on the subject of the Dark Continent. He told about the habits of the people; but the darkness and the soul-death of millions for whom Christ died he scarcely alluded to. The immediate effect was to raise a laugh; the ultimate result was to make them think Africa was a country to avoid.

The man who apologizes for foreign missions apologizes for his own conversion. We would have been heathen this afternoon had not foreign missions come to our ancestors in northern Europe. As Max Mueller says, "Christianity would cease to exist if it ceased to be missionary." "Christ is the propitiation for our sins, and not for ours only, but for the sins of the whole world."

In speaking in churches upon this subject there are two methods: the first to go to the church as an individual; the second method is to go out in groups. The Union Theological students last year divided themselves into seven groups. We scattered missionary information through the churches, and raised $5,000 for missions over and above what the churches were previously giving.

Secondly, we want to reach these people through Eye-gate: first, through missionary periodicals; second, through pamphlets or tracts; third, through missionary charts; and, fourth, through missionary books. Under the first point I want to name three periodicals: "The Missionary Review of the World," "The Missionary Echo," and "The Medical Missionary Record." We volunteers can secure the first for one dollar a year, the second for twenty-five cents a year, the third for fifty cents. Let us be sure to have these papers with us as we speak in churches, and have as many people as possible take them. Secondly, our leading Boards publish a large number of pan-denominational pamphlets.

The Baptist Board publishes, among others, three which I wish each of you could read: "China's Millions," "A Question of Ownership," and "The Bed Rock of Missions," by Rev. W. Ashmore, published at Tremont Temple, Boston. Then I would recommend that we secure as far as possible the pamphlets of the Student Volunteer Movement. The recent appeals from Japan, China, and India, I am sure, will burn their way into the hearts of the people in our congregations. Your address is once for all, but if you can leave something with the people to read, there will be a permanent impression among them. Mr. Kellogg, of Cornell University, has forty or fifty charts here with him. I heard last night of a man in one of the Western colleges who told him that the little chart that represents the 856,000,000 heathen by black squares had burned its way into his heart.

The last means by which we can influence churches and institutions is through missionary books, and I have a list here of twelve of what I consider absolutely essential missionary books. I would like very much to have you take down their names. 1. "The Crisis of Missions," by Dr. A. T. Pierson, $1.25. 2. "The Great Value and Success of Missions," by John Liggins, $0.75. 3. "In the Far East," by Miss Geraldine Guinness, an intensely spiritual book, which I hope every volunteer will read. 4. "The Centenary Report of Missions of the World's Conference," held in London, $2.00 for the two volumes. 5. "Medical Missions," by John Lowe, $1.50. 6. "The New World of Central Africa," by Mrs. H. Grattan Guinness, $2.00. 7. "China and the Chinese," by one we have with us, the Rev. J. L. Nevius, D.D., list price, $1.50. I can heartily recommend this book. And, also, in speaking of China, I would recommend a little book by Rev. J. T. Gracey, D.D., which costs only 15 cents, a capital work, containing a summary of the missionary work in China. 8. "India," the best work upon India, by Rev. J. T. Gracey, D.D., $1.00. 9. Upon Africa we all of course ought to read "Livingstone," by W. G. Blaikie, $1.25. 10. Also the life of A. M. Mackay," recently published by his sister, $1.50. 11. Upon India I would also recommend "The Life of William Carey," by Geo. Smith, $3.00. 12. On Japan, the best available book is "The Mikado's Empire," by W. E. Griffis, $4.00.*

I wish I had opportunity to name a number more, but I hope that we will secure these books and read them. If you have not money enough to buy the books, get your Band of volunteers to purchase them and put them in the volunteer library. We have a volunteer library in the Union Seminary, and I trust you will prevail upon your librarians to procure them.

It is not enough, however, to have missionary literature in our libraries. An appetite for it must be created, and here we can do a

---

* See List of Missionary Books at close of Report.

great deal of work. Instead of going to a man and asking him to read a book, ask him to peruse the most interesting chapter; for instance, the chapter on opium suicides, in " In the Far East," or " The Floating of the Dayspring," in " The Life of John Paton." I have a friend who has read " In the Far East " through three times, and says there are descriptive passages in it of such surpassing beauty as to rival Tennyson or Washington Irving. As some one has well said, " If disciples do not wish to flame with missionary enthusiasm, they must avoid contact with the heroic souls who have given their life to missions." And let us do all we can to get these facts before the churches, and we will have the missionary fire ; for I believe there is enough of the spark of love in our church members, if they had only the information before them. Fidelity to duty on our part means the evangelization of the world in the present generation. Lukewarmness on our part means another generation of millions lost. Fellow volunteers, what will eternity be for them, a joyous day or a starless night? Upon us more than upon any other class of Christians depends the answer to that question.

Woman's Work for Woman.

Miss Nettie Dunn, of the Executive Committee of the Student Volunteer Movement for Foreign Missions, presided over the Convention during the discussion of this topic, and introduced it with the following words: —

There is a beautiful illustration in the Bible; it is in the story of Ruth, as told in the second chapter of that book. Ruth said to her mother, " Let me now go to the field and glean ears of corn after him in whose sight I shall find grace." And her mother said, " Go, my daughter " ; and she went to the field and asked permission of Boaz to glean, and he said unto her, " Let thine eyes be on the field that they do reap, and go thou after them." And so food was provided for her, and a chance for the gleaning; and later on this lord of the harvest said, " Let her glean even among the sheaves, and reproach her not: and let fall also some of the handfuls of purpose for her, and leave them, that she may glean them, and rebuke her not." So she gleaned in the field until even, and brought in that night a wonderful gleaning as the result of that single day.

Dear friends, it is the story of Woman's Work for Woman. It was the men of our country who first took up the work in foreign lands. Thirty years ago the women of our nation began to say with Ruth, " Let me now go to the field," and they went; and they heard the Lord of the harvest say, " Let thine eyes be upon the field, and go out after the reapers." Thirty years ago the first woman found her way to a

Hindoo woman's heart, and up to the present day these women workers have been carrying the spirit of Christ into foreign lands. Thirty years ago there were no women's missionary societies on this continent; to-day there are forty-three different societies in different churches, and these societies are working in all the fields of the world, and I suppose they are raising nearly a million dollars a year and sending it out.

We have representatives of fifteen of these societies with us, and I wish some of you might read the letters that have come to us. We are to hear to-day from two of these representatives. The first of them is Miss Abbie B. Child, of the Woman's Board of Missions of the Congregational Church, who will now speak to us on —

Qualifications of Workers.

After all that has been said of the qualifications of workers, so well and so fully, by those who are so much wiser than I, it seems hardly best for me to do very much in this way; and yet perhaps, for a very few minutes, I might add some simple and I hope practical suggestions that may be of use to some of the women volunteers in this country. I understand there are one hundred of them present.

The first essential qualification I should mention would be that quality made so vivid to us by Prof. Drummond as the "Greatest Thing in the World" — Love; love for God and love for man as a foundation, and love for missionary work as the key-stone of the arch; a love for God and for His Son that will make one ready to obey His call wherever it may lead — to do His will whatever it may demand; a love for our fellowmen that will enable one to live year after year among degraded, ignorant women, patient, cheerful, untiring, trying to awaken the souls within them and lift them from the low plane on which they live; a love for missionary work that will make this the one thing in the world that one wants to do. Mere sentiment, any romantic ideas, any desire to see the world, can have no place here.

I believe the call to missionary work must come from the still small voice within. Like Elijah, we cannot hear the call in any short-lived fire of enthusiasm, kindled at a meeting like this, in any mighty wind of persuasion that comes from an eloquent speaker, nor in any earthquake of family life that sets one adrift upon the world. The thought may be born in one of these — it often is; but the real call comes from the still small voice that abides after these have passed away.

Love like this I have mentioned is born only of the Spirit, and will form a sure foundation upon which to rest the various other qualifications which go to make a successful missionary.

Among these we may mention : —

1. *Adaptability.* First, adaptability to circumstances : to be able to make the best of inconveniences great and small ; to be able to sleep on a tent floor or a comfortable bed ; to ride over a lonely mountain road, or to entertain a party of friends at home. Second, adaptability to people : to be able to get on with crooked sticks without unnecessary friction ; to be able to give up our pet schemes and theories.

2. *Versatility.* One never can tell what she may be called upon to do in the foreign field. She may find it necessary to teach men high in authority and of keen intellect, or the most ignorant woman ; to man a station ; to manage a hundred wild girls in a boarding-school ; to take care of a sick child ; to relieve a tired missionary's wife ; or undertake any kind of domestic drudgery. We love to look on missionary work as a high and holy calling, and so it is ; but not so high as to keep one from innumerable small kindnesses to smooth another's pathway. There was surely never a higher calling than that of our Lord, who came to redeem a lost world, and yet he was willing to labor at a carpenter's bench and to wash the disciples' feet.

3. *To know how to care for one's health.* From what I have seen I believe that to have the ability to take care of one's health is quite as important, if not more so, than to have vigorous health itself. To know the limit of one's possibilities ; to know when and how to rest ; how to select the most important things to be done and have strength of mind enough to leave some things undone, — may add years to one's life, and so to one's usefulness.

4. A qualification often mentioned is, *sanctified common sense* — one too important to be left out of any category. One must have common sense before it can be sanctified, and I believe it is a gift, but one that may be cultivated or destroyed. To sanctify common sense does not mean, I take it, to deprive it of any of its clear perception — its simple practical way of solving knotty problems ; it only means that these elements shall be intensified, and that it should be turned to a high and noble use.

5. This practical element, combined with *high intellectual training,* which we all acknowledge to be one of the first essentials in preparation for missionary life, makes a most desirable missionary. Just here let me say, that at least a year of practical experience before one leaves this country is most important. If one is to be a missionary teacher, let her teach in some school as like our mission schools as she can secure. If she is to do evangelistic work, let her spend a year in some Bible training school like the one under Mr. Moody's care in Chicago. If she is to be a physician, let her have a year's experience in a hospital.

6. As a sixth qualification I should mention a *steady persistence in well-doing*. Comets are very brilliant and interesting, but for reliable results we must depend on the fixed stars; and a comet could surely never represent the constant light and warmth of our Sun of righteousness.

7. A seventh requisite, which is so obvious that it need scarcely be mentioned in this presence, is a *spirit of prayer*. It is difficult to imagine any woman undertaking the foreign missionary work in her own strength. One man in a thousand might do it perhaps, but a woman never. When we stop to think what it is for a handful of men and women to go and settle down in a country with the avowed purpose of overturning the domestic, religious, even national, customs that have existed for centuries, surely no one would dare enter upon the work without a divine call, or take one step in it without divine guidance. With God all things are possible.

Mrs. N. M. Waterbury, of the Woman's Baptist Foreign Missionary Society, then spoke on the topic —

METHOD OF WORK AND NEED OF WORKERS.

The need of workers seems to be a foregone conclusion. You have recognized the need of workers, and therefore you are here to-day. There may be a little question still about the need of woman's work in foreign lands. Perhaps if I speak briefly of the methods of work you will comprehend why women are needed in this foreign mission work.

Our Missionary Union, after many years of single blessedness, no doubt, over parts of its work, united itself to the Woman's Board, which is auxiliary to it. One part of the work which the Woman's Board takes from the Missionary Union is the work among the children in foreign lands. We need women to do this work, particularly to go among the little children, to lead them and teach them and guide them. It is a wonderful work and a blessed work, this work of teaching the little ones of Christ, of educating them, of training them, of guiding them. Some one has compared it to that first miracle in Cana of Galilee, where Christ said, " Fill the water pots up to the brim." It was only water that went in, but wine that came out. And as we put the word of God into the hearts of those children, it don't mean to them what it will mean. God will turn it all into precious wine. This work for the children is women's work; and we want women who are willing to go out and gather in the poor little lost children of the world and lead them to Christ.

In India there is this peculiar state of things. The high-caste women are shut up in the zenanas. It would be a terrible disgrace and crime for a man to look upon one of these high-caste women. We need women for that work, which no man could do, however willing. That of course is peculiar to India; it does not apply to other countries. And yet, when we consider the millions of women in India, we must ask women in America to think of that phase of work. Then again, we have great masses of no-caste women throughout China, Africa, and India, — women who are as free to be about as the men. Why cannot women evangelize these women? They can occasionally hear the Word from men, but it comes to them with far more force from women.

If you were to go out with me into a little suburb of Madras, and to step into a little mud schoolhouse, you would see coming in fifty or sixty native women of the lowest caste, of the most degraded condition, coming in with their water jars on their heads and their babies on their hips, sitting down to listen for the first time to the story of Christ. They are not interested, but they have seen us come into the schoolhouse, and they come in. They sit down on the floor, and we do. We do not take up the Bible. You cannot understand how ignorant and degraded these women are; they must have something to catch their hearts and their attention.

At first, of course, as I went out, filled with methods and theories, I had certain addresses which I had prepared to deliver to these heathen women, and certain things which I thought would be very instructive and helpful to them. But somehow or other I did not seem to be popular in speaking to heathen women; they all slipped out, and I had to go home and wonder what was the matter. So I decided to let methods go largely, and to get my heart just as full of the love of Christ as it would hold, and go to these women as a sister and friend. I might take up the Bible and read a chapter to them; but in the meantime they are wondering: " What makes her feet black and her hands white? And what a queer dress that is! " And so they are discussing me and I am losing them.

Usually there are a dozen babies there. I pick up one of the babies — it is not an easy matter to pick up one of the babies, they are generally well oiled; but if you catch hold firmly and carefully you can get one up — and ask how old the baby is. " Six months." " What a remarkable baby," you say; and all the women crowd around to show their babies. I ask how many teeth the baby has. The mother opens the baby's mouth, and all the other mothers open their babies' mouths. They ask me if I have a baby. " Yes," I reply, " I have a little white baby over at the mission-house." Well, that is a great misfortune, they say; if I would only oil it and put it in the sun it would get black. So, after explaining to them that that is not my way of doing things, I ask them, "What are those scars all over the baby?" "Oh, yes," they tell me, "the other night the baby was possessed of an evil spirit, and we couldn't do anything, and we sent for a doctor and he burned it with a red-hot iron." I try to tell them how to help the baby, to come over to the mission-house and get a little bottle of pills that will drive the evil spirit out. So they come over to see my baby.

You think, What time she is wasting! We get impatient sometimes. I want to get the love of Jesus in their hearts, but how can I do it? At last the time has come; every woman — every mother, every sister, every grandmother there is interested. Then I say: "Keep still. Take up your babies and hold them still. I am going to tell you a story, but you must all listen. It is a story about a baby,— a wonderful, wonderful story. That is what I came to tell you. It is a little story about a baby." I needn't tell it to you, because you have heard it all your lives. But they had never heard the story of the little baby in Bethlehem, and they listened to it; and as they hear of the poor mother who had no place but a manger, and how the boy grew, and how his mother nursed him, and how he gave his life for them and their babies, they want to know more of this man who died for them. And so more and more we have followed Christ's method, and a little child has led some of these mothers into the kingdom of God.

There is other work, too: we want to train Christian women. Oftentimes the women say: "You have a good God, of course. We are bad, and we have a bad God." Then I can say, "Here are women just like yourselves; they came from that village over there, and from that temple, and they are Christian women." And the Christian women say: "Yes, my sister, a year ago we were like you. To-day we are worshipping this God. And he has saved us and helped us; and He has come to save you." So we find constantly a need of women to do the different parts of the work; and we need a great many more women.

THE VOLUNTEER'S PREPARATION.

Dr. Luther Gulick, of the Springfield School for Christian Workers, was unable to reach the Convention in time to speak on the first topic of this subject, and we present below a brief paper since furnished by him.

PHYSICAL QUALIFICATIONS FOR FOREIGN MISSIONARY SERVICE.

The following conclusions are the results of three generations of foreign missionary, and two generations of medical, service, united and studied with reference to the problem of the world's evangelization. I address missionary volunteers.

First conclusion: *You must be well.* The health of your body vitally affects your mental and spiritual conditions, and these usually determine the quantity as well as the quality of the work the Lord does through his servants. We may say that this is unreasonable, unphilosophical, illogical; but these are not to the point. The real ground of acceptance or rejection is whether the history of the Lord's work in foreign lands will bear it out. On this ground there is no room for discussion.

I do not say, nor do I imply, that one must be robust. Many a person delicate by natural inheritance has spent a long life of great usefulness by attention to the second point, which is, *you must know the laws of health.* I refer to hygiene, physiology, physical education.

In addition to the advantages year by year both as to quantity and quality of the work, mentioned before, it will add a score of years to your work at the time of life when, by your experience and influence, you are qualified to do your best work. A year of usefulness after twenty-five years of experience is worth several times as much as the first year when you have had no experience. Attention to this second point adds the years at the valuable end of your life. " My son forget not my law : but let thine heart keep my commandments ; for length of days and long life and peace shall they add to thee." This command and promise is literal, and not figurative. You cannot ignore God's laws about the body all your life and then be spared the punishment. It may, however, be visited most heavily on your children, if you are blessed with them, as exhausted physiques and that lack of reserve power of body which is usually seen in the children of the overworked.

The laws of the body are the same for missionaries as for other people. God demands obedience before sacrifice. There are to-day scores of consecrated men and women in this country whose hearts are in the foreign field, who are acquainted with the language and customs of those peoples, who have already won the confidences of the nations, and whom God has removed from these fields because they would not obey His laws about their bodies, and ignored the intimate relation that exists between their physical, mental, and spiritual conditions.

We say, "What a strange dispensation of God's providence," or "What an inscrutable leading." Being in the work of the Lord, the maker of law, does not free us from the obligation of obeying that law.

God wants us to carry the knowledge of His Son to the uttermost parts; the fields are white to the harvest. But He insists that we shall work in the lines that He indicates; and I firmly believe that *He*, and not we, are right in this matter. The man who overworks lessens the sum total of the work he can do, and so postpones the Day of the Lord.

One should be used to simple foods, simple habits, and independent of little changes in food and water, — all these can be cultivated. Knowledge of foods is invaluable. Englishmen going to India often keep on eating meat three times a day, and are visited with an inscrutable (?) dispensation of God's providence, in the shape of sickness. The climates of India and England are different and demand different foods.

I now place my argument on another ground. A prospective foreign missionary should cultivate a well formed, well disciplined body, because his body is an essential and eternal part of him. This is necessary in order to perfect manhood. ("As we have borne the image of the earthly, we shall also bear the image of the heavenly." — 1 Cor. 15 : 49.)

Christ's work is for the whole man (" For ye were bought with a price: glorify God therefore in your body." — 1 Cor. 6 : 20), and the missionary stands as an exemplar of that work to the people with whom he is. (" Ye are our epistle written in our hearts, known and read of all men." — 2 Cor. 3 : 2.)

The work of the Church at home and abroad is all tending back to the original plan as taught and practised by Christ, as work for the whole man — body, mind, and spirit.

In closing, your body must receive its due — not undue — share of attention, because it will enable you to do your best work, and because it is necessary, if you are to reach the best personal perfection which is possible to you, and which is our object in life to attain.

The Rev. F. F. Ellinwood, D.D., of the Board of Foreign Missions of the Presbyterian Church, treated the second division of the topic:—

THE INTELLECTUAL PREPARATION OF THE VOLUNTEER.

It is to my mind impossible to treat of the intellectual aspects of missionary work, without reference to the fact that there must underlie everything that belongs to the mind the great principle of the grace of God in the heart. Dr. Nevius told us this morning that there was in the conception of the Chinese no such idea as religion, but only teachings. In the great systems of India and of the Eastern world, those which we are specially confronted with in the great intellectual struggle, there is no idea of religion — everything is intellect, everything is knowledge, and that of the most speculative and metaphysical kind.

But in the missionary work we are ever to bear in mind that when we appeal to men darkened by sin, we must appeal to the whole being; for not with the brain, but with the heart, man believeth unto righteousness. And, therefore, in treating of intellectual preparation, we assume, first of all, that at the bottom and in the middle and at the top there must be consecration of the heart, there must be devotion to Jesus Christ, and every other department of the human soul must be considered with reference to that. If I were to put this thing in just the shape in which I would have it come clearly to your minds, it would be this: What you are to do in the preparation of the mind is wholly to be done with reference to the end in view.

There should, in the first place, be thorough preparation along all the lines of missionary work. A doctor should be thoroughly prepared, as was shown this morning, for the reason that if he is half prepared his work may bring injury. If his surgical cases are failures, they may only arouse the superstition of the people against him, and the failure of his surgery involves the failure of the whole prestige of the missionary work. So, if a man sent forth to preach the Gospel preaches it in a slipshod sort of way, showing that his mind has not been disciplined, that he is not master of the work he has in hand, that may operate against the cause, and he may do more harm than good. If he so imperfectly learned the language that he uses a word the very opposite of the one he wishes to use, arousing a spirit of ridicule and disgust in the audience, he has done harm.

In the second place, a man who goes out to the missionary field should understand the ground on which he wishes to work. What would a railroad company think of going into a country without studying its physical features? There ought to be just as much of that common sense, which we were told just now must exist before it can be sanctified, in all the processes and lines of work which concern the great missionary cause. Now, I know that I may perhaps arouse a little prejudice when I say that we must study the heathen systems which we are to encounter. And I would direct your minds, if you wish to see the principle of this, to Paul's instructions to young Titus, whom he made a bishop in Crete. Read the 8th, 9th, and 10th verses of the first chapter of the Epistle to Titus, where he warns the young man to prepare to meet opposition. That kingdom had been swept with the worship of Baal, the worst of the heathen religions, and he is told in that Epistle that there were men going about leading whole households astray.

There are just such men as that in India. I remember seeing one of the best missionaries I knew in India actually broken up in a bazaar mission by a man paid to do this work, and provided with all the sharp questions that can be gleaned from the keenest infidels, to puzzle the speaker and get the laugh of the crowd on him. I was told by a young missionary that he encountered such questions as this: "Do you say that God created this world for His own glory?" "Yes." "Well, did it add to His glory to create this world?" "Why, yes; His glory was promoted." "Did He then receive something that He didn't have before He created the world?" "Well, yes." "Well, was he then quite complete before? was He infinite, was He perfect before?" These questions were asked by a Sunday School scholar, a boy of seventeen. Another question: "You say God pervades the whole world?" "Yes." "He is in all living beings?" "Yes." "All things?" "Yes." "Well, then, is He not in that idol? and, if so, why do you forbid us to worship it?" These are questions put by professionals, for the very purpose of meeting the missionary and thwarting him. Do not learn the heathen systems for your own sake, to become a *savant;* but find out their inconsistencies and enormities and absurdities, that you may place instead of these the true word as it is in Jesus Christ.

We are told that Ambrose, Bishop of Milan, used to sit up nearly all night in prayer or reading. He had just two books which he used in those vigils; the one was the Bible, and the other the philosophy of Plato. You are shocked that a man of prayer, praying in the night watches, should have Plato, a heathen philosopher. Did Plato add anything to the Bible? Not at all; but his idea was to see the relations which existed between the profoundest of the world's philosophers and the blessed word of God. And it was by just the discriminating knowledge thus acquired that he won the power that enabled himself and others, strong men,— not a Salvation Army, but men who grappled with the greatest heathen problems the world ever saw or will see,— to conquer and sweep away all the gods of the Roman Pantheon, and rear there the love and light of Jesus Christ.

Another thing: study these systems that you may not do them an injustice. If a man blunders, if he gets up before an audience and shows that he is ignorant, if he depends upon ignorant denunciation instead of intelligent discrimination, let him beware lest he misrepresents, blocks the way, shows the people that he does not understand their systems, and therefore is merely trifling and blundering and doing harm.

In the second place, let him study the systems of the country, especially in India and Japan, for he may know full well that there are keen, educated young men there who know all about Christian principles; they have learned it in the mission school and elsewhere. They know all about their own systems. They know all the cheap thrusts of our modern infidelity. They know all that has been published here and there of the beauty and glory of Buddhism and Brahmanism. They are armed at all points. How is a missionary, who has given no thought to such subject, to grapple with such men? One of our missionaries in Siam was asked by a young Siamese prince, "What do you think of the 'Forty Mistakes of Moses,' by Ingersoll?" Another wrote of his astonishment at being met with arguments from Huxley from a man who had hardly a rag of clothing on.

Again, study these systems in the spirit of Christ. I wish we might have something like the "Present Day Tracts," published by the Religious Tract Society in London. I would not advise missionaries to give much time to the study of these systems, but I wish there might be put into the hand of every missionary a well prepared little tract with just the concrete pith of the argument against all these lines of attack, against all these allegations of Buddhism and atheism and Hindooism, something like Canon Taylor's "Mohammedanism." We must have some idea of these things; we must know where the main points are; we cannot go out as ignoramuses.

We must remember that this is an age of intellectual activity; that the rippling waves of error and truth are sweeping over all the world; that in India they are now using the English language, which we taught them as missionaries, as a vehicle with which to spread all the vilest French novels, translated into English, and all the English works of the same nature. I saw the other day a report from the English Vernacular Society of London. One of their agents had gone through the bazaars of Calcutta, and he found stores piled up to the very ceiling in the back rooms with cheap reprints of the vilest French novels. An American carried out almost a shipload of them to Siam; and it was found, as stated by one of our missionaries lately, that the Siamese of the higher class were withdrawing their girls from education, because they found that their education opened the way to them for the vilest novels of Christendom. They shrunk back; they said, "If this is civilization and this is education, we must withdraw our girls from it in self-defence."

Now, we must meet this state of facts, and supply India and Siam and Japan and China with the truth, and with the truth on its controversial side to some extent; and, far more, with that truth which is the very spirit and love of Christ, and which brings the heart into contact with Him, and which leads the Christian to say, as Paul said, with the same tact and overpowering love, "Whom ye ignorantly worship, him declare I unto you."

I was last week at Lockport, at the Young Men's Christian Association Convention. I was thrilled; I was spiritually benefited and lifted up. And I had my mind at the same time on this Convention, which I expected to attend. Perhaps some are here who were there; but I am impressed with the fact of the mighty power that God is raising up in the hearts and minds of young men. And now I want to ask that not only through your Volunteer Movement, by which you send out men to the field,—and I bless God for that Movement, I believe it is in answer to the prayers of Christians,—but what I want to say is, Multiply ways and means of spreading the truth. I do wish that we might have, among the young men of this country, a combined effort for flooding India and Japan and China with Christian literature, the brightest, tersest, most concise that you can find, along a thousand different lines. Send it out like the leaves of autumn, for it is comparatively few men and women that you can send, in proportion to the demand; and if Satan is flooding the heathen world with all the blackest, vilest literature, let us at least employ the English tongue, which we have established, as a vehicle for the dissemination of truth to as great a degree, and vastly more.

Question. Do you intend to convey the thought that only the best educated men should go as missionaries to India?

Answer. I believe, from the standpoint which I represent, that our best policy, with the limited means we have, is to send the most thoroughly educated men we can. I rejoice in every form of missionary effort. I believe in sending missionaries of different grades. But I don't think it would be good policy for us. I don't believe in sending out the young men who go out in business. I might differ a little from Dr. Dowkontt; I doubt whether those who go to support themselves should be labeled with the missionary work. Here is a young man who is partly supported by a Missionary Board and partly engaged in business. Men in that city will be disgusted and outraged by what they consider an injustice. They will say, "You are supported here by somebody, and you are breaking up the competition." I wish there were ten thousand earnest young men who would go out and simply engage in business and be members of Young Men's Christian Associations out there. But do not involve the missionary and the mission societies. A commission merchant in New York said to me, " Your missionaries are all in business to some extent, are they not? " " No," I said, " they are not." We find it absolutely necessary to make a point of that, to avoid evil questions. " But," he says, " I am receiving orders from a missionary." It transpired that in a few instances there had been such missionaries engaged in business, and the implication was that all the missionaries were engaged partly in business, and thus there was a false impression conveyed.

Mr. S. M. Sayford presented the next topic in the following words : —

Preparation in Soul Winning.

The ultimate end to which all Christian efforts converge is the winning of souls to Jesus Christ, in order to the establishment of His kingdom when He who is the Prince of the kings of the earth shall be King over all. The standard of the value of a soul is determined by the price that is paid for the soul's redemption. " For God so loved the world that he gave his only begotten Son that whosoever believeth in him should not perish, but have everlasting life." The gift involving sacrifice is based upon two most important considerations, — love and knowledge. We must love men for whom Jesus Christ died, and know that men need to be saved, because men are lost. We need to love God, who sent Jesus Christ into the world, and know Jesus Christ in order that we may bear witness of Him.

Now, there are just two things necessary in order that a witness may be faithful : first, that he knows that about which he is going to talk ; and, second, that he is truthful. And no man can testify concerning Jesus Christ unless he knows Him. Paul says, " I know whom I have believed, and am persuaded that he is able to keep that which I have committed unto him against that day." Blessed be God for the assurance concerning the safety of the man who trusts in Jesus Christ.

The doctrine of redemption or salvation is the impelling and propelling force of all Christian effort ; I mean, of course, aside from the sacred energy. I use the word impelling in the sense that it sends a a man, and the word propelling in the sense that it keeps a man going ; and I believe that that doctrine underlies all genuine effort to hasten the coming of the King in His glory.

This great Scriptural fact is the fundamental preparation for effective work in winning souls. Christ called men to follow Him that they might become fishers of men. And very soon afterwards we find Him in the synagogue teaching and preaching, and all men marvelled, because He spoke as one having authority and not as the scribes and Pharisees. So these men followed Jesus in order that they might become fishers of men. And we are not in the dark as to what Jesus Christ taught His disciples; for, in summing up just before He went back to glory, He says, in the last chapter of Luke's Gospel: "These are the words which I spake unto you, while I was yet with you, that all things must be fulfilled, which were written in the law of Moses, and in the prophets, and in the psalms, concerning me. Then opened he their understanding, that they might understand the Scriptures, and said unto them, Thus it is written, and thus it behoved Christ to suffer, and to rise from the dead the third day: and that repentance and remission of sins should be preached in his name among all nations, beginning at Jerusalem."

Now, my dear friends, I do not believe, to start with, that the Gospel of the Son of God can be improved upon. I believe the Gospel is the power of God unto salvation as much to-day as it was when these words were first uttered. A new Gospel is some other Gospel. A mutilated Old Testament means, sooner or later, a mutilated New Testament; a mutilated New Testament means a mutilated Gospel before long; and we have no warrant in the word of God that any other Gospel is the glad tidings of salvation or that any other news than that can save lost men to-day.

Now, in preparation for soul winning, we need to study the Bible. I have not the time to make the distinction I would like to make here, but I can sum it up thus — to study the Bible in order to find Christ rather than to lose Moses. You know what that means. Christ says, in the fifth chapter of John, the 39th verse, "Search the Scriptures; for in them ye think ye have eternal life: and they are they which testify of me." Paul, writing to Timothy, commended Timothy because he knew the Scriptures: "From a child thou hast known the Holy Scriptures, which are able to make thee wise unto salvation through faith which is in Christ Jesus." And then follows the statement, "All Scripture is given by inspiration of God, and is profitable."

Now, I would sum up the preparation on the theoretical side in just these three statements: First, come to Christ, in order that you may follow Christ. Second, learn of Christ, in order that you may know the doctrine of salvation. Third, pray for the power of the Holy Ghost, that you may preach in demonstration of the Spirit and with power. Now, that brings me, just for a few moments, to the practical side of the question in distinction to the other, and that has to do with the handling of men. I dread this subject, because I believe there are men and women here from foreign fields who have been handling men, who are infinitely better qualified to discuss this question than I am. But, since the fact has been emphasized that men are men all the world over, and that all the world over there are men lost away from God, without help or hope, who need Jesus Christ, I will nevertheless venture to speak.

This preparation for soul winning begins when the man comes to Jesus Christ, and never ends until the man is crowned with Him in glory. It is a preparation that you cannot afford to put off until your feet touch the foreign soil: if so, you are losing golden opportunities every day, the like of which you will never have beyond the walls of these institutions of learning. Somebody says, "But I cannot talk to a man on this subject in college, because we know each other so well." That ought to be one of the best reasons in the world why you could win a man to Jesus Christ. Seven-tenths, possibly, of the men who make this excuse cannot press this question upon the attention of men they know, because, in all human probability, they have not been living right before men who do not profess what they profess. We who are vessels need to be sanctified in some such sense as the vessels of the Church are sanctified; we who are temples for the indwelling of the Holy Ghost need to be sanctified or dedicated in some such sense as these temples made with hands are sanctified or dedicated — set apart for holy service, set apart for a holy life.

I believe that no man here can receive the power of the Holy Ghost which Jesus Christ promised when he went away unless the man is clean. I do not forget the beautiful illustration which Dr. Gordon used with reference to the emphasis that is laid upon the need for a man to cleanse himself. I do not forget that, nor do you, when he spoke of the two ways of emptying a tumbler, one to turn it upside down, and the other by putting quicksilver in and crowding the water out gradually. But how about the man who has those things about him that he is not willing to give up for Christ's sake? "Grieve not the Holy Spirit of God whereby ye are sealed unto the day of redemption."

Up in the hills of New Hampshire, some time ago, I had my attention called to one of those little neglected farms. There was an old dilapidated building on it. I went through to the little woodshed in the rear, and there I saw a running stream of cool water. Its source was up on the hill; it was constantly running. There was a tin cup there, and in the cup there were some stones. Now, then, I might have poured water in that cup from then until now, and the stones would remain, and in that sense the cup never would be full, and it never could be filled with water until the stones were taken out. And it is with these stones in our hearts and lives that we must grapple, and by the grace of God cast them out, in order that we may be clean for the Master's use. And when we are, there is simply this one thing left for us to do, and that is to study man.

Somebody suggested on this platform to-day that it would be a good thing for a man to spend some time in an industrial institution. I remember when a divinity student of Yale said to me, "How is a man, crowded as I am, going to get into contact with men personally?" I said : "A man passed here a while ago, while I was waiting in your college hall, carrying a hod of coal. I said to him, 'You have a fine institution.' He said, 'Yes; they are a nice set of men.' I said to him, 'Are you a Christian?' He set down his coal hod and answered, 'You are the first man that ever asked me that question.'" There was a man for whom Jesus Christ died, a janitor in the divinity school, never approached on the subject of religion by those whose end in in life it was to save souls for Jesus Christ.

Go and meet some man and touch the tender spot in his heart. Does it pay? you say. Yes, it pays over and over again. When Stratton touched a drunken man under the lamp-post years ago, in Boston, and said, "Young man, there is a better life for you than this," the man replied, "How do you know?" Then Stratton pointed him to this better life, and started him in the preparation for that marvelous career, which was embodied in the late John B. Gough, that man who brought rays of sunshine to hearts and homes in many lands. It pays to win any man to the love of Jesus Christ, it does not make any difference where he is. Study men; learn how to approach them. What a beautiful illustration was that given us to-day by Mrs. Waterbury! Get on the sunny side of man, and then when you have reached him tell the story of the Christ who came to seek and save those who are lost.

After 4 p.m. the Convention broke up into several conferences held simultaneously for the discussion of the following phases of foreign missionary work : Medical, Educational, Evangelistic, and Industrial. A conference upon woman's work for woman was held at the same time, and conducted by Miss Nettie Dunn.

Evening Session.

The evening session of the Convention opened with a brief song service, conducted by Mr. Smith. The devotional exercises were conducted by Mrs. Steven, of the China Inland Mission, speaking more especially upon the theme —

The Spiritual Preparation of the Volunteer.

I feel, dear friends, that this subject that has been given to me, the one of spiritual preparation for foreign work, is the most important subject that could be given to anybody; and why the Lord has given it to me I am sure I don't know. In the first place, what is our work to be? Our work is to be that of witnessing. The Lord Jesus said, " Ye shall be witnesses unto me." That is to be our work.

In order that we may prepare ourselves to witness for Jesus, it is absolutely necessary that we shall sit much at His feet, that we shall learn of Him of whom we are to witness, because unless we know Him of whom we witness, and unless we have been brought into personal contact with Him, we cannot witness about Him. By sitting at the Master's feet I do not just now mean in prayer meetings, or in church gatherings, or in public meetings of any kind, but sitting at the Master's feet to know Him. How do we best learn to know people? Not in the busy crowd, not in the great gatherings in convention, but when we can be alone together the heart speaks to the heart; then we come to know a person. And it is only so that we can know Jesus. I do feel that this sitting at Jesus' feet, away from everybody, getting low down at His feet, listening to His voice, is the only way in which we may know Him and get the necessary power to witness.

Then, as a result of sitting at the Master's feet, will follow two very necessary things in preparation for foreign work, or any work the Master gives us to do. The first seems to me to be emptying. We want to be emptied of self, of our own opinions. You remember how the Lord Jesus told the disciples, when He gave them their great command, that they were to go to Jerusalem and stay there until they should be filled with power from on high. When He told them to go forth and preach the Gospel to every creature I have often thought how they must have longed to go then; but he said, "tarry."

We are told that there was a time in the life of Moses when he evidently thought that he was the proper man to deliver Israel. He supposed that all his brethren would understand that the Lord was going to deliver them by his hand. But the Lord had to deal with him. He had to tarry. He had to come to understand that he could not do anything at all. He had to be thoroughly emptied. And, unless we are emptied, the Lord cannot fill us with the Holy Spirit. But oh, dear friends! if we become humble in spirit and want to be emptied, we will be emptied, and He will fill us with power. The strength we have to do this service will be all His strength; the love we have for those dark souls will be His love. He will give us His patience in dealing with them. What will He not give us, what can He not do for us? There are two things, it seems to me, we have to understand. In the first place, that we can do nothing, and that we are nothing; and, in the second place, that we can do all things. We are nothing in ourselves; we are weakness itself; but, oh! may He make us weak enough so that His own strength may be put in us; and then we can do all things through Christ who strengtheneth us. Oh! may He grant in all the service He shall give us to do that first and foremost may be His glory; and then, if that is so, He will use us, and He will work through us, and we shall have the power, and souls will be brought to Him.

Rev. George W. Chamberlain, D.D., of Brazil, then addressed the Convention on —

The Spiritual Crisis in the Occident.

I do not know who painted that map [indicating large map above the platform showing the distribution of the different religious systems of the world], but, as I have looked upon it, and especially upon the Occident, I have thought it must have been some descendent of Bezaleel whom God inspired. I am not responsible for the wording of the topic as it has been announced, but I accept it — "The Spiritual Crisis in the Occident." From the Land of the Rising Sun to the going down thereof beyond the Golden Gate, His name shall be great. There is a crisis in the Occident. "There is a tide in the affairs of men which taken at its flood leads on."

As shown upon that map in an enlarged scale [indicating a map of Brazil] is the part of the Occident from which this crisis utters its voice to the volunteers. It crowds itself into a cry, " O la! vem ca!" If that is not your mother tongue it is the mother tongue of many a brother; and it is addressed to you from your brother of the Latin tongue: " O thou there, come here!" Your land is bathed in sunlight. It has the color of gold on it, the light of the Sun of righteousness. And then to the south of you look at the blood, the black in red, the voice of your brothers' blood crieth from the very ground. [The map referred to showed red as the color of those parts of South America where the Roman Catholic religion prevails, and black those parts of

Brazil inhabited by heathen Indians.] I am aware that those who have possessed that part of this Occident world may find reason of offense; and, not only that, but many of you will take offense at the truth, not because you are not of the truth, but because Christian charity operates in the hearts of many of God's elect to persuade them to try the experiment of the fable of the man who brought the frozen snake to his heart and warmed it. And it is not only a crisis in South America and Mexico, it is a crisis in our own country in regard to the system which arrogates to itself the name of the Holy Mother Church, but a church which is dry of the milk of the Gospel. The author of "Our Country," a book which you have all read I trust, in the first chapter of the book says, that what has transpired in our country in the last century is without precedent and must remain without a parallel, because there are no new worlds to be discovered.

When a fellow missionary of mine read the book in the mountains of Brazil he said, "It makes one's hair stand on end to see the problems which confront our Church at home." Yes; but it ought to make the very blood in your heart curdle to think that we have in the South, in the territory of Brazil, a theatre prepared by the hand that fashioned the earth, for the reception of a heathen population, for the enactment of the same drama, and that that drama involves for the Christian Church a facing of those problems, with no Plymouth Rock behind us, and no Hugenot blood in our veins. And you have thrust out into that fiery furnace a few of your volunteer brethren, — twelve in the whole country, ten in Brazil, — and you expect them to quench the fire that has been consuming those nations three centuries.

At all the conventions I ever attended among my fellow Christians at home, I have heard little reference to this Occidental land, to which the Lord of all lands in the earth calls upon us to give the Gospel.

Two hundred and twenty-nine of your number are already in Asia, thirty-three are in Africa, twelve in South America, eleven in Mexico, two in Central America, two in Cuba, five among the Indians to the north of you. I could not help saying to Dr. Storrs awhile ago: "You call yourselves the American Board. Why do not you put an oar to us in the South?" Put it in their power and there will be more. Let there be means and men will come. But why should they go? Does the cry, "O thou there, come here," touch you? Why, if it were nothing more than "an infant crying in the night and with no language but a cry," it would touch every mother's heart here. We would only need to hear it without those walls to awaken compassion in the heart of every mother's son here. It is the cry, not of one infant, but of all the infants born into that land; it is the cry of the men and of the women. How can I prove it? They may not be conscious of that cry; they may not have voiced it in words; but some one has voiced it right there in the colors of the map. What means that black in red? The indigenous population, I suppose. There are a million of them in Brazil alone, so estimated. What do they know about the Gospel? They have been surrounded by that red color for three centuries, representing a church which says it is the Christian Church, charged with the mission of Christ to the nations. I have answered that question repeatedly.

I met an old Brazilian at the mouth of the Amazon ninety years of age, who knew much of the Indians. I said, "Can you tell whether there has ever been any portion of the Gospel translated into the general tongue of the Indians? "No," he replied, "I am interested in the Indians, but I have never known of any part of the Gospel being translated into their language. I have a catechism over two hundred years old, translated into their tongue by the Jesuits." He says: "Take the book and use it. I am too old to do anything more; take it and do something for the Indians." As I opened it on the high seas between Para and New York I came upon a page with these questions: "How many places are there to which the soul at death can go? There are four. What are they? Hell, purgatory, limbo of the fathers, limbo of the children. What is hell? Hell is a fire in the center of the earth to which the wicked go at death. What is purgatory? Purgatory is a fire above that of hell to which the souls of the holy go that they may get satisfaction for sin for which they did not get satisfaction in this life. What is the limbo of the fathers? It is a cavern above purgatory to which the souls of the holy fathers went formerly, before that Jesus Christ was manifested in the flesh to take them out." On the margin of this catechism some one had written, opposite the definition of the limbo of the fathers, words in Portuguese which translated read, "It is now for rent." I read that to a friend in New York and he said, "It will do for the brethren of the new theology." The catechism continued: "What is the limbo of the children?" O ye mothers hear! "It is a cavern above the limbo of the fathers, into which the souls of little children who died without baptism go, a land of darkness and of the shadow of death, to wander forever."

Is that an obsolete doctrine? As you ride through the roads of Brazil and pass by any cemetery you will see little catacombs outside of the walls of the cemeteries, and you will inquire what they are. They are the tombs of children who could not go into holy ground because their souls had gone to limbo. They died without baptism, and they cannot go to heaven. They are buried in stone like the stony heart of the holy mother church that tells this to the mothers to whom Christ said, "Let the little children come unto me."

Is that confined to this church in South America? No, no! If the artist had been a little truer, there would have been streaks of this very red fire of purgatory running all through this yellow [referring to the United States, which was colored yellow on the map, as indicating the predominance of Protestantism]. It is taught here. You do not believe it perhaps. Some of you have read, " Our Christian Heritage," by Cardinal Gibbons, and you are persuaded that that is what Rome teaches; and you are inclined to be very charitable to the church that teaches after all the truth. Rome is Babylon; Rome teaches both things; Romes faces about; Rome confounds men, she confounds the very elect. That is not the book that Cardinal Gibbons wrote for his own church; he wrote it for you. He wrote another book, " The Faith of Our Fathers," which is both; it has two faces. You find that Rome is *ubi semper eadem*, here and everywhere. People tell you Rome is different here from what it is in South America. It is the same difference you will notice in a ship sailing with every stitch of canvas, straight on her course into port, as she has done in South America, and has cast her anchor, and the same ship beating up against head winds, obliged sometimes to tack and run back on her course. It is her own boast.

Now, what does the red in that map mean? Not only the fire of purgatory for the souls of the holy, but the fire for the word of God. Let me voice the cry again of an old gray-headed Brazilian, who said to me in 1865, in San Paulo: "Young man, what was your father about? My father died without knowing there was a Bible in the world. You say you have had it always. Why do you not have compassion, why do you not have a fellow-feeling? My father was a religious man. He taught me all that he ever knew, but he never said " Bible " to me. He died without knowing there was such a book; and here it is in my hands now, and I find that he was wrong." I said to him : " My friend, when my father and those who lived with him attempted to put this book into your father's hands, it was contraband in the custom house. It was only lately that the civil arm has broken the ecclesiastical in this respect, and the word of God is coming up the mountain ranges. What are you going to do?" " I shall see that my boys shall have no complaint of me. I know it is the word of God, and approves itself to my conscience." I saw him a few years ago, a leader in the presbytery at San Paulo. He came to represent a church in his neighborhood, and he said: " Now I can say, ' Lord, let thy servant depart in peace, for mine eyes hath seen thy salvation.' My boys " — he had twelve and a daughter — " my boys are all married. My grandchildren are growing up in the knowledge of this book, and now I am ready to go home." I said: " Senor Henrico, what you have done is for your own children. Remember the children about you." "I shall take care of that as long as the Lord keeps me alive," he replied. And he does; wherever he goes the Bible goes in his pocket, and he gives it to others or reads it to them. He is a representative of the white population. If I were to put old Henrico Gomez on this stand you could not distinguish him from any Anglo-Saxon in this land.

I have spoken of the Indian. What other classes are there there? We have two millions of black freedmen, sons of Brazil, now free, but many of them natives of Africa, speaking the lingo of their own people, remembering the scenes of their childhood in Africa, and yearning to go back. A million of Indians, two millions of Africans, ten millions of Portuguese, and their descendants. They mingled in the early colonial times with the Indians, and we have the mestizoes. They mingled with the negro in later times, and formed the mulatto class. We have every shade of color in Brazil; we are cosmopolitan. We cannot draw the color line at our communion table or anywhere else; if you drew a color line it would be a zig-zag streak of lightning which would knock everybody down. In describing the condition of these thirteen millions of Brazil, I describe the condition of the rest of South America and of Mexico. In speaking of their condition I have only represented to you their need, and that is a voice, — silent it may be, unconscious to them, — the voice of your brother's blood, and it crieth from the very earth.

But that is not the only crisis. What is a crisis? Look at your dictionary; spelt it with a *k;* think of the Greek — to separate, to divide, to determine, to condemn. You look under crime, coming from the same root — to separate, to determine, to decide; it is a crisis. How closely they are related, crime and crisis. The failure to respond to the crisis at this time of the Lord's judgment, when He is manifestly expressing His judgment as to what His Church ought to do, will become a crime from this day forward if this Volunteer Movement does not imply also the giving of the Gospel of Christ as freely to our brethren of the rest of this hemisphere as we have received it from our forefathers. You and I can never say again, as I said to the old man who first asked me why we had not had compassion, we can never say again, that there was no freedom, for, by the judgments of the Lord which have been in the earth in the last few years, there is now absolute freedom, so far as the republic of the United States of Brazil is concerned, and there is almost absolute freedom in regard to the rest of the land; that is, there is no limit upon the giving of the Gospel to them except the limit of our will power, of our volunteering power. When the judgments of the Lord are abroad in the earth the inhabitants should learn righteousness. What has the Lord been saying to us in these last eighteen months? Why did he thrust eighteen representatives of the South American governments into the very eye of this nation in October and November of 1889? And why, on the very day of their opening their session for consultation, did the telegraph tell us that there was no more a throne on this continent? Think! Between the rising and the setting of the sun, God had allowed the tides to come together, — liberal, conservative, and republican,— and they had rushed together at His bidding, and they lifted the last throne on this continent, and floated it clear over the Atlantic Ocean, and it will never come back; and with it they floated the hopes of Rome as to her domination, yet it hastened to bless the republic. The Archbishop of Bahia, within three weeks after the babe was born, sent the papal blessing to them; that meant, " Bless me; do not cut off my revenue." But when the revenues were cut off by the government determining that there should be thenceforward no state patronage, that every one should have the right to express his opinions without prejudicing his rights as a citizen, the church began to curse, not openly but inwardly, and issued a proclamation that unless the constitution suffered modification they would find themselves confronted by the apostolate, as the twelve bishops called themselves and the twelve millions of Roman Catholics; and they began to form their clerical party. But they found themselves so weak that they did not dare to put one man in nomination. The elections came on on the 15th of September, the convention met on the 15th of November, 1890, and the constitution was adopted on the 24th of February, 1891, amid the acclamations of all. On the 25th of February they elected their President, under a constitutional regime copied closely from our own, and superior to it in points already recognized as defective in ours.

What does this mean? We cannot separate Jesus Christ from politics; He puts up whom He will and puts down whom He will. " Be wise therefore, O ye kings, be instructed, ye judges of the earth; serve the Lord." What does it mean for you? How shall they call upon Him whom they have not known? But you say, Are they not Christians? were they not baptized in the name of the Father, Son, and Holy Ghost? But what does that mean? Men confront me with that argument, and say they baptize in the name of the Father and of the Son and of the Holy Ghost. Of course they do. Did you ever know the forger of a note to be careless in imitating the signature. The question is, Does it represent bullion? is there anything back of it? Who is the Father? A Jupiter Tonans, with a thunder bolt ready to hurl upon you? Who is the Son? Nominally a mediator, but displaced by the saints — they have not enough days in the calendar for all of them, so they have the Day of All Saints. And not only this host of obstacles, but above all the mother of God: to her you must appeal, whether in South America or here or anywhere where that system dominates. Why? Well, in the minds of the people it is sifted down to this plain logic: What kind of a son would he be if he did not obey his mother? But does this lie only so in the minds of the people? When the twelve bishops of Brazil returned from the Vatican Council they held a jubilee, and the bishop of the diocese of San Joseph said to the assembled priests and students: "The church is happy to have for a universal patron so powerful a one as St. Joseph. These are troublous times for the bark of St. Peter, and we need a strong arm on the helm, and St. Joseph is *duas vezes omnipotente*. He is the putative father of Jesus Christ, and the legitimate spouse of the mother of God. It is written in the Gospel that Jesus was subject to His parents. And the legitimate spouse is obedient to her husband." If that had been picked up by one of our reporters we might have stood in some doubt as to the accuracy of it. But it was published in the ultramontane organ "O Apostolo," and gloried in, and it represents what that dominant church calls the truth.

Need of the Gospel of Christ there is. Is there a supply? That depends upon you. Is there a demand? Oh! if I could carry you there and confront you with the hungry-eyed people who want to know all about it, you would know whether there is a demand for the Gospel. Need? Yes. Demand? Yes. Supply? Twelve men. For what? Consider that without touching any other portion of South America you have in Brazil, a territory equal to that of the United States; that you have not only that 13,000,000 of people there needing the Gospel, but inevitably in this generation millions yet to come to whom we must minister the Gospel. Slavery is gone. Brazil is as hungry for labor as a dry sponge for water. It is going to gather in men from every quarter of the Orient, where there is a superabundance, and we are to confront there these problems which make your hair stand on end at home, notwithstanding all your resources of churches and other societies of the Christian Church. All of these problems are to be thrust upon us within a generation. Do we need you? Yes; if we had you all down there you would find work. And the cry to each one of you is, "O there, come here!" When I heard that cry first, it was uttered just at this point [indicating on the map], half way between Rio Janerio and San Paulo, on those mountains. It was the cry of one man lost on the mountains, and it brought up the mountain side twelve Brazilians. That man voices the cry of 13,000,-000 to you, out of the way they are, not for a night, but for eternity, unless you succor them with the word of God.

Rev. Judson Smith, D.D., of the American Board, addressed the Convention on —

THE SPIRITUAL CLAIMS OF THE ORIENT.

Young Christian friends of the Volunteer Movement, it has been a great pleasure to me these days to sit here with you and share in your deliberations, catch the spirit that animates you, and come a little closer to the purpose that fills your hearts, and to note how your eyes and souls look away from these scenes to the distant lands whence that call is that has raised your hearts and caused you to put name and purpose to this Movement to which you belong. As I have sat here and noted the numbers, the spirit, the strength of the Movement, I have drawn a contrast in my mind with a movement like this in its interior aim something more than a century ago; for the Volunteer Movement for Foreign Missions did not begin in 1886, at Mt. Hermon; indeed, it did not begin at the time of which I speak. But a century ago there was a movement full of interest, fascinating to study, instructive to you, young friends, to-day.

Go to Northamptonshire in England; look in upon the humble home there where a young man sat upon the cobbler's bench and gathered patiently, laboriously, the facts about the world of his times. And, that he may impress upon himself and upon others more distinctly the facts as he ascertains them, he makes a rude map, — sketches the countries of which he reads, — and as he gathers his facts writes them in — the people, their habits, their religious convictions, and their needs. And that map hangs before him day by day, its facts filling up, the world becoming more and more distinct to his view, impressing his mind and teaching his heart. And when others come into that shop of William Carey, he does not speak to them of the gossip of the day, but he turns their thoughts to that which fills his own soul, and repeats the facts he has ascertained, and seeks to impress upon them the spiritual needs of the wide world. And, as his eye follows land after land, — these are heathen, and these are heathen, and these are heathen, — his mind is overwhelmed and his eyes gush out in tears. My friends, there is instruction as well as fascination in that wonderful story, the beginning of the missionary interest in William Carey, which raised up the English Baptist Missionary Society, and at length brought him, the first volunteer of that movement, out into India to the splendid career as a missionary which he there ran.

The course he followed, I take it, is that which you have followed. That which moved you has been, not so much the difficulty of Missionary Boards, as another difficulty, not distinctly uttered in human speech, but wafted on the night air, speaking of spiritual destitution among the millions and hundreds of millions that dwell upon the face of the earth and know not God. You have heard the voice of China's millions, a voice that is not articulate, but that to the Christian's heart appeals more resistlessly because it has no cry, because the hearts that speak it are not yet sensible of all their need.

The fact of heathenism, which was the great fact in all William Carey's studies, that shaped his life to that marvelous career, is to-day just as appealing and just as dark as it was to him. Geographically it is spread all over the face of the earth wellnigh as broadly now as then. It is a greater fact than it was in his day. The heathen population of that day, under his estimate, was 430,000,000; but even with a just estimate of the facts of his day, the heathen population of the world to-day is greatly in excess of what it was in his day. We reckon it up at over 850,000,000. The heathen population needing the knowledge of God, who make their appeal to the Christian people of to-day, are more numerous now than then — not that missions have failed, but the population of the world has increased, that of heathen lands equally with the population in other lands.

Now, for a moment, let us pass over in our thought the facts which are so familiar, which we have often studied. I wish to turn your thought specially to the heathen peoples of our day. They are the people among whom the Bible and redemption through Jesus Christ are not found. I do not say they are the people among whom God is not known, for He hath not left himself without witness to any people. They are the people among whom the Bible, Jesus Christ, and redemption through him are unknown, where false religions and idolatry prevail. We understand that very well. They include 850,000,000 — the greater part of the population of Asia, the vast bulk of the population of Africa, considerable portions of the populations of America and the Islands of the Sea. We may well follow Carey's own method to impress the thought upon our minds; and as the eye passes from continent to continent [indicating map], from nation to nation, and from people to people, and we recall that these are heathen, 200,000,000; these are heathen, 250,000,000; these are heathen, 350,000,000,— what can words express of the thought that comes before us? Well may our hearts sink under the weight, and our eyes, too, flow down with tears for the waste, the weary waste, that is in the world in which we live, where light is for us in noonday brightness, but where these millions — more than half the population of the globe — are in midnight gloom. They know not the God whom we worship. The Bible that reveals Him, that brings home the truth to us, is to them an unknown book. Jesus Christ, in whom our life centers, from whom our light comes, with whom are wrapped up all our blessings and all our hopes, is unknown to them. Let us look a little more closely into this fact of heathenism — the condition and the needs of the heathen world. There is a tendency in our day,— I think we are all sensible of it and come under its influence to some degree,— a tendency to idealize the condition of the heathen and the heathen world. We know them so much better; we have looked into their condition in various ways. Ethnologically they are interesting to us. We know their language and literature in the same way; and in a merely scientific view there is much to attract attention and to divert attention from the central fact upon which Christian thought fixes and toward which Christian sympathy is directed. I have heard the people of Japan spoken of in terms that would at once, if there true weight were to be received, awaken in every one's heart a desire to go that he might sit at the feet of a people so polite; they are so cultivated, and possessed of everything the human heart could wish. But how false is that idea. The Japanese are sunk down in spiritual death; they know not Jesus Christ; their life is not moulded by His Spirit; they have not the word of God. They are heathen, and they need the salvation of Jesus Christ. The very term "heathen" is often thought to be a reproach. The Japanese do not wish to be called a heathen people, and their so-called friends oppose the name. They say, "Do not speak of them or of the Hindoos as heathen people; you may speak of them as un-evangelized." I think that influence overspreads the Christian world to some degree to-day; and I think that so far as it has weight it dampens missionary enthusiasm; for a people that do not greatly need the Gospel are a people that we do not greatly care to seek out and supply with the Gospel.

That which moved Carey was that there were thousands of millions sinking into death without the light of Christian knowledge, having no hope and without God in the world. They are there to-day: they are in China to-day, they are in Japan to-day, by the million and the hundred million, without a ray of the light that shines on us, without one whisper of the Gospel that comes to us full-toned and sweet and resistless. Life for them has no future that can inspire desire. Life has for them no aim that can lift up to noble purpose. Heaven, they know it not. Heathenism, I suppose, to-day is essentially the same that it was in our Saviour's day. I know that the conditions of people differ greatly. I grant at once that the Japanese or Chinese or Hindoos are a cultivated people relatively; that the African tribes and the people that inhabit the South Sea Islands have sunken low relatively. But I know, also, that at the heart of the life of them all there is the want of the knowledge of the true God, of love and faith and hope that lift up man and make him truly the child of God and the heir of immortality.

What was heathenism in our Saviour's day? Read the first chapter of Paul's Epistle to the Romans, and you have an inspired description. Paul was writing to the Romans, the most cultivated people of his day, the heirs of the glories of Grecian civilization as well as of the civilization that Rome itself had nourished and carried forward. He writes to them and he speaks of the condition of that people, and you mark the depravity which he depicts and the awful fruits of that depravity, the enmities, the jealousies, the hatreds, the unnatural passions, the devouring lusts, the hopelessness, the blackness of despair that rests upon a people that know not God. But Paul, you will say, is an interested writer, a disciple of Jesus Christ, and perhaps he exaggerates. Go then to Horace, the poet of the Augustan age, and read what he says of the very Roman world of which Paul writes. Read the satirists of the day, the historians of the day, and you will find the colors with which Paul paints the condition of the Roman world are not too glaring. Read Ulhorn's "Conflict of Christianity with Heathenism," the first two chapters, if you would have in a later form a lively sense of the condition of the heathen world as it was when Christianity came. Heathenism is, I suppose, essentially the same fact that it was among the Germans, the Britons, the Scandinavians, when the Gospel went among them. What bloodthirsty, cruel, coarse peoples they were! We go to Central Africa to-day to find their parallel. Heathenism in Africa is what heathenism was in those countries. And we know what it was, — a record of crime, of a people without light, without uplift, without hope, without prayer, without the inspiration which Christianity alone can kindle in the human heart.

But we have heathenism described in our own day. We need not go even back to those remote days. Travelers, missionaries, have been in the midst of heathenism as it exists to-day, and we know what their testimony is. I do not mean the travelers that stop a few days at a port and come home and write their record; I mean men like Stanley, who have gone into the heart-darkness of the earth, and have told the truth that they have seen with their own eyes. Read Stanley's "In Darkest Africa," and imagine the life of the tribes through which he passed, devouring one another, without a gleam of the light celestial, and yet capable — and this is the most interesting thing in Stanley's testimony — capable, as he believes, of the best things, if only the culture of heaven shall come. Read Mackay's account of the beginning of his work in Ugunda; how after the friendship and the delightful exterior of King Mtesa, with whom he had so much to do, had been penetrated a little, he found him a bloodthirsty king, who, without a thought, would sacrifice two thousand subjects in a day. Read what Judson reported of Burmah when he went there. Read what Carey reported of India when he went there to do his work. Read what Williams tells of the South Sea Islands, where he lost his life. Go to the stories that were brought back from the Hawaiian Islands seventy years ago: a Christian nation in the accepted sense of the term, seventy years ago occupied by a people pagan, barbarous, bestial, sunken beyond hope. Look at the Fiji Islands: fifty years ago pagan and cannibal, but now redeemed and sitting in the beauty of the King.

There is no moral destitution, no moral desolation on the face of the earth, that for a moment begins to compare with that which broods over the lands of heathenism. I am not saying that every heathen mind is as dark as every other; I speak of the general fact, whether in India, China, the Islands of the Sea, or darkest Africa. Go to darkest London, it is hideous enough; it should be impossible in a Christian city. Go to darkest New York; it should be impossible in the light of this nineteenth century and in America. But darkest London set down in China would shine like a candle of light in the darkness that is about it. Darkest New York set down in Africa would be shedding abroad, by comparison, the light of the Kingdom in the midst of that dark land. In England, in London, in New York, in America, Christianity is dominant; it breathes through all literature, through all public sentiment; it is expressed in architecture, in art of every form, in life, in institutions. But in Africa there is nothing like that, in China there is nothing like that; it is a great wide sea of human life apart from God, hopeless, sinking down in death and dark despair. Those who come the nearest to it know best what an abyss it is; those who have lived among it come back to us to tell how stifling it is to live in the midst of heathenism, how nothing but the grace of God enables a man to labor in the hope of the coming Kingdom.

I think I have already indicated the need by what I have spoken regarding the condition of heathen lands. What do they need? Why, we begin to say, they need better modes of dress, better homes, better forms of industry, a greater variety of occupations — a thousand things. I grant it all; they need them all undoubtedly, in a sense. But we have not touched their deepest need. We may take the telegraph, steam, electricity, everything that we possess, and if the Gospel has not gone before, if it has not opened the way, if it does not open the way, if it does not furnish the permanent condition for these arts, they are useless. They will not lift up a nation; they will not maintain themselves in the midst of a people that know not God.

What these people need is just that which in the early day went into the old corrupt society of Rome and leavened it, wellnigh to the preservation of that decaying empire; that which went into the virgin soil of England and lifted it out of barbaric night, step by step, century by century, to the noonday of Christian civilization in which she sits and is mistress of the world to-day. That is what these peoples need — the Gospel of Jesus Christ, not culture. Rome had culture, and she fell. Greece had culture, and she fell. Culture could not save those nations, nor can like culture save the nations of to-day. It is redemption that the lost world needs; it is the evangel of goodwill to men, peace on earth, the words that calm the weary heart wherever the Gospel is preached.

Missionary work has been established in nearly all these heathen lands of which I speak; we are not at the very beginning. Carey stood much nearer the beginning of this work. Step by step India, China, Japan, the Islands, and Africa, have been opened. There is scarcely a land on the face of the earth to-day that is not accessible to the Gospel of Jesus Christ. I know there are great portions of the world where the Gospel is not found. I know of the fifty millions of the Soudan, where no missionary is, and of Thibet, where there is no missionary. But the gates there are open; the triple bars are broken and the highway is building; and this missionary work not only has been introduced, but it has made progress.

I am not of those who think the Gospel is to be once sounded around the world and that then its errand will be done. I believe the Gospel is to be preached the wide world round, generation after generation, until the nations are born into the kingdom of Jesus Christ. I believe that China is to become a Christian nation in as high a sense as the United States is a Christian nation to-day, — the great bulk of its population gathered into churches, living in Christian homes, the movement of life there led by Jesus Christ. I think that a revolution is to come to India; it has begun. It is to come to Africa; it has begun in that great continent. Give the Gospel time enough. There is power enough in it to redeem the human race; and that is God's promise concerning it, and that is the inspiring hope which is to dwell in our hearts, and to make us patient to labor underground, generation after generation, in the faithful expectation that the generation will come that shall see the structure so founded rise in beauty, to the glory of God and the salvation of the race.

But, as to the success which the Gospel has already achieved, I refer to the 3,000,000 adherents of Christian churches and the fact of the Bible translated already into 300 tongues, so that nine-tenths of the human race, might, if they would, read the word of God in their native tongues; I also refer to the 6,000 missionaries. The number is not so great as 400,000, but it is 6,000 better than nothing. And 3,000,000 are not many compared with the thousand millions yet to be reached; but a century ago there were none of these 3,000,000.

3,000,000 in a century!—let that process go on. In not so long a time the 3,000,000 will be 30,000,000, and in another period not so long, 300,000,000, and in another period not so long the 300,000,000 will be the entire multitude on the face of the earth that know not God. The progress of missions has been so great already, that if the same forces operate along the same line with the same increase, we can look hopefully for the conversion of the world, I know not whether in this generation—the evangelization of the world may be achieved in this generation; the conversion of the world may come two, or three, or five generations hence; I cannot say how many, but it is coming. The Christian population of the earth to-day is multiplying faster than any other: in India this is true, in China it is true, in Japan it is true. In 1877 there were 13,000 converts in the Protestant missions of China; in 1890, more than 36,000. Population in China has not grown like that.

But, despite all this, we face the fact to-day that great as the success of missions has been so far, the results yet to be reached are vastly in excess of former results. I refer to statistics in the Missionary Review, but will not vouch for their accuracy. In India the work of missions has been prosecuted for one hundred years. We have about 900 missionaries, one to 275,000 souls in that great empire. In Africa, where missions have been prosecuted for some seventy years, we have about 600 missionaries. In China, where mission work has been prosecuted for eighty years, there are 600 missionaries; this of course means ordained missionaries, or one to about 650,000 of the population. Those are the three countries where the mass of the heathen people is found; and see what the missionary force is at present: one to 275,000 in India, one to 450,000 in Africa, one to 650,000 in China. The work is just begun. It is a dawn that promises a glorious noon; but it is a dawn, it is the beginning of the movement, and you, young friends, have come to the kingdom at a glorious time.

I have sketched the condition of the heathen world as I have on purpose not to discourage or dishearten you by the greatness of your task; but rather that you may face the facts and brace yourselves in the Lord to the mighty and difficult and long problem which you attempt, in the assurance that He who has given the word of command will also give the strength, and in due time will give the victory. The Shanghai Conference called for a thousand men within the next five years for China, a very modest request. The missionaries did not say all that was in their hearts. They measured their requests by what they supposed to be the readiness of Christian lands to respond. I understand the China Inland Mission proposes to call for a thousand additional men for its own work in the next five years. The other societies ought to put in the thousand additional called for by the Shanghai Conference. And that would mean that every man who goes there should have his wife; and that would mean some 4,000 in five years. India needs as many as China. Were her missionaries to voice her needs, they would not fall short of the call of the Shanghai Conference. Africa, could her missionaries speak, would say she too must have her thousand in this five years. 6,000, counting the wives of missionaries, and single men, makes up the entire foreign missionary roll to-day. That should be doubled in two years; we want it quadrupled in five years; and let the good work of multiplication go on, as the Boards at home promote and the Boards abroad invite.

And now I come to the last point, and I speak to you who represent the institutions of learning in the United States and Canada — Christian America. What is the part of America in this great work? It is significant to notice the part that America already has. Of the 200 foreign missionary societies about 70 belong to America; more than one-third of the foreign missionary societies, of the laborers, and of the money that go abroad come from America. This is a suggestion of what is the divine purpose regarding our relation to this work. We have come to it by the leading of that Divine Providence that still leads on. We are well able to respond to the call. Our colleges and seminaries were never so full as now. Thousands of our choicest youth, the best material for missionaries, are in our schools. You are their representatives, 500 strong; you are here representing more than 6,000 of those who have heard the call and have responded. The potency of America to respond to her part of this great work that opens abroad is demonstrated. I rejoice in the signs of the times. I know no event of modern missions more impressive, more full of promise, than this Student Volunteer Movement.

Again, wealth, which constitutes the sinews of missionary work, how it multiplies in our land! You who heard those remarkable addresses last evening do not need that I shall more than touch upon the theme. There is money enough here to set this work, not simply upon its feet, but to multiply it tenfold immediately, without drawing upon our resources. Here is the immediate problem resting upon the Church; the problem rests not a little on you to solve. You seek to go to the foreign fields. It is for you to raise the money, to stir the churches. Were the churches ready to send Judson and his companions abroad? No; but the young man appealed to the churches, and the appeal drew out the resources needed. Your appeals are needed in the churches of the land to-day. It is the call of the hour. There has never been such a call since the world began; there has never been a day like this in Christian times before, — the wide world open, the opposition that we have met giving way, the false faiths with which we grapple yielding and preparing for flight, our youth rising up to go where the open doors summon, and the wealth of the land more than sufficient for all the need. In this close grapple of the Gospel with the sin of the world, through slow progress, defeats, and successes, we begin to find the opposition that we have met weakening, the forces that have barred the way dispersing. And out of the open visions we may hear the inspiring word of the Master, " Surely I come quickly ; " and in the midst of our toil and strife it is for us to answer, half a prayer and half a shout, " Even so, come, Lord Jesus ! "

FOURTH DAY, SUNDAY, MARCH 1.

Morning Session.

The consecration meeting was conducted by Mr. Robert E. Speer, who said : —

Fellow students, this is our holy hour. The Lord Himself consecrates this morning time by prayer. It was on the first day of the week, the day after the Sabbath on which He healed Simon's wife's mother and all the diseased people who were brought to Him at the sunsetting, that in the morning, rising up a great while before day, He went out into a solitary place and prayed as we need to pray. May it be with the quietness, and, in some sense, the loneliness that marked Him. And may He teach us His great longing too. We have said to Him this morning, "If ever I loved Thee, my Jesus, 'tis now." As in our song a moment ago we stood before the bleeding One, we told Him we were conscious we could not repay His gift with drops of grief; and I trust we all meant it truthfully when we said we would give our hearts, our lives, ourselves — all — into His hands. Was this the first time we have talked thus to Jesus, or is this contrite kneeling at His feet an old scene in our lives? How often are we to die to the world and to self and to come anew into the life of God? There was one Calvary for Christ; there must be one for each of us. And so now, just a few minutes at the beginning of the stillness of this consecration hour, I want to speak of something in the life of our brother Paul which may help to make our position before Jesus, not merely momentary and passing, but permanent and abiding — his three ambitions.

The word which Paul uses to signify "being ambitious" is translated differently in the Old Version in each of the three passages where it occurs. The Revised Version translates it uniformly "making it my aim." But we shall learn most of what was in the old missionary's devoted heart if we keep the words just as he wrote them — "I am ambitious."

The first of these three ambitions is in the fifteenth chapter of Romans, the twentieth verse: "Yea, so have I been ambitious to preach the gospel, not where Christ was named, lest I should build upon another man's foundation. But, as it is written, To whom He was not spoken of, they shall see: and they that have not heard shall understand." Almost all of us here this morning have been given by the Holy Spirit a share in this desire of Paul's; but perhaps we have not made it an ambition. An ambition is a mighty thing. I remember with tears before Him this morning some that I used to have that were terrible in their power and their unwillingness to yield to any obstacles. Not many of us here have escaped awful struggles with these things when the Lord was leading us into the secret of His presence. Shall we not transfer all the power and passion that used to be in these old desires, transfigured with the glory of our new devotion, to this ambition to preach to those who have never heard His name? There are obstacles of home and friends, of selfish longings or worldly temptations, in the way of every one. Nothing but an overmastering ambition will carry us over these into the lightless lands. There are mournful and discouraging voices on every side. It is enough to say boldly with Paul, " I am covetous of the *honor* of preaching the gospel where Christ has not been named." We are told over and over that ambitions are worldly things. It depends on their end and spirit, fellow students. If the end is in Him and the spirit is of Him, we need not be afraid. Why did Paul yearn to have this privilege? " Lest I should build upon another man's foundation." He was building a house of gold and silver and precious stones, and he did not want to run the risk of having his work ruined by building on a foundation of wood and hay and stubble, which some one else had laid. Or, was it that the number then, as now, of those willing to build on the stones which others have laid was large, while few, very few, walked after the example of Him who " must preach in other cities also," or of His servant who was forever passing into " regions beyond " ? Oh, my fellow students ! is this passion strong enough within you to build on foundations which your own hands have laid, to let your lips syllable the Name in absolutely unillumined countries? If it is His will, may the good God, the great Giver, quicken in us strongly this great ambition.

Paul's second ambition lay deeper and broader even than his first. It is in the Second Epistle to the Corinthians, the fifth chapter and the ninth verse : " Wherefore we are ambitious, that, whether at home or [absent, we may be well [pleasing to Him." That dear Friend, who came not to be ministered unto but to minister, and who gave His life a ransom for many, — let us remember it was "for many," — realized this perfectly in His life : " He that sent me is with me : the Father hath not left me alone ; for I do always those things that please Him." This was the witness which the Holy Ghost bore of Enoch that " God translated him, for before his translation he had this testimony that he pleased God." Paul's Christian life began this way : " It pleased God to reveal His Son in me that I might preach Him among the heathen." And so begun, the passion grew upon him, that whether at home in this body or absent from it and present with the Lord, always he might be well pleasing to Him. Let us test our lives on this touch-stone to-day. Am I here this morning only to please Him? Did I become a volunteer only to please Him? Are the thoughts in my mind and the loves in my heart just now pleasing to Him? Aye, am I living my life solely with reference to pleasing Him? And now we see why Paul was ambitious to preach where Christ had not been named. It was because he coveted the honor of pleasing Him. It may be that some of us who have been cherishing these two ambitions may have to give up the first; we cannot give up the second. I trust it may not happen; but suppose He should hold us back, " not permitting " us, are we ready in this to be well pleasing in His sight? If this sharp sword cuts as it is pressed against the displeasing things in our hearts, let us endure it quietly; we shall be better men and women when the pain is past. And as we let the Purifier do His work within us, it is added joy to remember the truth which John knew so well, that afterward we shall have increased power in prayer. " Whatsoever we ask we receive of Him, because we do those things that are pleasing in His sight."

And now, lastly, will you turn to the First Epistle to the Thessalonians, the eleventh verse of the fourth chapter: " And that ye be ambitious to be quiet." It is an echo of the Lord's words, " I am meek and lowly in heart." " Be ambitious," says Paul, "to put on that ornament of which Peter speaks, even a meek and quiet spirit." He did not mean that they were to be idle, for he added in the same verse, "and work with your own hands." It was not that they were to stop thinking, for had he not told the Corinthians that, far from that, they were to bring every thought into captivity to the obedience of Christ? Were they to refrain from speaking with their lips? Not so long as men remembered that He said just a little while before He was parted from them, " Preach the gospel to every creature." None of these. Be ambitious to have your life full of that breathing stillness, that holy quietness, which filled His. Oh, my fellow students! how noisy these rough, boisterous lives of ours have been. In our prayers this morning shall we not ask that that loving Voice, which spoke peace to the tumultuous waters, may quiet also the turbulence of our souls?

May it be to the glory of our gathering for these few days that every soul shall gain these three ambitions, and shall keep them until death as the controlling and molding principles of life. I pray that the third one may be realized in this hour; for He who was a man of sorrows and acquainted with grief, who as a lamb before her shearers is dumb, so opened not His mouth, who pleased not Himself, but did always the things that pleased His Father, learning obedience by the things that He suffered, who said of Himself that He was meek and lowly in heart, He knew and loved and lived this quiet life. And would it not please Him, — and to please Him was the object of the second of these ambitions, — would it not please Him, who came to give the garment of praise for the spirit of heaviness, and the oil of joy for mourning, if we should clothe ourselves also with the ornament of a meek and a quiet spirit? As we spend the rest of this hour in prayer, may our petitions and our thanksgiving be increasingly trustful in their expression of the new longings growing up within us.

Afternoon Session.

Counsel was given to volunteers by returned foreign missionaries in the form of testimony or exhortation, and called by the moderator " a nugget meeting."

Mrs. S. B. Capron, thirty years in the Madura Mission, India, said : —

I have only a word to say to the volunteers. I want you all to ask yourselves, are you able to repeat yourself in others? If you are not, the sooner you learn the lesson the better. The greatest work that you will do on the foreign missionary ground is to do your best work through the native catechists, pastors, teachers, schoolmasters, and schoolmistresses. Now, if you are not willing or able to repeat yourself in others, I beseech of you make the experiment now, before you are on foreign missionary ground. For the natives, from the pastors down, will every one of them read you through and through in less than three weeks, and know just about what manner of spirit you are. And if you would like a suggestion as to how this may be done, just in the sphere where you are, notice whether any one comes to you within three or four weeks' space of time and says to you, " What you said in the meeting the other night helped me." Has any one said that to you? Then take courage. Then find five or six children and see whether you can make an impression on them and get them to doing things. If you can, take courage from this beautiful passage in Hosea, " They that dwell under his shadow shall return." There is no shadow without sun, and the Lord expects us to be able to do this for Him on foreign missionary ground. If you have an idea that you are going to do the same work there that evangelists do in this country, you will find yourself mistaken. You must repeat yourself through thirty or forty people, who will do the work among their own people better than you, single-handed, possibly can.

Rev. Frank Gates, nine years in Turkey in Asia, said:—

There are two classes in the Turkish Empire, Mohammedans and nominal Christians, but from our standpoint these two classes are one. They differ in creed and agree in practice. A Christless Mohammedanism and a Christless Christianity both need one redemption. I want to say to-day that you may just as surely expect opportunities to sow God's seed in the work of teaching, and God's blessing upon that work, as in any other.

Last year a revival wave swept over Turkey. In Mardin we were longing for a blessing. Before the week of prayer we arranged subjects for the week of prayer. Then we gathered together all our helpers and all the Christians we could get, and prayed for a blessing; and the missionaries met at noon and prayed for a blessing. The week passed, but the blessing didn't seem to come. We said, "We can't give it up." We began to hold meetings in the schoolhouse, and still we prayed, and at last the blessing came. The schoolboys came forward one after the other and professed Christ.

God's Spirit uses God's word. Why should you expect God's blessing upon His word and preaching, and not expect the Word you had sown, looking in the eyes of those young men in the class-room, to bring forth the fruit of conversion? Why should you expect that the Word you teach day by day should be fruitless, and the Word you preach to a vast multitude should be blessed? Christ's teaching by the wayside was the most fruitful of all his life. In others the Spirit worked, but it was educational work to them. One Mohammedan saw on the wall a text, "Ye are not your own; ye are bought with a price." He asked what it meant. We told him. He went away thinking about it. It was seed sown. Another, a nominal Christian, said: "What, Christ alone saved so many men in all the world, and no need of the saints? It can't be"; and he went away thinking. It was seed sown, not harvest gathered. But in those students that had been taught the Word day by day it was harvest. The last class went out all Christians but four or five. It is these men, with God's word sown in their hearts, that must do the work. You must train these men, and bring God's Spirit into contact with them.

Rev. J. P. Jones, twelve years in the Madura Mission, India, said:—

A word of appeal and of warning. For the last few years of our mission we have sent tearful, heartrending pleas for men, and we have found very little response. In behalf of the mission I wrote a year ago, "Send us eight men to fill vacant places in our mission to-day." For three years we have sent for a man to take charge of the high school in Madura. For years we have sought for two men at Kossa-molo at our normal school and theological department, with 400 young men studying there, but we find no response. Come over and help us; come as soon as you possibly can. Come with the word of God dwelling within you, and it will be a rich blessing to us, and I am sure that through us you will bless that whole field, where we have 2,000,000 souls dependent upon us.

A word of warning. Test your consecration before you come. Some come before they have tested it. What does it mean? Am I really prepared to go out there and be in the minority? Can I stand with Christ alone among those heathen people? Can I listen with patience, can I listen with divine resignation, to the voice of those people, despising our religion, blaspheming our Lord, calling us names? Can you, when you leave all these blessed associations, all these influences of support and strength and comfort to you, can you stand with Christ alone, and feel even in your solitude that you are in your right place, full of His Spirit and prepared to make known His name to those people? I know some have had to come home who had not tested their consecration before they went. Test it every day. See that your life is hid with Christ in God, and standing there you can do gratefully, joyfully, the service of Christ among these heathen people.

Rev. J. P. Graham, a missionary of nineteen years' service in Western India, said: —

It has been assumed and asserted also that the native Christians of India are "rice Christians." As a witness, I must say that I have seen some that are "rice Christians"; but, made indiscriminately, this assertion is a false and a cruel slander. For instance, I have seen a native Christian woman, after she had given a tenth of her month's earnings to the service of the Lord, come forward, and as a special thank-offering give one-fourth of her monthly earnings in addition. I remember one occasion when one of our missionaries had lost a little child, a native Christian woman offered up the prayer that the parents might be able to think of their little child not as lying in the dark grave, but as playing around the feet of Jesus in heaven. Such a sentiment could only come from the heart of a Christian mother. I have seen a native Christian woman go week after week through heat and dust and mud and rain, to tell others that they might learn of the Saviour; and she gave up only when her own strength failed and she was laid upon the bed of death. And at last when she died, she died in the peace and assurance which only those can have who are certain that to be absent from the body is to be present with the Lord. I know a young man who was assaulted by his father and terribly beaten, because he had become a Christian. And when a companion who had suffered with him brought suit against the father and the father was condemned, the young man came forward and redeemed his father by paying the fine which had fallen upon him. I remember one of our native Christians who was taunted by his companions that his God allowed him to live out under a tree for three or four months, "while our God," they said, "gives us houses to dwell in." But he remained under the tree, remained comforted and contented by the assurance of God's presence with him. The result at last was that almost all his family and all his neighbors were brought into the Church of Christ through his influence and example. Now, let me ask you, Are these men "rice Christians"? The Spirit of God dwells in them as well as in those who have offered themselves to take the Gospel to them.

Rev. M. J. Coldren, ten years a missionary at Orissa, India, said:—

I think ten years of experience has brought to me the fact that the one thing most important for a missionary is to have positive assurance in his soul that he is there at the order of God. I believe the experiences through which I have passed, had it not been for that one fact, would have brought me back home within three years from the time I left. That is one of the important things. Be positive, be sure; ask of God some tangible evidence, if need be, upon which you can risk your life, country, and everything, and then, amidst all the trials and oppositions that may come, you will find that you have a sure refuge. There are times when a missionary would doubt whether he was able to keep on with the work before him, and he would return to his home, if it were not for this assurance in his soul that the Lord really wants him.

After I went to India, I spent six years in Balassua, and then was changed to open up a new station. As I came into the new district, surrounded by 400,000 heathen with no other missionary except my wife in all that boundary, with over 3,000 villages to look after, I remember one evening we were talking over the prospect of success. In the village where we lived there was not a Christian, and every influence was against us, except in a social way; as far as our religious life was concerned, they all desired we might leave the place. As my heart was full I walked out and sat under a mango tree in front of the house. And as I thought of these things, the clouds became darker and darker, and I came to understand then what I had not thought before I left. I used to have a kind of idea that missionaries were angels, or something like that, but I found that they were men. And as darkness gathered I began to feel discouraged. I looked up in the agony of my soul and said, " O Lord, who is able to stem this mighty tide of heathenism until success and victory shall shine forth ?" And then the Spirit came to me and said : " If you will live in this village for twenty-five years a straightforward, honest life, it will have a grand influence upon these boys and girls that are now coming on. And if you will add to that, every day, an earnest, honest, consecrated Christian effort for the salvation of some poor soul, for twenty-five years, that life of yours will shine out in the surrounding darkness like a beautiful star in the dark night." And I said : " O Lord, it is enough. I will make the effort; you give the victory." And from that day to this never has there been a discouraged hour to me. But I have made the effort; I have pressed forward, and, blessed be His holy name, we have a large number of Christians, and a still larger number of children in our Christian schools being educated in this great work. Consecration, then, is the essential thing.

Rev. R. Winsor, twenty years at Sirur, India, said : —

You have heard of the work that there is to be done. You have heard of the impression that we are able to make upon the pagan mind. Some may doubt whether it is possible to reach the heart of these people, so to impress them, so to imbue them with the idea that there is something beyond and outside of this as to make it possible for them to receive what we offer them. But go into the zenana and read to those women, who for the first time in their life have ever heard anything like it, the story of the prodigal son. Speak of the young man as he sets out from home, and as he comes to himself in the foreign land, and then, finally, as he returns to his father and the father comes out to meet him; and then say that that means God's divine love, God's forgiving love for those who come to Him, and there is immediately awakened in those people a new idea, and those women have been moved to tears, — a thing unusual. Never by their own religion are they moved to tears; and it opens to them something beyond what they ever conceived before, — divine love to a lost race. That idea of love is not found within the covers of those eighteen ponderous Hindoo Bibles. What do they say ? You at home sing with volume and feeling, " Tell me the Old, Old Story "; but not so with these women, not so with these people, — they say : " Tell me the new, new story. Tell me again the new story." And so earnest are they about it that they will not let the missionary go until she promises them that she will return. I want to say to you, fellow students, one thing has interested me most intensely as I have looked at you. We have been together; we have had a most delightful season. But the cold world will come upon you; and, remember, we are going into our land of Moriah, and God will call our Isaacs. And you may not know what your Isaac is; but we are to bind it to the altar, never to be retracted. And if God in some way causes you to bind a sacrifice to the altar, He will make some provision by which His own providence through you shall be met.

Rev. John M. Allis, Santiago, Chili, seven years, said : —

For convenience I have noted down two or three things that may be helpful. These are conclusions that I have reached from my own observation in regard to missionaries, and I put them in the form of counsel.

1. Cultivate your piety. You have nobody to depend on for that work but yourself. 2. Keep informed about home plans of work. You will find they will be very suggestive and valuable. 3. Learn your own denominational methods. Some people go out without knowing them, and often find themselves in a muddle. 4. Master the language. Men have failed simply because they have missed at the beginning. 5. Be self-reliant. You have nobody but yourself to depend upon, humanly speaking. 6. Go out married. And, in connection with that thought, select somebody suitable for the work; for I have known missionaries fail from that lack. 7. Submit yourselves to your brethren, or learn how to do so. 8. Take care of your own physical nature. No man should sin against his physical nature and think to escape the consequences by prayer. 9. Don't suppose that your mission is to change social customs which do not involve immorality.

Rev. George L. Mason, Huchow, Eastern China, ten years, said : —

What we need in China — and I speak of a field of about 400,000 people, in the city and out, and probably there are a hundred other fields of that kind unoccupied in China — what we need more than anything else there is preachers. In our section there is opportunity for speaking, for making public addresses on moral questions; and we can gather audiences in the evening, week after week, so that there is a greater need there for public preaching than for personal work. And what we need, more than book-makers or schoolmasters, is the man who believes in the Gospel as the great regenerating medium. Go out there and preach, brethren; and you who stay at home and hold the ropes, who must deny yourselves, and cannot have this privilege of preaching the Gospel among the heathen, what you need is to feel, and act as though you felt, that you are the Lord's, and take the time to pray for us. Send us some telephonic message by way of the throne, and get a blessing in your own hearts. I met an old man in New England in my boyhood. He wrote to me after I had gone away, "Every day since you have been gone I pray for you." I am not sure, but it would seem to me I might have made shipwreck of the faith there if there had not been earnest prayer in my behalf. Sometimes we get so absorbed in the routine part of mission life that we do not have the time for the daily, earnest, personal contact with the people that is needed. Resolve that you will preach whatever else you do; and you at home, that you will pray for us, whatever else you do.

Mrs. Jennie Fuller, of Akola, India, of fourteen years' experience in that field, said : —

It is not what you do as a volunteer that counts, but what you let Christ do for you. I remember that after years of disappointment at what I had not done, I said to an old Christian that I was a failure, and he said, "Praise the Lord," because when I became a failure then Christ could make something of me.

Mrs. D. Z. Sheffield, of Tungchow, China, twenty-one years in China, said : —

We have heard of the volunteers over in China, and the question came to us, Is this Movement as deep as it is broad? One could not sit in this Convention day after day without knowing that God is here, that this is a tide that is advancing and will never end ; and here it is, because God's laws have been obeyed. This is an age when mothers have been learning the privilege of consecrating their children to the Lord. This is the age of women's missions. I wish to emphasize these two thoughts. First, you need to learn to live in an atmosphere of prayer. Your supply of grace must be from moment to moment. The other thought is in regard to soul winning. This is to be your life work. You want to be experts ; you ought to do better work than we have done who went out twenty-five years ago. You have had Christian Endeavor Societies and Young Men's and Young Women's Christian Associations to train you. You are going to love those souls just as truly as you love the souls of your dear friends in the school-room and in the hall. First you will begin to work for them for the love of Christ, but it will not be long before you begin to do it for them. It makes me homesick to think that some of you are going to see China before I do. We would like to have all the 6,000 volunteers in China, but we are not going to be selfish, we are only going to claim our third. This waiting time is precious ; make the best use of it possible, so that you can take your best selves to your work.

Rev. F. A. Steven, of the China Inland Mission, seven and a half years in China and Upper Burmah, said : —

Not pity for the perishing so much as obedience to Christ should be our motive in going to the heathen. Christ has said, "Go ye into all the world, and preach the Gospel to every creature." The Gospel was prepared and issued for the whole race, — not for Anglo-Saxons and Jews alone, but for the whole human race. It is like a letter bearing a superscription that is handed to us for delivery; and it is in that attitude that Paul recognized himself as standing when he said : "I am debtor both to the Greeks and to the barbarians, both to the wise and to the unwise. So, as much as in me is, I am ready to preach the Gospel." The postman is dishonest, is defrauding the government, is defrauding the individual to whom the letter is addressed, if he keeps it back. Let us be faithful messengers in delivering our message.

The command is to all; it came to that little Church on the mountain top as the representative of the Church of all ages. That is the general command, — I speak now to others besides volunteers, — that general command embraces you, if you love the Lord Jesus, old and young, and you cannot get out from under the binding force of that general command unless you have a specific command to you as an individual from the Lord to stay at home. Are you quite sure that you have got it? Are you quite sure that you are needed at home more than yonder? that you have a word from the Lord to stop at home? Are you quite sure that you are unfit to go, that you are too old to go? Are you quite sure that you have exemption from the general command? God is light; Christ is the Light of the world. To His disciples He said : "Ye are lights in the world." "As my Father hath sent me into the world, even so have I sent you into the world." The Light of the world came to shine forth the light. The lights in the world are sent to shine forth the Light of the world. Where should the light shine? In the darkness, surely. Where is your light shining to-day, my brother, my sister? Is it shining where it is doing most for God's glory? If not, will you not seek and covet as a grand prize from God the permission to be placed where your light will do most to dispel the darkness? If you covet after this fashion you will get the missionary blessing, even if He ultimately says to you, "Stop at home and be content."

Rev. W. R. Lambeth, M.D., of Kobe, Japan, nine years in China, five years in Japan, and son of a missionary father and mother, said: —

Three different nuggets in three different forms:

First, a missionary needs grace, grit, and gumption. Gumption to take care of himself, to keep out of others' way; grit to stay upon the mission field for life; grace to love poor human souls, though darkly visaged,— however evil the eye or vicious the mouth, to see there a soul upon which is the impress of Almighty God his Father.

Again, this nugget: "Apart from me ye can do nothing." It teaches us humility; it is no use to go to the field without that. Another part of it: "I can do all things through Christ who strengtheneth me." Still another part is this: "This is my commandment, that ye love one another, as I have loved you." Let the bond between the humility upon the one hand and the ability upon the other to do all things for Christ, be that of love, and that love for others, even as Jesus has loved us.

The third is this: "Opportunity and importunity" — importunity for enduement of power. We cannot save the lost or lead souls to the Master without the power of the Holy Spirit working through us and constraining human souls. Let us seize every opportunity to give the Lord Jesus Christ to dying souls.

Rev. Mr. Hayes, seven years in Soochow, China: —

This meeting has reminded me so many times of that meeting held on the other side of the globe last May. 430 missionaries met together and prayed for an increase of the force. They sent out an appeal for 1,000 missionaries in the next five years. I see the answer to the prayer of our Saviour. I see an answer in the faces before me to the appeal from the missionaries there. Volunteers always make the best soldiers. Christ loves a cheerful giver; he loves cheerful service. Two things I wish to bring before you: One is, that while you look forward to the great work before you, don't forget this little phrase, "Whether, therefore, ye eat or drink, or whatsoever ye do, do all to the glory of God." The second, I wish each one of these volunteers would try to lay hold on his or her individual church; get your support from your church if you can, or get as much of it as you can. Let each man or woman of you interest some church, or as many individuals, in yourselves personally, as you possibly can.

Miss Meta Howard, M.D., two years in Seoul, Corea, said: —

We want in Corea, first of all, educated missionaries to translate the Bible. We have only one book of the Bible fully translated. We want some one to help us write a dictionary, so that every missionary who comes there may not have to begin at the beginning. We want some one to translate some religious books. We want some one, above all, who is apt in learning the language and preparing books for these translations; and no one can be so apt as one who has been disciplined by college and especially by the study of several languages before he goes there.

We want men, and the field is open before them. There is not a door in Corea closed to a missionary, and though the inner doors are closed to men, they are open to women. So, really, more doors are opened to the women than to the men, because they are all opened to the women. I never went to a house to treat a woman but first I was invited to visit the men's apartments and visit with all the relatives they might collect; and so I had more opportunities to do evangelistic work than any other missionary in the country.

We want women. We have girls' schools, and we have had wonderful success in this line. The girls come to us by the hundreds that we cannot take in; and one wonderful success is that in five short years of work we have been able to graduate one girl from our school who has married an official, and yet can go out on the street and preach the Gospel from house to house. Not another Corean woman who is a real wife, and especially whose husband is in an official position, can do such a thing as that.

Rev. Henry Forman, of India, six years engaged in theological seminary work, said: —

The kingdoms of heathenism are the kingdoms of Satan, and it is wickedness in high place and low place you go to reach, and not simply to correct mistaken ideas. If you go you must work among such surroundings. You must be healthy,— above all, healthy in mind and spirit. But in order to be healthy, you must observe God's laws for body, mind, and spirit.

Here rises the great question of cheap missions. I urge upon your earnest thought this side of the truth, of which heretofore some have been losing sight. God has created you, your good and lawful appetites as well as your capacities for work. A home, a happy, elevating home, is one of God's best gifts, to comfort, to cheer, to lift up when disheartened, to lighten when oppressed. It is our Father's own provision. Disregarding this provision, some have made shipwreck. A comfortable Christian home does not decrease your influence in India; I earnestly urge that it increases it. Right provision for wife and children is God's will; to fail in this is to deny the faith. I have seen sad examples of this in conscientious, earnest men and women, who have darkened their own lives and the lives of those who called them father and mother.

Some of you think of the cheaper method of missions as the highest type of mission work. Let me refer to my brother, who is known and loved by many among you. He earnestly tried this, with a view of starting such a mission in India. His conclusion was that he forfeited the respect of the natives, decreased his influence, and injured his work thereby. Yet I recognize that men's gifts differ; only, 1 urge, let not one man put a burden on another because he himself does not feel it to be a burden. I know a lady who can go into a Hindoo's home and enjoy the food, while most ladies would be made sick by it. The difference is not in their piety; it is in their stomachs. A manner of life may be easy for one that would be very, very hard for another. Choose that manner of life in which you can be healthy and at your best. Your lives are too precious to be hampered for the purpose of saving a little money which church members here could easily supply by spending less of their millions for tobacco and kid gloves.

Rev. Geo. A. Wilder, of Natal, South Africa, said: —

I must admit that when I was out in Africa and heard that 5,000 young men and women had volunteered for the foreign missionary work, I was astounded,— I was hardly capable of realizing it; I thought a wave of missionary sentiment had passed over the United States. But since I have been in your midst I have learned, and now believe thoroughly, that this Movement has a level head and a warm heart, and is a truly spiritual movement.

In the number of qualifications that have been enumerated here, one has been left out, and that is missionary heroism. I believe that each one of you is filled with this spirit. I believe that before me is a body of young men and women who are heroes, and they are the stuff of which heroes are made. I believe that there are to be developed here Livingstones and great men of whom we shall hear — great because they have the Holy Spirit of God in their lives which are there shining in the darkness of heathenism. In South Africa, as I light the lamp in the evening, various animals and insects come around — moths, beetles, and occasionally a bat, and on one occasion a serpent. So I say to you who are going out to the continents that are in darkness, go there with the light of the Spirit of God in your hearts, and let that Holy Spirit burn and burn brightly, and burn hotly too, and there will come from the votaries of the rites of Asia, from the serpent worshippers of Africa, those that will come to the light they see in you. And you, in the name of Him who died for you, will be able to command the winds and the waves and the devils, and they will obey you.

Mr. C. J. Lafflin, three years on the Congo, Africa, said : —

In Africa we want at once some well-trained workers. We want
all kinds and conditions of workers there, but especially do we want
well-trained, strong, healthy men. Sickly people are not wanted there:
in every case they are practically useless, and often worse than useless.
But whether we go to Africa or to China, I believe the main thing for
us to know is, where would Jesus have us be. I think I am the youngest missionary of this company, but I say this, that what I have done I
have done through God out there. I feel that when I am working
there I am upheld by Him daily ; and if I had not a firm conviction
that I am called of Him to go there, I would certainly never return.
I advise nobody to go there unless they are positively sure that God
has called them to the work. Make sure that you are where God
would have you be, and make Him first in everything.

Miss Ella J. Newton, twelve years in Foochow, China, said : —

The memory of this Convention will be very precious to us foreign
missionaries when we go back to our work, for we shall feel and realize
that the young people of the Church of Christ have taken up this work
of the evangelization of the world, and what these young people take
up will be done. I want to leave just one thought with you, dear
friends. The inspiration of these meetings will largely fade away.
The romance of missionary life will not last very long. But the love
of Christ filling our hearts will help you and me, will help us all, to
stand alone with God in the dark as well as in the light, when everything seems to go wrong and we are discouraged on every side, will
help us all through the days to come, until victory crowns our work.
I am glad God let me go to China ; I am glad for the hope that I may
spend the rest of my life there ; and I promise a hearty welcome and
all the work you can do to every one of you who will join us there.

Mrs. J. N. Cushing, Rangoon, Burmah, said : —

Just one word to those who are in a hurry to go quickly to their
field of work. Remember that if you are to evangelize the world in
this generation, there are a great many unlearned, unwritten languages
for you to dig out. You must have the ability to dig out the language,
construct an alphabet, translate the Bible, make a dictionary, do all the
preparatory work, before your brothers with less preparation can come
and be evangelists in that language. Be patient, therefore, and prepare yourself thoroughly. Spend as long as the Lord will have you
in perfecting your education before you start.

Dr. Nevius, of China, American Chairman of the famous Shanghai Conference, said : —

There have been so many references made to this Shanghai Conference that it is hardly necessary for me to speak of it much in detail. The appeal has been made to you on paper, and formal action was taken in that conference before it adjourned, requesting those connected with it who were going home to England, to Germany, to America, to appeal in person on behalf of that conference, and by word of mouth to bring home this appeal to you. And this seems a very fitting presence, before those who have specially given themselves to the work of Christ in foreign lands, to present this appeal formally.

I will say just a word about that conference. As you have heard before, it was made up of over 400 missionaries, about one-third in the Chinese Empire, representing most of the denominations in Protestant Christendom. It was the second Protestant conference held in China, the first being held in 1877. Its session covered on the programme ten days, but the business required that the time should be extended to twelve days. The addresses were limited, those who opened subjects to ten minutes and the others to five and three minutes. It was full of business; it was full of results. It was a grand conference: but above all it was full of the evidence of God's presence. I can say, truly, that I never felt the communion of saints to such an extent as at that conference. There were veteran workers, considerably older, several of them, than myself, who had been nearly fifty years in China, a few survivors of that company that first entered the eighteen provinces nearly fifty years ago. A great many results were reached, to which I will not refer, excepting simply to say that we determined to have one common version of the Bible in not only the classical language of China, which covers all China, Japan, and other surrounding nations, but in the different dialects of China.

But this one conclusion to which we came, and in which you are specially interested, with reference to the appeal, was one arrived at with a great deal of solemnity and prayer. I shall never forget the moment when the vote was taken on that subject. I think it was a rising vote. It was deliberate, prayerful, solemn. It was said last night that it was a modest appeal. I feel that it was a modest appeal. It was the minimum — 1,000. What shall we do with 1,000? We shall then have only one missionary to 200,000, or a married man, a minister and his wife, to 400,000 of the population of China. We will only be able to establish a central mission in 200 out of 1,700 walled cities of China. Suppose our additional thousand, with the thousand already on the field, to be so distributed among the provincial capitals and the *Foo* cities of China — eighteen provincial capitals and one hundred and eight *Foo* cities. Suppose we have in each of these three ordained missionaries with their wives, one medical missionary and his wife, and two single missionaries. Allow me to say here, I believe in single missionaries. Leave it with God. Don't lay the burden on any one whether they should be married or unmarried: we want both kinds. Settle it according to your circumstances and God's guidance. Suppose, then, that we have three ordained missionaries, one medical missionary and his wife, and two single missionaries in each of these different centers. In each center they would have a resident population in the city where they reside of from 50,000 to 1,000,000. Under the jurisdiction of that city they would have nine walled cities of the third class, containing populations varying from 50,000 to 300,000 or 400,000. Each one of those nine walled cities of the third class would have connected with it perhaps a score of market towns with populations varying from say 3,000 to 20,000, and each one of those market towns would have connected with it villages and hamlets containing populations of from a few hundred to several thousand. This 1,000 is for male missionaries of the highest kind of qualifications and different grades of qualifications. We want, however, as many lady missionaries besides.

Rev. J. T. Gracey, president of the International Missionary Union, said : —

I come to bring you, in these few minutes, the greetings of the International Missionary Union, and to thank you for sending us a delegate at our last annual meeting. In the providence of God we have established an annual meeting of all the missionaries of the United States and Canada whom we can reach, in a sort of world's missionary conference. We want the address of every missionary of whom you know, whether recently at home or many years at home. We have the post-office address of about 500 returned missionaries, and that 500 missionaries ought to stir this continent. You have had a little sample of what an International Missionary Union meeting is for a week. I come to ask you to send us other delegates this coming year. Come down and spend a week with seventy-five or a hundred returned missionaries, discussing and presenting the various sides of the problems which interest them and interest you.

I have been very glad to be with you. And I am glad of one thing — that you are international as well as inter-denominational. There is one thing I want to say that I don't think has been sufficiently emphasized by the Protestant Church of the United States. I don't think you have quite realized the high, thorough, and perpetual protection which the British flag gives to missionaries whenever they need it. I am an American of the Americans, and not a Britisher, as you might suspect; but I know scores of times when I would have been torn into a thousand pieces, so to speak, but for the force of the British flag. And the whole American missionary force has the full protection of the British flag accorded to it that it affords to its own people. So I am glad you are international. The fact is, in this missionary work you cannot be national.

Now just one thing that is a nugget. If you do not remember anything else that has been said here, you had better remember this. The Revised Version of the Old Testament, reads, Isaiah 64: "God worketh for him that waiteth for him." It will take you a good while to understand that. "God worketh for him that waiteth for him." I waited ten years under the deepest and profoundest conviction, that stirred my soul to its depths every day, before I dared open my mouth about going into the foreign missionary work. Collins, the founder of our China mission, wanted to go, but he hadn't any money. Finally he wrote to Bishop Gaines: "I must go to China. Engage me a passage before the mast. My own strong arm can send me there and sustain me when there." But the Board sent him. Don't be afraid to wait; God works.

Don't be a pessimist ever. It would not seem as if that was necessary here in this presence with this motto [indicating the motto of the Convention]. Don't be discouraged. The oldest missionaries are those of the largest hopefulness. I went ashore once on the island of St. Helena, and as I went up I heard music. After a while I found it was music that came from three half-castes of some sort sitting at a fruit stand under an umbrella. It was sweet, low music, a chant; and when I got nearer I found they were chanting the grand old doxology of the English Church: "Glory be to the Father, and to the Son, and to the Holy Ghost. As it was in the beginning, is now, and ever shall be, world without end, Amen;" and the sweet, low music of it blended with the low music of the sea waves as they splashed over the shore. And as I stood on that island, 1,700 miles away from any continent, I stamped my foot and I said, "That is it." The islands of the sea have caught the sound, and it shall sweep upon every part of the breeze, until, wherever ships and carriages reach, wherever the sky covers and the earth sustains, wherever there is sunshine and rain, wherever there is blood and flesh, there will be none who do not say, "Glory be to the Father, and to the Son, and to the Holy Ghost. As it was in the beginning, is now, and ever shall be, world without end, Amen." And let all the people say "Amen."

Evening Session.

The first address of the evening was given by Robert P. Wilder on —

THE PERILS AND PRIVILEGES OF THE STUDENT VOLUNTEER MOVEMENT.

In the fall of 1883, Messrs. Van Kirk and Langdon, of the Senior class, and myself, of the Junior class, were sent by the Philadelphian Society of Princeton College as delegates to the Inter-Seminary Missionary Alliance Convention, held that year at Hartford, Conn. At this convention the thought came to Mr. Van Kirk that there should be, as he expressed it, "an organization of those who had definitely decided that it was their duty to go to the foreign field, in order that they might encourage and enlighten one another, and do more effective and aggressive work in behalf of the cause." Upon our return from Hartford, we three met and considered the formation of a mission band in Princeton College, to which should belong men pledged for foreign service.

My father counselled and encouraged us in this effort. In conversation with him I learned of a similar society at Andover Seminary, of which he was a member. It was a secret organization — secret, doubtless, because public sentiment was then hostile to foreign missions. Father informed me that "The Brethren" society of Andover Seminary, to which he belonged, was organized at Williams College about 1808, probably at the place where the famous "Haystack Meeting" was held. When Samuel J. Mills, James Richards, and other founders of this society, left Williams College, they carried the documents of the society with them to Andover. In the constitution are found the words: "No person shall be admitted who is under any engagement of any kind which shall be incompatible with going on a mission to the heathen." "Each member shall hold himself in readiness to go on a mission when and where duty may call." These words suggested to my father a pledge for a similar society, which we contemplated organizing at Princeton. Five of us met in the front parlor of my house and appointed Messrs. R. W. Van Kirk and John N. Forman a committeee of two to draft a constitution for the Princeton Foreign Missionary Society. This committee was heartily in favor of the pledge suggested, and embodied this pledge in the constitution, the second article of which read as follows: "Any student of the college who is a professing Christian may become a member by subscribing to the following covenant. 'We, the undersigned, declare ourselves willing and desirous, God permitting, to go to the unevangelized portions of the world.'" "The object of this society," according to the constitution, "shall be the cultivation of a missionary spirit among the students of the college, the information of its members in all subjects of missionary interest, and especially the leading of men to consecrate themselves to foreign mission work." Mr. R. W. Van Kirk was chosen president of the society, and I was elected to the office of secretary.

The meetings were held at my house at least once in three weeks. I can remember, as if it were but yesterday, the fellows sitting in a semi-circle, facing the folding doors upon which was extended the map of the world. I can see father's earnest face kindle as he tells us of Mackay's work in Formosa, or gives the latest news from the Dark Continent. I can still hear his urgent appeal to those of us who are pledged and to the few who had not yet signed the covenant. He would point to his thirty years' experience as a foreign missionary, and press home the Scriptural argument for missions, the need for workers, and the privilege of personally entering the service. From his talks Forman and I secured many of the arguments which we used later in our intercollegiate work. After his appeals, the old missionary would withdraw, and we would kneel in prayer. In an adjoining room, unknown to any but myself, there was another praying. When the service was finished, we two would slip off together and talk it all over. God alone knows how much those meetings in our parlor owed their success to my sister's prayers.

Most of the sessions were conducted by us students. Some of these meetings were intensely interesting. I remember that at one service one of our members said, "Woe is me if I preach not the Gospel to the heathen." As soon as he finished, Forman jumped to his feet with the words: "I know why Curtis feels so. Over his bed hangs a chart with the black squares representing 856,000,000 of heathen. Any man sleeping with such a chart at the head of his bed must decide to be a foreign missionary or have a nightmare every night." Fred. Curtis is now in Japan, two of our members in China, one in Bulgaria, two went to Syria, two in Siam, one in India, one headed for Africa. You ask what led these men to decide? Largely personal work.

The first recruit whom God gave me writes from Peking, China, as follows: "It was only when, in my walks and talks with you, I found that you would agree with me in holding that, when carried to its logical extreme, it was the duty of every Christian to be a foreign missionary, if God permitted, that I could rest in the conviction that I was bound to go. I was then quite in the dark as to my future; but I think I remember one walk toward the southwest with you when I was persuaded to make that statement and form one of the band. I signed about January, 1884, two and one-half years before the famous Mt. Hermon meeting was held."

This society at Princeton, though a college organization at its inception, was thrown open to divinity men also. Many of our members belonged to the Theological Seminary. Through the fall of 1885 and spring of 1886 my sister and I met, night after night, to pray for a widespread missionary movement through the country, asking God to give us the privilege of helping in such a missionary revival. Not even our parents knew the burden resting on our hearts. When an invitation came to address a convention at New Brunswick that seemed one answer to our prayers. At last Mr. Wishard came to Princeton, and urged the claims of the Mt. Hermon Summer School. As a result of his appeal, I abandoned plans to teach during the summer, and started for Mt. Hermon. Before leaving Princeton, well do I remember my sister's saying, " I shall pray for a great missionary revival among the college students where you are going." Her prayers were answered. 100 men at Mt. Hermon turned their faces toward foreign fields. Then Tewkesbury, of Harvard, suggested a tour through the colleges and seminaries. Three of the four men selected for this work were unable to go. I felt the need of a companion, and thought at once of Forman, who was one of the founders of the foreign missionary society at Princeton. We started in October, 1886. God condescended to bless the work done then by Forman and myself, and subsequently by Speer, Cossum, and Miss Guinness, until there are now 6,000 volunteers enrolled, of which number 350 have sailed.

I have dealt thus at length with the organization of this band, for three reasons :

1. It furnished the pledge of the Student Volunteer Movement. The covenant that the 6,000 volunteers have signed is almost identical with that found in the constitution of the Princeton College Foreign Missionary Society.

2. From this society went out the two men, J. N. Forman and myself, who inaugurated the Student Volunteer Movement for Foreign Missions among the colleges.

3. This society furnished us the idea of organizing volunteers into bands in the colleges and seminaries, and suggested methods of conducting band meetings.

So much for the origin of our beloved Movement. It is another monument to answered prayer. The little beginning at Princeton has assumed intercollegiate and international proportions.

But what shall the future bring this organization? is the question you ask. The same comes to me as I am about to leave this Movement, with which I have been officially connected since its inception. Shall it die as did the Andover society? What are the flaws in it? What the weak points? For three days we have been turning our batteries upon it too see whether it can stand the fire. Secretaries of the leading missionary societies and returned missionaries have helped us in this work of friendly, but frank and forcible, criticism. If a more effective movement could be started, your speaker would be the first to help it. The speedy evangelization of the world was the crowning motive leading us to begin the Student Volunteer Movement. We have given time and strength to it. Thus far it has seemed to be the best organization for this purpose. But if a better one is found, we shall throw this one overboard. True love is not blind to faults. Faults there are in the Movement. What are they? They are not in the organization. That seems to be nearly perfect. By uniting our Movement with the three leading student organizations — the College Young Men's Christian Association, the College Young Women's Christian Association, and the Inter-Seminary Missionary Alliance — we have given it permanency and patronage and a limitless field in which to expand. Through its advisory committee we have given the Movement the counsel, co-operation, and confidence of older and wiser missionary workers. No one, so far as known to me, has criticized adversely our organization.

What then are the perils? They are not from without. To be sure there is not money enough in the treasuries of our Boards to send us forth. The A. B. C. F. M. has ordered a retrenchment of ten per cent. in Japan. Neither it nor any of our missionary societies feel able to send forth a large number of volunteers.

1. Here is our first peril. Shall we yield to this adverse gale? Some say: "Yes. We have given our lives to the work. The churches should give at least their money." This is true. The wealth of American Christians is estimated at $11,000,000,000.

But because churches are disobeying Christ's last command, is it any reason why we should? Should the heathen be allowed to perish because our church members purchase flowers to adorn earthly temples, when the money is needed to win souls for the heavenly temple? The Protestants of New York City give in a single year $100,000 to floral decorations, while their work suffers retrenchment. But these Christians are answerable to their Master. We must not plead their sin as an excuse for ours. Students in one of the leading theological seminaries said to me: "It will do no good for us to apply for foreign service. Two of our best men applied, and were rejected for lack of funds. They were far superior to us." To such I answer, Do the Boards say, "Go ye into all the world and preach the gospel to the whole creation"? If so, then the Boards' dictum should settle matters. But it is Christ who commands this world-wide campaign. A Christ-sent man no empty Board treasury can stop. Dr. Herrick Johnson well expressed it when he said, "Young man, if the Board is in your way, bore a hole through the Board."

But, you answer, if the Board refuses me is that not a call of God for me to remain at home? That depends upon the cause of their refusal. If you are refused because of ill health, mental or spiritual incompetency, the probability is that you are unfit for foreign work. But even here the Boards are fallible. One of the best foreign missionaries was rejected by three Boards. Yet he went abroad, and God used him. But almost invariably the missionary societies are wise and just in handling such cases.

If the Board rejects you because of lack of funds, do not interpret this as a call of God to stay at home. You say, How can I be sent? First, pray to Him whose is the silver and the gold. Then go to your home church where you are known and loved, tell the pastor and people of your purpose, and doubtless they will raise your salary. The churches are ready and willing to give if appealed to by young men whose lives are consecrated to the work. We heard yesterday from a volunteer who raised $5,000 in six weeks. There is plenty of money in the churches. But the average church member does not know of the needs abroad nor of our purpose to go. Let us come to the churches having as our theme the highwayman's motto, "Your money or your life," saying the needs are so great, the command so urgent, we have given our lives — will you not give your money? I am glad, for two reasons, that our Boards lack funds. First, so that the faint-hearted and backboneless volunteers may be weeded out. If such a small obstacle as lack of money paralyzes a man, how will greater obstacles on the field affect him? Second, so that we may be compelled to address the churches and give them facts and fire. Think what it will mean if scores of volunteers make a thorough canvass of the churches informing them upon foreign fields and prevailing upon each church to support at least one volunteer. Of course, in such cases the volunteers should be sent out under the various denominational Boards, and their support should pass through the Boards. The coast is clear for us to do this church work. The leading missionary societies favor the plan and will further us in our efforts. So this lack of money is our extremity if we are weak-kneed, but our opportunity if we are strong in the Lord and true to our pledge.

2. The second peril is from friends. Some wiseacre will come to a volunteer and say: "You are too good a man for foreign work. The home field needs men of piety and brains like yourself." A student told me that before he entered college it was his purpose to become a foreign missionary. While in college his professors said to him that he was too good for such service. Continual dropping told. Finally

he was flattered into feeling that his rare ability was too precious to be wasted on the heathen. After leaving his flattering friends at college and entering a divinity school, he began to recover from the malady and joined the Volunteer Movement. He saw that his brain was not unusually massive, and that even if he possessed great talents the foreign field could utilize all his ability.

A professor in a leading divinity school told a senior that he was too able a man for foreign service. What do such professors mean? Shall we send inferior men to grapple with Neo-Buddhism and infidelity in Japan? Are any too brilliant to deal with the subtilities of Hindooism or the modern philosophic-religious cults in India? If any man before me holds this view, a month's contact with the Somajists or theosophists in India will knock out his conceit. Yes, even the most degraded in Africa need the best. The most ignorant need as teachers the clearest thinkers. England's ablest scholars, Bishops Patteson and Selwyn, found their talents taxed to the utmost in their work for Polynesian savages. Our Saviour did not hesitate to preach a matchless sermon to the fallen women of Samaria. One well says, " It would be a sad day for American Christians if they should ever deserve Nehemiah's reproach, ' Their *nobles* put not their necks to the work of their Lord.' "

Friends occasionally take a different tack. They magnify difficulties of language and dangers of climate. They counsel caution and urge our unfitness for foreign work. They argue thus : All cannot be sent since there are 6,000 volunteers. Let those better qualified go. I deny the premise. The church can send more than 6,000. If American Christians give one per cent. of their income there will be money enough to send 20,000. 6,000 would hardly suffice for Africa alone. They would be a mere handful among the 200,000,000 who people the Dark Continent. Can we not, should we not, send 20,000 volunteers abroad during this generation? Is it too much to ask of the 12,000,000 communicants at home? But friends say you are unfit to be one of this number. They may be right. Pray over the matter unselfishly. Find out your unfitness and overcome it. If it be intellectual unfitness, study and discipline your mind. If it be physical, endeavor by careful diet and daily exercise to overcome this obstacle. If after careful training you are still unfit, you can work at home with the satisfaction of having done your best to go. If the defect is a spiritual one, then halt. Move not a step until this unfitness be removed. By prayer, study of the Word, and practice in soul winning, this defect can be overcome. Before applying again to the Board, however, try to test your spiritual gifts. It is better to burst the gun at Birmingham than on the Afghan frontier. Several of our ablest missionaries were regarded by friends as unfit for foreign service. Do not let the question be decided by a " What say your friends? " but by a " What saith the Lord? "

The most serious peril under this head is that presented by home ties. The winds of opposition from father and mother have changed the course of many a man who has weathered other gales of fierce opposition. You say, Are we not told, " children obey your parents " ? Yes, but complete the verse; it reads, " obey your parents in the Lord." Are we obeying them in the Lord if they interfere with our doing the Lord's work? How did Christ deal with this subject? (Matt. 10: 35–38; Matt. 12: 46–50.) Was Asa a disobedient son? He removed his mother from being queen because she had made an idol in a grove. He put God and His cause first, his mother second. Can we allow a mother to be queen in our hearts if she interferes with duty to Christ? When Christ called James and John they did not argue about filial duty. " They immediately left the ship and their father and followed Him." Rev. Edward Judson writes of his father: " The Rev. Dr. Griffin had proposed him as his colleague in the largest church in Boston. ' And you will be so near home,' his mother said. ' No,' was his reply, ' I shall never live in Boston. I have much farther than that to go.' The ambitious hopes of his father were over-thrown, and his mother and sister shed many regretful tears." If God says " go," no home tie is strong enough to be valid. Should I not consult with my parents? (Gal. 1: 15–17). Let God, not your parents, settle this question. You should pray for them and give them the facts. If consecrated they will in time feel the force of Christ's command as do you, and will bid you " God speed " in the work. But what if parents are financially dependent upon me? If you are an only child and the support of an aged father or mother rests upon you, then you may be exempt. But if there are other children in the family, you are under no more obligation than they to support parents — yes, not so much.

There is a question more difficult than this to decide. It presents a serious problem. Many of our volunteers have faced it, and some have fallen before it. It is a delicate subject, but in dealing with our perils I must deal with this. If the first commandment means any-thing it means that God and His service must be dearer to us than the dearest earthly tie. So firm was William Carey on this point that when his wife refused to accompany him the answer came, " Go I must or guilt will rest upon my soul." Many sad complications would be avoided did volunteers live up to their pledge. One said to me not long since that his fiancée refused to accompany him. With my whole soul do I pity that man; but the fault is largely his own. Had he, from the first, made it evident to her and her friends that it was his unflinching purpose to go, he would have avoided this complication. The out and out volunteers run but little risk in this direction. Dr. Judson wrote as follows to his fiancée: "May this be the year in which you will take final leave of your relatives and native land, in which you will cross the wide ocean and dwell on the other side of the world among a heathen people. We shall no more see our kind friends around us or enjoy conveniences of civilized life, or go to the house of God with those that keep holy day; but swarthy countenances will everywhere meet our eye, the jargon of an unknown tongue will assail our ears. We shall see many dreary, disconsolate hours, and feel a sinking of spirits, anguish of mind, of which now we can form little conception. O, we shall wish to lie down and die! And that time may soon come. One of us may be unable to sustain the heat of the climate and the change of habits. In view of such scenes shall we not pray with earnestness, 'O, for an overcoming faith?'" Strong language, you say. Yes; but it required a strong woman to do the work. If strong, his words would not daunt her. If weak, she had better be daunted. Write such a letter to your fiancée. If she be thoroughly consecrated, it will nerve her to new consecration. If she is unwilling to go find out the fact as soon as possible, leave her, and thank God for your escape from a union which would defeat His plans.

One volunteer hesitated to go because his mother-in-law opposed it. Imagine a man in the United States Army telling his officer that he could not go to a western army post because his mother-in-law objected! Oh! for men like Zinzendorf, who will say, "I know of only one passion, and that is He."

3. The third peril is *self*. This explains why so many volunteers cool off. The lack of money in the Boards, pressure of friends and relatives, are perils; but the chief perils are in the volunteer's heart. At some meeting the missionary fire was kindled and he signed the pledge. If the fire is not kept up the fault is his own. You say that he decided under excitement. That makes no difference. Excitement is often a God-send. Hear Dr. Judson's statement upon this subject: "My views were very incorrect and my feelings extravagant; but yet I have always felt thankful to God for bringing me into that state of excitement which was perhaps necessary in the first instance to enable me to break the strong attachment I felt to home and country. . . . That excitement soon passed away, but it left a strong desire to prosecute my inquiries." Whether "excitement" is followed by such a "strong desire" depends upon yourself. Do not say that God allowed the flame to wane. Have you fed the fire? Information is the fuel. If the fire has died for lack of fuel the fault is your own, since there

is an abundance of missionary literature at your hand. But throwing on fuel is not enough. Look well to the draft. Knock out the clinkers of self which clog up and deaden the fire of consecration.

Unless careful men, our professional courses of study will chill us. Those who are familiar with medical students know that many of them are callous. This cannot be if the heart is warm. Even theological men will bear me out when I say, that the business-like scrutiny of the Word, examining it with the microscope of textual criticism, is a chilling operation unless we constantly approach the study with bowed heads and scan the sacred pages reverently. Here is your peril. Let not the fire of consecration cool under your professional studies. He that holdeth the seven stars in His hand, who walketh in the midst of the seven golden candlesticks, commends many things in the Ephesian church — its labor, its patience, its abhorrence of evil. Why then does He threaten to remove its candlestick? Because the church had left its first love. Why? The calls are more urgent now than when they volunteered. Witness the ringing appeal from the Shanghai Conference for 1,000 men. Why has the first love lessened? Is it because our love for Christ has lessened? He says, "If ye love me, keep my commandments." If His last command means less to us now than when we first volunteered, it is because we love Him less. "Lovest thou me? ... feed my sheep." If we are less anxious to feed the sheep wandering through all the mountains of the world, it is because we love the Shepherd less. Is not Christ saying now, as in the days of Ezekiel, "My flock was scattered upon all the face of the earth, and none did search or seek after them."

But some volunteer, completing his course of study, says, "Should I not wait upon God for grace and guidance?" That depends. What do you want guidance for? If to determine what foreign field should claim you, well and good. But if to determine whether you shall go abroad or stay at home, remember that question was settled when you signed the pledge. You have decided once for all to go unless God blocks the way. Do not re-open that question. But should I not pray for grace. God never gives grace for futures. We all have more light than we live up to. To get more we must use what we have. Then there are crises when any delay is unjustifiable. Notwithstanding the many adversaries opposing, a wide door and an effectual is open to us.

What are our privileges? They belong to two classes,— those before sailing and those after reaching the field.

1. Those before sailing :

(a) We have the personal privilege for preparing for the largest possible service. Throughout our courses of study we have the assurance that every bit of knowledge can be utilized in the foreign field.

Are you a skilled mechanic? Read Stanley's description of Mackay's work in Africa: "A high solid workshop in the yard filled with tools and machinery; a launch's boiler was being prepared by the blacksmiths; a big canoe was outside repairing. There were saw pits and large logs of hard timber; and quiet laborers came up to bid us, with hats off, 'good morning!'" And, best of all, about 2,000 Christians, of whom Stanley says, "Such fortitude, such bravery, such courage! it is unexampled in the whole history of Africa — just the fortitude I had read of in books of the martyrs of the early church." Remember that Mackay was an explorer, ship builder, sailor, doctor, peacemaker, diplomat, teacher, and preacher. What larger field do you want for your varied talents? Oh! that is Africa, you say. Of course all kinds of talent can be used there. Come to India. There you can learn of a missionary who works in indigo factories, supported his family, and, in addition to that, earned $2,500 worth of property for his mission. You find this same artisan invited to teach Bengali, Sanscrit, and Marathi in the government college. You may see him superintend thirty-four translations of the Bible, or parts cf the Bible, into as many different languages, besides doing a stupendous amount of evangelistic work.

Can you use the axe as well as the pen? Both kinds of skill are needed abroad. Knowledge of printing, blacksmithing, ship-building, carpentry, medicine, journalism, book making, all can be utilized in this magnificent work to which we look forward. A volunteer writes from Africa, "we are very anxious to get a young man, a layman, to come to see to our *transport* business." As the German proverb states, "All kinds of nets are needed for all classes of fish." We have all classes of work abroad, and every talent, can, if consecrated, be utilized. Here is a work for which no man is too great — none too small — if the heart be filled with the Holy Ghost; a work in which the weak things, base things, and those despised have been used. And, as we study and think of this work, how our hearts and minds expand! The millions who cling to great ethnic faiths troop into our sympathies until our thoughts broaden, our love deepens, and we too have begun to love the world somewhat as God loved it. Oh, the personal privilege of preparing for the work of foreign missions!

(b) But there is a public privilege for us prior to going abroad:

First, to secure volunteers. Next to going yourself comes the pleasure of getting some one else to go. Secure another man to enter foreign service and your life is doubled. Prevail upon fifty, and your life is multiplied fifty-fold, if they turn out to be as good workers as yourself. There is a Kansas volunteer in our midst who has secured 130 recruits, an Ohio man who has been instrumental in obtaining 150 other volunteers. Think of the privilege. I do pity the men who go abroad empty-handed, and cannot point to a single man having decided as a result of their efforts. Think of the privilege of receiving such a letter from the Dark Continent: "I am thankful to God for the Inter-Seminary Alliance. . . . Glad I met you there. . . . From the number you addressed, in my seminary, —— is in Micronesia, —— is in Japan, —— is in Turkey, —— is on his way to Zululand, and I am here." Do not let Forman, Speer, and Cossum have a monopoly of this privilege. What would you think of having a man from China write: "I owe to you my being here. As a result of a walk with you over the college campus, I signed this covenant and joined the band." Such letters I prize among my choicest treasures.

Secondly, we have the privilege of arousing the home church to a greater interest in the work of missions. You say, that is presumption. We should follow, not lead, the Church. But God has worked differently. If Martin Luther had waited for the Church to lead, where would have been the Reformation? If William Carey had waited for the Church to lead, where would have been modern missions? Prof. Austin Phelps speaks as follows of the first missionary revival in America, 1810 to 1812: "Foreign missions from this country had their birth, not in the churches, not among their ministers and wise men, but in Williams College and Andover Seminary; not among the people who were to support them, but in the hearts of those who were determined to go supported or not supported. It was youthful foresight that detected that early dawn. It was youthful faith that read the promise of the meridian. The fathers smiled, and the wise men shook their heads at the dream of the young men, but now the room where they met for prayer and the grove where they walked in counsel have become shrines."

"Rejoice, O young man, in thy youth!" God chose a young man to arouse England, and he did it, though only after twelve years' battling. God chose a young man to arouse America to assist in the world's evangelization. Is He not calling us to stir the church of America to finish the work of world-wide evangelism? It is in our power to stir Canada and the States from Toronto to Texas and from Nova Scotia to the Pacific. Think what God did through the one man Wesley. What can He not accomplish through 500 men and women if we let Him use us! Think of the churches and the institutions which we represent. How can we accomplish this? The way in which Jerusalem was kept clean was by having every man sweep before his own door. Let each one of us sweep away from his own church and institution whatever ignorance and indifference there is to this, the greatest work of the nineteenth century.

2. After sailing:

First, the personal privilege. We can enter upon the grandest work given men to do. A work which the greatest Apostle coveted: "Unto me, who am less than the least of all saints, is this grace (privilege) given, that I should preach among the Gentiles the unsearchable riches of Christ." Do you wonder that a volunteer writes from Africa, "There is such joy in this service that I almost pity those who have to stay at home"? As we enter the foreign field let us remember that we are treading in the footsteps of the greatest men of the church. Schwartz, Carey, Livingstone, Martyn, Judson, Hannington, and a host of others are watching us. Seeing "we are encompassed about with so great a cloud of witnesses, let us lay aside every weight, and the sin which doth so easily beset us, and run with patience the race that is set before us, looking unto Jesus, the author and finisher of our faith."

Secondly, by sailing we have the privilege of strengthening the home church. One says, "As metaphysics may be called the pure mathematics of Theology, so missions are its practical application, and are destined to play an important part in correcting the vagaries of theologians, as practical engineering has done in the domain of theoretical mechanics."

Thirdly, we have the privilege, after reaching the field, to co-operate with missionaries and native Christians in a forward movement to speedily evangelize the world. It is the privilege of being at the front in what may be the final charge. We must admit that the world can be evangelized in this generation. Whether it shall be depends largely upon us, the students of North America. Courage, fellows! If God could evangelize through missionaries our ancestors, the skin-clad Britons and the naked savages of Germany, He can use us to evangelize any existing heathen nation. But, to accomplish this, one thing is essential. With it success is assured. If the student volunteers receive this fire from on high our land will be illumined and the dangers of distant lands be dispelled. "And there appeared unto them cloven tongues like as of fire, and it sat upon each of them. And they were all filled with the Holy Ghost." We volunteers need this fire.

1. Effects of baptism of the Holy Ghost. (1.) Boldness. Acts 4: 29, 31. (2.) Utterance. A cringing coward, when filled with the Spirit, faces the whole populace of Jerusalem. He looks upon those before whom he denied Christ. The audience was unfavorable, his message distasteful; but the Holy Spirit gave utterance, and there followed an effect unknown in the history of the world. The same day 3,000 were converted.

Paul asked Christians to pray "that utterance may be given unto him," and utterance was given. He and Barnabas " so spake that a great multitude . . . believed." Paul the scholar, Paul the learned, Paul the philosopher, prays for utterance. What does this mean? Have we not heard men speak elegantly and learnedly, yet the words did not move hearts nor mold lives. They were "faultily faultless, icily regular, splendidly null." Why? The speakers lacked unction. They did not possess this utterance of the Holy Spirit.

Mary and Elizabeth had this utterance. Whitfield possessed it. One says, "It is utterly impossible to assign a natural reason why Whitfield should have been! the means of converting so many more sinners than other men. Without one trace of logic, philosophy, or anything to be called systematic theology, his sermons, viewed intellectually, take an humble place among humble efforts."

2. Who can have this baptism of the Holy Spirit? Not only the Apostles, not only the seventy — even the women — all. This is our heritage as much as it was Peter's. We should have more power than he had, since we have the same promises and the light of his example.

3. How can we obtain this baptism of the Holy Spirit? " God has spoken, yea, twice have I heard this, that power belongeth unto God." To Him we must look, and to Him alone. But there are several conditions we must fulfil before receiving this power.

(1). Bible study. Peter was not ignorant and unlearned as far as his Bible knowledge was concerned. His sermon at Pentecost was made up entirely of quotations from the Old Testament Scriptures and applying these passages. The early disciples were thoroughly familiar with the doctrines and promises of the Word. Christ had taught them how to use the Sword of the Spirit. (John 14 : 26.) He cannot bring things to our remembrance unless we first store them in our memory.

(2). Faith. It is better to have too much faith than too little. It is better to be too hot than to have a Laodicean lukewarmness. Stephen was "full of faith and of the Holy Ghost." He was "full of faith and of power." See how the word faith is emphasized. Do you suppose that God will give us a Pentecostal outpouring of His Spirit if we are so "narrow " and " proper " as to practically deny the possibility of another Pentecost now? As we go abroad let us remember the words, "According to your faith be it unto you." "He could not do many mighty works because of their unbelief." Let us expect a Pentecost upon the foreign field.

(3). Eye single to God's glory. He will not give His glory to another. When Uzziah "was strong, his heart was lifted up to his destruction." If we preach for " effect," to win admiration, the Holy

Spirit will not fill us. Can we truthfully say with Zinzendorf, "I have but one passion, and that is *He?*"

(4). Waiting, eager waiting upon God. (Luke 24 : 49.) They tarried ten long days, though the world needed them. Let us never, never dare to leave for foreign service until endued with power from on high. Nothing but prayer will give us this power. Remember that they were all with one accord in one place. Fellows, if we long for this baptism let us all meet with one accord *daily* around the mercy seat. There is a power in united supplication. Let us pray at the noon time daily for this power.

Then note that they were eagerly waiting upon God. They must have had that prayer meeting very early in the morning; for after they had received the baptism of the Holy Spirit, and after the news had spread and the crowds had assembled, it was only nine o'clock in the morning. And only the hungry and thirsty shall be filled. (Jer. 29 : 13.)

If we go from this Convention filled with the Holy Spirit, what then? A missionary revival will sweep through Canada and the States, and the world will be speedily evangelized. What then? When the Tabernacle was finished it was filled with the glory of the Lord. When our work of preaching the Gospel to the whole creation is finished, "the earth shall be filled with the knowledge of the *glory* of the Lord as the waters cover the sea."

FAREWELL MEETING.

After a period of a few minutes, made impressive by silent prayer, the farewell meeting, which was given up entirely to the volunteers, was begun, and included brief addresses, in which were presented the needs of various lands and peoples, and also testimony from students and others of the chief impression of the Convention or the dominant purpose formed while at Cleveland.

Mr. H. G. Bissell, of Hartford Theological Seminary, said: —

Friends and volunteers, I have no introduction, I have no statistics, and I have nothing humorous to say. India needs first of all the Gospel of Jesus Christ. India needs that Gospel through yourself personally, individually; and no country can get the Gospel of Jesus Christ without wholesouled love on the part of Christ's disciples. I speak not only as one who has lived there, but as one who has come to love the people; and I shall never feel satisfied unless I can go back and work among them. And to those of you who desire to go, let me say, that if you do truly desire to go and work among the people of India, no one can prevent you.

India needs the Gospel first for the young men and the boys. The young life of India is waking up to Western thought. Don't think that India is in the background. India's thought is coming to the front, and can shortly stand up alongside of Western thought. It needs the Gospel for the young girls; it needs it — God pity them — for the desolate widows of India: it needs it for the men who are going downward every day because of the superstition and the ignorance which weigh so heavily upon them. Go to no country unless you love the people of that country with the deepest and sincerest love with which God has endowed you. Come to India and you will find places there to demand any kind of talent. I have been there as a boy in my father's family, going around with him from district to district, and I say that any kind and all sorts of talent may be used in India for its evangelization. And, in facing this great truth, which seems almost impossible, I comfort myself with these three thoughts: God's greatness, Christ's redemption for the world, and the vacant field. Face the three and come along.

Rev. Kajinosuke Ibuka, vice-president of the Meji Gakuin, Tokio, Japan, said: —

The needs of Japan are many and great; but, above all, Japan needs Christ. The leading men of Japan have been carried away with your civilization, and the Japanese government has adopted one system of your civilization, and has introduced one improvement after another, the last thing being the adoption of the representative form of government; and our first parliament is in session now. But what is the rest of the civilization without the religion of Jesus Christ? Indeed, it is a serious question if the introduction of Western civilization into Japan without the religion of Christ will not be a positive injury. The greatest need of Japan, let me repeat, is Christ. But Christ needs His messengers to carry His Gospel to the people of Japan. And so the next need of Japan is men, men like Christ, filled with the Spirit of Christ. A great deal has been said about the intellectual preparation of missionaries, which is true; but, after all, it is the life of men, the Christlike life, that is needed. We do not ask for many. We do not ask for 1,000, we do not ask for 500, we do not ask for 300; we ask for 100 young men, full of the Spirit of Christ. And with those 100 young men, with the force already on the ground, the whole empire of Japan, with its 40,000,000 people, can easily be evangelized, God helping us, in this generation. There is not the least doubt about it.

Twenty-five years ago Christianity was prohibited in Japan. When I became a Christian, in 1873, it was high treason to the empire to profess Christianity. When I joined the church of Yokohama that was the one solitary Japanese Christian church in the whole empire. But now, thanks to God, we have more than 300 churches throughout the whole country, now we have about 35,000 Christians in the country. God has removed one difficulty after another, and has opened the door wide, and tells His people to come in and and take possession of the land for Christ. Will you not come to Japan and preach the Gospel to the Japanese people. And with your help, and the forces already on the ground, I repeat, God helping us, that I think the whole country may be easily evangelized in this generation. May God grant us His blessing!

Mr. Mott: —

There is one race to which we owe more than to any other, concerning which we have said comparatively nothing in this Convention, and I have asked Mr. Slomans, a converted Jew, to speak to us a few minutes upon his race.

Mr. Wm. Slomans: —

Nineteen hundred years ago the dear Lord Jesus, before leaving this world, bade adieu to those watching disciples upon the mount outside the city. Remember his words in Acts 1: 8, " But ye shall receive power, after that the Holy Ghost is come upon you: and ye shall be witnesses unto me both in Jerusalem, and in all Judea, and in Samaria, and unto the uttermost part of the earth." It has not been carried out, dear friends. There are to-day 12,000,000 Jews in the world, about the same number that were in the world when Christ lived; and how little has the effort been made to tell them the story about their elder brother's death for them. I heard to-night that in Cleveland alone there are 5,000 Jews, and not a tract distributed upon the streets among them to tell them about Jesus. Dr. Freshman, in New York, is doing a marvelous work in this direction. Successful work is in progress in Boston and Chicago. Cleveland has no such work. The motto of this Movement, "The Evangelization of the World in this Generation," I believe to be a reality; I believe that you and I will see the successful carrying out of that motto by the help of God. And I will tell you how we can hasten it — by getting God's own children to see the reason. God has given the Jews the wealth of the world for a reason,— namely, to extend His cause; and I tell you, dear friends, it is our incumbent duty to tell those despised and rejected Jews the story of the Cross. We have heard a good deal about education, industrial work, and other work among the heathen. The Jew does not need any industrial work, does not need any educational work, because they have these. They are not pagans; they are not heathen. They need Christ. There are none of you in whose faces I look but have heard the story of the Cross and seen its radiance. You have power to tell them of Jesus. If this Convention does not result in anything else, if it only puts a desire in your hearts to lead a child of Abraham to the Cross, it will have accomplished its mission.

Mr. E. E. Helms, of Topeka, Kan., speaking on Africa, said: —

I believe if Jesus Christ were here to-night, and could point to that picture [indicating the map of Africa], he would say there is only one place in this universe darker than that spot, and that is the land of the blackness of darkness forever. I heard a man say not long since that the social sin had honeycombed the city of New York. It has eaten the heart and soul and body of Africa. You can magnify Mohammedanism, and Romanism, and Catholicism, and a thousand other things; but it is the social sin with which the devil is cutting the throat of Africa.

I heard a gentleman a short time ago describing the greatest army that ever marched. He spoke of Napoleon's army of five hundred thousand with which he swept down upon Russia; and of the five millions which Xerxes brought down to sweep Greece; and of Sherman with his army fifty miles wide marching on to the sea. And I said, surely it is not true. The greatest army ever in march would make a procession 150,000 miles long and ten men deep, sweeping toward the sea of destruction, in rags and filth and witchcraft and sin and idolatry down to death — 8,000,000 last year, 250 since we have been in this hall, We have sung and written and talked about Africa long enough; and if the Lord stood here to-night He would say, "Let somebody go." Africa needs heroic men. If Jesus Christ were here He would say to you that it means sickness, starvation, death, to go to Africa. But it meant death for Him to come down to this world. It meant death for Paul to go to Rome. To-night Africa pleads and Africa dies; and Jesus Christ from the heavens pours down into your heart His Spirit, with these burning words, "If ye love me, keep my commandments," — which means, save Africa.

Then followed a brief statement from volunteers expecting to go to foreign fields within the next twelve months, telling where they intended to go and why. A few only are given: —

"I want to go to Assam, India, because I believe I must go."

"To the Telegoos, because they are perishing for the Word of Life."

" To Burmah or to India, I am not positive which — but to preach the Gospel of Christ, because I believe it is the power of God unto salvation for every one that believeth."

" I am going to the Soudan, because it is the darkest place in the world."

" To India, because I was born there and saw the needs of the young men and young women there with my own eyes."

" I am going to Corea, because I believe that is the country which needs me most, in the medical work."

" I am going to Brazil, because there are millions there — 2,000,000 of native Africans, and a native population of 12,000,000 — without the Gospel of Christ."

" I am going wherever God wishes me to go, because He commands me and has given me a call to take hold."

" I am going to Bulgaria, unless the Board wants me to go somewhere else, because I was born there and know the needs of that field."

" I expect to go to India within the next twelve months, because I believe it is the key to Asia, and the vast masses of the unreached millions are still in Asia."

" I expect to go to China, because I believe it is the Gibraltar of missions.   One-third of the human race are there, and most feebly equipped with missionaries."

" India, I think.   ' Woe is me, if I preach not the Gospel of Christ.' "

Mr. J. A. Sinclair, of Queen's University, Canada, then spoke, as follows, concerning the Volunteer Movement in Canada: —

I did not know I would have to speak to-night until I came into the hall, and consequently I am afraid I cannot pack as much into two minutes as you Americans can.   There is one thing I must say, and that is that I think we delegates from Canada have received a great deal of inspiration from our contact with the Americans.   I think the closer relations we can have in spiritual matters, especially regarding the world's evangelization, the better.   There is no danger of too much competition there, because the more competition in spiritual matters the more benefit every one receives.

Your chairman has asked me to speak regarding the Volunteer Movement in Canada.   He and Mr. Cossum are better prepared to speak of it than I ; but I can speak of the Movement in our own institution.   In the first place, I made the remark a little while ago that this Movement must have had its origin in Heaven, because so many different places claim it. If the Volunteer Movement did not start in our University at Kingston, we claim that the plan of each institution sending its foreign missionaries started there. We had already planned to send two missionaries when we were brought into relations with this Movement. You have already heard the chairman say that ten per cent. of the Canadian volunteers had already reached the field, against five per cent. of Americans. I am proud of that. We are slower than Americans, but when we do get started we have momentum.

In reference to our impressions from this Convention, I think its aims have been grandly attained. The Convention has brought the volunteers into contact with the Mission Boards and with the veterans from the foreign field. I feel that the Volunteer Movement is now on a firmer and more intelligent basis than ever before. The contact with the veterans has shown us how wonderfully God sets His seal on the work of foreign missions. There may be a great deal of enthusiasm in reference to volunteering for the mission field, but when you come down to solid facts it means much to leave father and mother and home and friends and home influences. But when we hear one after another coming and saying, as one lady did this afternoon, " I envy you because you are to be in the foreign field before me," what stronger testimony do we need? May God bless the Volunteer Movement!

Mr. Mott: —

We would like now to hear from a great many of the delegates. Confine yourselves now to two facts: 1. Mention where you are from. 2. Take your choice of one of two things — the dominant impression which this Convention has made upon you, or the dominant purpose which you have formed while here.

Among the responses were the following: —

" Oberlin. Go to India."

" Syracuse University. An indefinite purpose to give my life to foreign missionary work changed to a definite purpose for that work."

" Ohio Wesleyan. I have been impressed with the needs of Africa, and expect to give my life to that work."

" Muskingum College. More volunteers. I feel the need of becoming thoroughly consecrated."

" Adrian College. My chief impression has been my own insignificance."

" Yale University. The immense power of prayer."

" Woodstock College. A profound conviction that this work is of God."

" Bucknell University. I am convinced of the fact that the motto of the Volunteer Movement can be realized."

" Gettysburg Theological Seminary. I don't look at this matter as so great a sacrifice as I did before. I look at it as a work of love and a work of duty."

" Richmond College. My purpose is to strive to please God."

" Ohio Wesleyan University. Going to China as a self-supporting physician if possible."

" Olivet. Have decided that I will hand in my name to the Student Volunteer Movement."

A question as to how many present had reached this decision to hand in their names to the Student Volunteer Movement during the Convention brought quite a number present to their feet.

" I wish to say that the address this evening changed my mind. I did not know how to leave my mother, because I loved her so; but now I believe that I love Christ more, and the love of Christ constrains me."

" The impression on my mind is the great opportunity I have for laboring in the churches during the year and a half before I go."

" Marietta College. Fully convinced that if I do my part I need not fear but that I shall succeed."

" Bucknell University. I came looking upon that motto as a grand but unattainable idea. I go home feeling that it can be realized."

" Andover Theological Seminary. My immediate purpose is to revive that missionary society which we had at Andover."

" Oberlin. I will find a church to send me."

" I have had a desire since I was eight years old to go to Africa. I have had that desire strengthened."

" Cornell University. I intend to interest in missions every heart I can."

" Ohio Wesleyan University. I want to spread more light in Africa."

Mr. S. M. Sayford said: —

I trust that in prefacing these remarks I may be permitted to say
a word to the delegates in the way of a very brief bit of personal
experience, by which I wish to illustrate the value of personal effort.
An old man in Lockport, New York, writes me that he has been praying for the success of this Convention. Seventeen years ago he was a
commercial traveler. The speaker was a merchant in Western Pennsylvania. He came into my store one day. I said to him: "It is just
my beer hour. Come over and have a drink with me." "Thank
you," he said, "I don't drink. Will you read a little book?" He
handed me a little tract on intemperance. I read it over my social
glass. In the afternoon the commercial man sold me a bill of goods,
but never referred to the tract. A month afterwards, meeting me on the
street, he asked me if I had read the little book. I said yes, and
he gave me another on profanity. I promised to read it, and read it.
Two months and a half later, selling me a bill of goods, he asked me if
he could have a word in private with me in the little office. We went
back into the little office, and he said, "My dear fellow, do you believe
in prayer?" I said, "My mother did." "Do you believe in prayer?"
I said, "Yes." "Well, I have a little book here; it is not a tract, it is
what I call my prayer list. I have only the names of men here who
have allowed me to pray for them. Will you put yourself down?"
I said, "What do you want to pray for?" "I want to ask God to
make you a Christian." I had heard many a sermon, but nothing that
went to my heart like that. It is worth something to win a man to
Jesus Christ; and if I am worth anything to the colleges of this country to-day, and through them to this Volunteer Movement, humanly
speaking, you owe it largely to that commercial traveler who now, at
eighty years of age, can yet pray for the blessing of God on this Volunteer Movement. Go home and do personal work, and fit yourselves
for the foreign field.

There are two or three things for which we are particularly grateful. First of all, we are indebted for the very generous hospitality of
the citizens who have given their homes and entertainment in the hotels
of this city, and thus have cared for us and given to us comfort and
pleasure. And to many of us Cleveland must be added as one of the
many green spots we find in doing the Master's work.

Next, we are indebted to the press for their faithful and generous
reports of the doings of this Convention. And then we are indebted
in a special way, and I don't know but what all this indebtedness comes
directly or indirectly to the citizens, because you would not have any
press here if you did not have citizens. And when I express the
gratitude of this Convention to the Young Men's Christian Association

of Cleveland, again we are expressing our gratitude to the citizens, for it is through their generous contributions that this magnificent building stands here, a monument to the glory of God, pointing the young men of Cleveland to the Lamb of God that taketh away the sins of the world,— a building more perfect in its appointments than any I have seen in the wide, wide land, with many new features that make it pleasant, cosy, comfortable, home-like. And you, friends, in giving this magnificent building to the Young Men's Christian Association, have brought the young men of all classes in this beautiful city to where they can have no excuse whatever for want of Christian fellowship and the benefits that come from united Christian effort.

And last, but not least, we express our gratitude to the friends who were moved last night to make an offering unto God in special gifts to the Volunteer Movement. My dear friends, we have reason to believe that what you did last night you did for Jesus' sake. And when I counted the hundred — no, there were ninety-nine, and a friend put in the other — pennies only out of all this audience, I said, " I doubt not that these pennies, even perhaps more than these dollars, were given for Jesus' sake." And we want to thank, with this class that gave last night, the dear friends who are going to give this week; because Mr. Goodman is to receive checks and pledges for the furtherance of the work that is represented in this successful and far-reaching Convention.

May God accept all our offerings, whether of money, or of effort, or of self, and help us all when we give, whatever we give, to be quite sure that we have given indeed ourselves unto Him, — these bodies a living sacrifice, which is our reasonable service. May the fragrance of this Christian gathering linger in this city when we have gone, and may the recollection of these blessed days in which we have sat together in the heavenly places, kindle anew the devotion and loyalty in the hearts of God's people in this city, and result in days to come in bringing to their number many more who shall further God's word, and, with the eye of faith fixed on the King, work with these delegates till Jesus comes.

Mr. Wilder then read a letter from a Cleveland minister, who had been in attendance upon the sessions of the Convention, and had been moved to take the volunteer pledge for foreign mission work.

Mr. J. L. Taylor said : —

Mr. Chairman and delegates, when you came to this city, you came with the idea of bringing yourselves in contact with the veterans from the field, and with the Board of the churches, in order that you might more fully equip yourselves for the work. Perhaps you thought of Cleveland; but I can tell you that the other night when I said that we as citizens of Cleveland and members of the Young Men's Christian Association appreciated the honor of having this Convention held here, I hardly knew fully what I was talking about. To-night I not only appreciate the honor, but I lift my eyes to God and thank Him that He has brought you among us. We certainly feel very grateful; and I wish that you had before you a more worthy and representative citizen to tell you all that you have done for us as Christian citizens of Cleveland. But I am a son of the same Father as you are, and I can tell you what you have done for the Christians of Cleveland.

You have shown us what the work of the Holy Spirit can do. You have opened up unto the citizens of Cleveland more fully than ever before what the words " consecrated " and " sanctified " mean. We have heard a great many missionary addresses, but there is one sentence that I heard this morning that made all of these facts sink into my heart, and that is this: " I expect to be on the field next year." If we can have a person talk to us, and present the facts of the needs of the foreign field, who feels those needs deeply enough to go himself, we feel there is something in those facts.

And so, while all of us in Cleveland shall not go to the foreign field, we also feel that you have stimulated this desire in our hearts, that as Christian people we shall more thoroughly consecrate ourselves as stewards of the Lord Jesus Christ. You are going from us to-night and we may never see you again; but, as we bid you farewell, you may know that you have taught us not only to be looking for our Lord Jesus Christ, but that we may help to hasten His coming. And so, as I said, as we may not see you again, in some glad day we both will hear the shout when we shall be gathered up to meet Him in the air, and so shall we ever be with our Lord.

Mr. F. S. Goodman says: —

I hardly know what to say, dear friends, but there is one word that I think will be a kind of key-note to anything I may say, and that is the word " opening." I regard these closing days of the past week and this first day of this new week as the real opening of this building. For the last four weeks we have had this building filled with people, but I say this is the real opening of this building. At our last State Convention a year ago, Mr. Mott dashed off for us in three sentences a motto for the State work of Ohio: " Hide the word of God in your heart. Tie yourselves to one man. Fix your eyes on the uttermost parts of the earth." And this new building, I thank God, has been opened to the uttermost parts of the earth.

The second opening is this: you have opened the minds of our people. A month ago we called a committee together to provide for your entertainment, and not a man on the committee knew anything about the Student Volunteer Movement. You have opened our minds now.

Third: I praise God that you have opened our hearts a little bit. I thank God that there are men here to-night who will go home, and who know where they can invest money for the King where it will pay.

Miss Nettie Dunn said : —

Dear friends, we have been brought together here by 'a common purpose, even a life purpose. We had made upon our hearts long before we came the impression of God's Spirit that we must go to the unevangelized, and we have had that impression followed by deep convictions, which we could not avoid, that we must go. And I hope that during this Convention we have had those convictions deepened. A woman said to the young men in Boston the other day in an address, "Be a positive element in society." Let us be a positive element in the Christian Church, going forth to these unevangelized lands filled with positive conviction.

A word to the women volunteers. There are a hundred thousand young women in our American colleges to-day; fifty thousand of them are Christian women, and only one or two thousand are volunteers for the foreign field. There are between four and five million Christian young women in this country, and only this handful going out to this great and needy field. In our colleges is there not a great work for us to do yet? Just a few things we can do, and do right away: Organize thoroughly in every college and in every association in our States. Plan to multiply ourselves, each one of us, a hundredfold within the next year. And then, let me say to you, will you not pray especially that a successor to Miss Guinness be found to work among us? May we not pray that a young woman can be found to go up and down this land laboring as Mr. Speer and Mr. Cossum have been doing, and working among the young women? I thought all through these years how my friend, Grace Wilder, in India, has been pouring out her heart to God. Shall we not pray in the same way for the young women of America to be saved, and the young women on the other side to be won to our Christ?

Mr. W. H. Cossum, Traveling Secretary of the Student Volunteer Movement, said: —

This Convention will adjourn to-night, and you will go back to your colleges and seminaries. To-morrow morning you will have to have a quarrel, possibly, with the ticket agent over these certificates. You will have a long ride on the railroad train, and you will be tired when you get back to your college. You will have some lessons to make up, and a great many things to check the high tide of feeling in this Convention to-night. Set your teeth together to-night before you go to bed, and determine that with God's help, after you get back, that you will carry out the principles you put down in your note-book. Go and emphasize the organizations which are there in your colleges; work through them, perfect them. Do the cold work, the uninspiring work. If there is any one thing that has made this Movement, it is cold facts, heated possibly by men who have spoken them. Go home and emphasize the channels through which these facts are presented. Emphasize this organization; let that burn itself into your heart.

Another thing for the volunteers. Do what you can do to further the Movement as volunteers. If every one of these 6,000 volunteers, by the grace of God and active service, gets another volunteer, just one — some of you have four or five years to do it in, some two or three, some one — if you each get one volunteer, there will be 12,000 instead of 6,000. God help each one of you to do this between this time and the time of your sailing. Then inform yourselves. Fill yourselves with facts; make yourselves foreigners; and use all the influence in the church that God has opened up to you, remembering that there is a great deal you think you will do now that possibly you will not do if you do not dedicate yourselves to it with a firm will to-night, and ask God to help you.

The closing remarks of the Convention were made by Mr. R. E. Speer, as follows: —

There was an evening in the life of our Elder Brother when, the Lord's heart grieved at the death of His friend John, he climbed a mountain side and sat alone to pray. And when the evening was come and the Lord was alone praying, He had to turn His steps down from the mountain top where He was alone with His Father, that He might do His peaceful work among the troublesome waves of the sea. At my own home in Pennsylvania, just above the village, there is a hill where one may go day after day alone and sit down in the silence of the Lord's own presence, the sights of the town still moving fast below, and yet all the while the restful peace of the Lord's own life around him. And yet, when the hours are gone, the steps must go down again, and the roar and the noises and the daily tasks fill our ears and our lives again, instead of our loneliness with the King.

My fellow students, these days of our joy have come to their even time now. We have had the pleasure of them and the richness of them, and to-night we must look into one another's faces for the last time before our feet go down once more to walk the paths where not one with another, but each one with our Lord, we shall walk apart, and yet together. I am very sure that as we go down there are many things that will stand before us that will naturally cool us. There are many things in the midst of which we may find great difficulty in still keeping this tenderness, this sweetness, that God has given us in these days. And I am very sure that, come what will, sooner or later there will be more hindrances than one put in our way before we may lift up the light of the face of Jesus Christ in the world's dark places.

There are just three thoughts in my mind to-night about these hindrances, at which for just one moment we might look. We had better remember that to the devoted soul a large hindrance means only increased devotion and prayer. I think we must remember, secondly, that the need of this world of ours, and the unobeyed voice of Jesus Christ, call in these days for a blindness to hindrances like that which marked the lives of those who saw the Lord in the flesh. And I think we ought to have confidence, in the third place, that if we know the need of the lost ones, and if we love Him who laid down His life for us and for them, we shall not be apt to make the mistake of walking in any pathway where Jesus the Master cannot walk with us.

I should like to say that, as we have tarried here, our hearts have been knit pretty closely to those with whom the Lord has thrown us in contact; and in the hearts of most of us to-night there are some desires we should like to speak to you a little while about. We are pretty sure we have learned to love a great many of you, and that it is the one desire of our hearts, especially for these who in the next twelve months hope to turn their footsteps into the regions beyond, that you should love them. In the years to come it will be a great joy to us to remember that the first night that we met with those who entertained us in this first meeting of ours, we won the hearts of those who, in all the years to come, will work with us for Him who loved us and laid down His life for us.

May I say, my fellow students, yet once more, gathering up for just one moment the lines of these thoughts which are rising in our minds, that there are three things for each one of us which should mark our lives from this day forth? First, may we from this time be holy ones, holy even as He was holy, and holy not when we reach the field only, but holy now. It may be that the words that we speak this last night may have faded out of our minds; it may be that the deeds we shall do outwardly this coming year may not be very strong as men count deeds of strength; but the *lives* that we live from this day forward shall either glorify or grieve Him. We may remember the words of Professor Drummond, of Dr. Livingstone, how many a time he had passed through tribes of Africa where David Livingstone had gone before, and at the mention of the good doctor had seen the savage faces brighten. They had not understood his words, but ,they knew the language of love in which he spoke to them, and they never forgot it. Fellow students, may we learn among other things this year the language of the Lord's tender love. May we be changed from glory to glory, even as by the Spirit of the Lord, until He molds us into the likeness of His own character. And, in the second place, may we from this day forward be men of prayer. May our lives from this very moment be nothing but an outbreathed prayer. There is one man here to-night who will remember, as I speak of it, that years ago we used to sit Saturday after Saturday, and whichever one would think of it first would say: "1 Thessalonians 5: 25, to-day — 'My brother, pray for me.'" May it be this coming year that as our hearts form a wish it may be quickly laid at His feet; that as quickly as our hearts gain a motive it may be handed over to Him; that as quickly as we see anything that our brother needs we shall find a delight in asking God to give it to him. And the last thing, my fellow students, is this — it has been emphasized more times than one; it is the yearning prayer of every heart here to-night: that besides being holy ones and men of prayer, we are to be in this world, more than all else, the living powers of the King. " Without me ye can do nothing." " I can do all things through Christ who strengtheneth me." " So then we are ambassador's for Christ — in Christ's stead." " As my Father hath sent me, even so send I you."

And now, fellow students, it is pretty hard to put in this cold language of ours the words of farewell that our lips must speak to-night. It is pretty hard to think that now, once for all in this world, we sit down together at the feet of Jesus Christ. It is pretty hard to remember that never again will those of us who have met here to-night meet as we have met now, until at last in the Upper City we sit down at His feet forever. And perhaps the best thing we can do to-night is, just in the silence and the stillness and the sweetness of that holy place in our lives where you and I live alone with Christ Jesus, to commend unto God and the word of His grace every volunteer who, with life devoted to Jesus Christ, shall sooner or later have the rare joy of holding up the life and death and the blood of his Lord before the world.   And then —

> "Sunset and evening star,
>   And one clear call for me,
> And may there be no moaning of the bar
>   When I put out to sea.
>
> But such a tide as moving seems asleep,
>   Too full for sound or foam,
> When that which drew from out the boundless deep
>   Turns again home.
>
> Twilight and evening bell,
>   And after that the dark,
> And may there be no sadness of farewell
>   When I embark.
>
> For though from out the bourne of time and place
>   The flood may bear me far,
> I hope to see my Pilot face to face
>   When I have crossed the bar."

REPRESENTATIVES OF MISSIONARY SOCIETIES.

Rev. J. G. Bishop, Dayton, Ohio.   Missions of American Christian Convention.

Rev. H. N. Cobb, D.D., New York City, N. Y.   Board of Foreign Missions of Reformed Church in America.

George D. Dowkontt, M.D., New York City, N. Y.   International Medical Missionary Society.

Rev. F. F. Ellinwood, D.D., New York City, N. Y.   Board of Foreign Missions of Presbyterian Church of U. S. A.

Prof. H. H. Harris, LL.D., Richmond, Va.   Foreign Missions of Southern Baptist Convention.

Rev. William McKee, Dayton, Ohio.   Foreign Missionary Society of United Brethren Church.

Rev. A. McLean, D.D., Cincinnati, Ohio.   Foreign Christian Missionary Society.

Rev. J. N. Murdock, D.D., Boston, Mass.   American Baptist Missionary Union.

Rev. J. O. Peck, D.D., New York City, N. Y.   Missionary Society of the Methodist Episcopal Church.

Rev. O. D. Patch, Cleveland, Ohio.   Free Baptist Foreign Mission Society.

Rev. D. C. Rankin, Nashville, Tenn. Foreign Missions of Presbyterian Church in the United States.

Elias Rogers, Toronto, Canada. Foreign Mission Board of the Friends' Yearly Meeting of Canada.

Rev. George Scholl, D.D., Baltimore, Md. Board of Foreign Missions of Evangelical Lutheran Church (G. S.).

Rev. Judson Smith, D.D., Boston, Mass. American Board of Commissioners for Foreign Missions.

Rev. F. A. Steven, Toronto, Canada. China Inland Mission.

Rev. A. Sutherland, D.D., Toronto, Canada. General Board of Missions of the Methodist Church.

R. R. McBurney, New York City, N. Y. Foreign Mission Committee of the International Committee of Young Men's Christian Association.

REPRESENTATIVES OF WOMAN'S MISSIONARY SOCIETIES.

Mrs. H. Benton, Cleveland, Ohio. Woman's Foreign Missionary Society (M.E.), Cincinnati Branch.

Mrs. A. G. Bergen, Evansville, Indiana. Woman's Board of Foreign Missions (Cumberland Presbyterian).

Mrs. S. B. Capron, Chicago, Ill. Woman's Board of Interior. (Congregational).

Miss Abbie B. Child, Boston, Mass. Woman's Board of Missions (Congregational).

Mrs. J. N. Cushing, Philadelphia, Pa. Woman's Baptist Foreign Missionary Society of Pennsylvania.

Mrs. George D. Dowkontt, New York City, N.Y. International Medical Missionary Society.

Miss Annie Geisinger, St. Louis, Mo. Woman's Board of Missions of the Southwest (Presbyterian).

Mrs. Dr. Gerould, Cleveland, Ohio. Woman's Board of Missions of Christian Church.

Miss Julia Haskell, Cleveland, Ohio. Woman's Foreign Missionary Society (Presbyterian).

Mrs. Juliana Hayes, Baltimore, Md. Woman's Board of Missions of the M.E. Church, South.

Miss Lizzie J. Lloyd, Niles, Ohio. Woman's Foreign Missionary Society.

Mrs. L. K. Miller, Dayton, Ohio. Woman's Missionary Association (United Brethren).

Mrs. RICHARD C. MORSE, New York City, N.Y. Woman's Board of Foreign Missions (Presbyterian).

Mrs. ELLEN G. REVELEY, Cleveland, Ohio. Woman's Foreign Missionary Society (M.E.), Cincinnati Branch.

Mrs. L. G. ROMICK, Delaware, Ohio. Friends' Board of Foreign Missions of Ohio.

Mrs. N. M. WATERBURY, Boston, Mass. Woman's Foreign Missionary Society (Baptist).

RETURNED MISSIONARIES.

AFRICA.

C. J. LAFFIN,	Congo Free State.
Rev. W. S. SAGE,	Rutofunk, West Africa.
Mrs. W. S. SAGE,	Rutofunk, West Africa.
Rev. GEORGE A. WILDER,	Natal, South Africa.

BRAZIL.

Rev. G. W. CHAMBERLAIN, D.D.,	San Paulo.
Rev. JOHN M. KYLE,	Rio de Janeiro.

BURMAH.

Miss ISABELLA J. WATSON.	
Miss J. E. WISNER,	Rangoon.

CHILI.

Rev. J. M. ALLIS,	Santiago.

CHINA.

Rev. Mr. BEACH.	
Mrs. BEACH.	
Rev. A. A. FULTON.	
Rev. J. N. HAYES,	Suchow.
Rev. GEORGE L. MASON,	Huchow, East China.
Miss ELLA J. NEWTON,	Foo Chow.
Mrs. MARY H. SHAW,	Tung Chong.
Mrs. D. Z. SHEFFIELD,	Tung Cho.
Mrs. F. A. STEVEN.	

COREA.

Miss META HOWARD, M.D.,	Seoul.

INDIA.

Rev. M. J. COLDREN,	Orissa.
Mrs. EMMA J. COLDREN,	Orissa.
Rev. J. W. CONKLIN.	
Rev. HENRY FORMAN,	Lahore.
Mrs. JENNIE FULLER,	Akola.
Rev. J. P. GRAHAM,	Sangli.
Rev. J. P. JONES,	Madura.
Mrs. J. P. JONES,	Madura.
Rev. G. L. WHARTON.	
Rev. R. WINSOR,	Sirur.

JAPAN.

Rev. W. R. LAMBETH, M.D.,	Kobe.

TURKEY.

Rev. C. F. GATES,	Mardin.
Mrs. E. D. MARDEN.	

CORRESPONDING DELEGATES.

WILLIAM ALLISON, St. Paul, Minn. Young Men's Christian Association.

J. M. ARCHIBALD, Buckville, Ont. Young People's Society of Christian Endeavor.

GILBERT A. BEAVER, Harrisburg, Pa. Assistant State Secretary Young Men's Christian Association.

Rev. R. H. BENT, Philadelphia, Pa.

J. M. BERKEL, Madison, Wis.

Miss ANNIE M. BRUGH, Bakersville, Pa.

F. H. BURT, Chicago, Ill. Assistant State Secretary Young Men's Christian Association.

H. L. CANWRIGHT, M. D., Battle Creek, Mich.

Rev. CHARLES B. CHAPIN, Schenectady, N. Y.

MYRON A. CLARK, Kansas City, Mo. Assistant Secretary Young Men's Christian Association.

W. H. COSSUM, Traveling Secretary of Student Volunteer Movement for Foreign Missions.

C. J. DOLE, Painesville, Ohio.

Miss NETTIE DUNN, Chicago, Ill. International Secretary Young Women's Christian Association.

Prof. RANSOM DUNN, D.D., Hillsdale, Mich.

Mrs. Dr. DUNN, Hillsdale, Mich.

Miss HATTIE E. DYER, Scranton, Pa. State Secretary Young Women's Christian Association.

Rev. C. H. FENN, Tonowanda, N. Y.

GEORGE S. FISHER, Topeka, Kan. State Secretary Young Men's Christian Association.

Rev. A. J. GORDON, D.D., Boston, Mass.

Rev. J. T. GRACEY, D.D., Rochester, N. Y. President International Missionary Union.

LUTHER GULICK, M. D., Springfield, Mass. Young Men's Christian Association Training School.

Miss THIRSA F. HALL, Chicago, Ill. International Secretary Young Women's Christian Association.

E. E. HELMS, Topeka, Kan. Assistant State Secretary Young Men's Christian Association.

J. M. HUDSON.

Miss ANNA L. INGELS, Oakland, Cal. Secretary California Tract Society.

Miss M. BELLE JEFFERY, Jackson, Mich. Secretary Young Women's Christian Association.

Rev. J. G. JONES, Cleveland, Ohio.

Miss S. C. KRIGBAUM. Young Women's Christian Association.

Miss ONA KUDER, Mt. Vernon, Ohio.

ARNOLD J. LATHAM, Chicago, Ill.

CLARENCE H. LEE, New York City, N. Y. Secretary International Committee Young Men's Christian Association.

Miss VIRGINIA MASSIE, Baltimore, Md.

W. R. McINTOSH, Toronto, Ont. Canadian Intercollegiate Missionary Alliance.

Miss MARION METCALF, Elyria, Ohio.

JOHN R. MOTT, New York City, N. Y., College Secretary International Committee Young Men's Christian Association.

Rev. ALEXANDER N. O'BRIEN, Topeka, Kan.

Rev. A. T. PIERSON, D.D., Philadelphia, Pa.

WILL E. REED, Cincinnati, Ohio. Intercollegiate Secretary Young Men's Christian Association.

Miss EMMA REEDER, New York City, N. Y. State Secretary Young Women's Christian Association.

Miss N. RITZENTHALER, Akron, Ohio.

Rev. EDWIN P. ROBINSON, Orchard Park, N. Y.

S. M. SAYFORD, Newton, Mass. College Evangelist.

Miss LIZZIE M. SATTLER, New Philadelphia, Ohio.

Rev. J. F. SHEPHERD, Akron, Ohio.

E. L. SHUEY, Dayton, Ohio.

Miss EMMA SILVER, Kalamazoo, Mich. State Secretary Young Women's Christian Association.

ARTHUR J. SMITH, Somerville, Mass. Evangelist.

G. C. SMITH, Springfield, Ohio. Executive Committee Inter-Seminary Missionary Alliance.

Miss CORABEL TARR, Chicago, Ill. International Secretary Young Women's Christian Association.

Rev. J. A. THOME, Marysville, Ohio.

EUGENE UNDERHILL, Philadelphia, Pa. Secretary Intercollegiate Young Men's Christian Association.

Mrs. M. A. WALKER, M.D., Toledo, Ohio.

Miss EMMA J. WALTON, Clyde, Ohio. Young People's Society of Christian Endeavor.

J. CAMPBELL WHITE, New York City, N. Y. Secretary International Committee Young Men's Christian Association.

Miss LOUISE M. WILCOX, Fredonia, N. Y.

E. J. WITT, Chicago, Ill.

Miss BLANCHE ZEHRING, Delaware, Ohio. State Secretary Young Women's Christian Association.

STUDENT DELEGATES.

NEW BRUNSWICK.
Mt. Allison College (1), *Sackville.*
LEONARD, S. C.

NOVA SCOTIA.
Acadia College (1), *Wolfville.*
KEMPTON, A. C.

ONTARIO.
Albert College (2), *Belleville.*

EMBERSON, R.	GODBOLD, W. H.

Huron College (1), *London.*
BROWNLEE, WM. F.

Knox College (2), *Toronto.*

GOULD, WM.	GRANT, W. H.

McMaster Hall (2), *Toronto.*

CHUTE, J. E.   MCDONALD, A. P.

Queens University (1), *Kingston.*
SINCLAIR. J. A.

Trinity Medical College (3), *Toronto.*

BARBER, H. L.   SMITH, E. G.   THOMPSON, J. J.

University College (1), *Toronto.*
SCOTT, J. S.

Victoria University (2), *Cobourg.*

AGAR, Miss E. E.   AGAR, GILBERT.

Woodstock College (1), *Woodstock.*
LANGFORD, O. G.

Wycliffe College (1), *Toronto.*
LEA, ARTHUR.

QUEBEC.

McGill University (1), *Montreal.*
READ, F. W.

McGill University Ladies' Missionary Society (2), *Montreal.*

BEAN, ELIZABETH S.   WILLIAMS, ANNIE.

ALABAMA.

Selma University (1), *Selma.*
LOVELL, Miss A. H.

ARKANSAS.

Hendrix College (1), *Conway.*
GODDARD, O. E.

CALIFORNIA.

Pacific Bible School (1), *Oakland.*
BURRUS, GEORGIA A.

CONNECTICUT.

Hartford Theological Seminary (1), *Hartford.*
BISSELL, H. G.

Wesleyan University (2), *Middletown.*

DUKESHIRE, WM. B.   RAYMOND, R. W.

Yale Divinity School (2), *New Haven.*

EWING, G. H.   FAIRBANK, EDWARD.

Yale University (9), *New Haven.*

BRONSON, OLIVER H.   KELLER, FRANK A.   SHAW, AUGUSTUS F.
BROWN, ALPHONSO B.   LEVERETT, WM. J.   WATERMAN, W. G.
HUNTINGTON, DAN'L T.   PITKIN, HORACE T.   WHITTEMORE, W. C.

DISTRICT OF COLUMBIA.

Howard University (1), *Washington.*

WEATHERLESS, N. E.

ILLINOIS.

Baptist Union Theological Seminary (3), *Morgan Park.*

GOUDY, B. F.   MERRIFIELD, I. N.   YOUNG, W. M.

Bible Institute (4), *Chicago.*

BARNES, EMILY.   HOOKER, W. C.   SLOMANS, WM.
CHRISTENSEN, HULDA.

Chicago Medical College (1), *Chicago.*

SEYMOUR, W. F.

Eureka College (1), *Eureka.*

JONES, SILAS.

Knox College (1), *Galesburg.*

LARKIN, RALPH B.

Lake Forest University (2), *Lake Forest.*

HOUSE, HERBERT E.   VANCE, E. E.

McCormick Theological Seminary (2), *Chicago.*

BANDY, C. H.   SWALLEN, W. M.

Monmouth College (1), *Monmouth.*

KLENO, J. G.

Northwestern College (2), *Naperville.*

SCHLUTER, H. C.   TAYAMA, H. M.

Northwestern University (8), *Evanston.*

BATTERSON, ELVA.   LOUTHAN, O. W.   TOMLINSON, W. F.
COBB, GEO. C.   STAHL, JOSEPHINE.   WALLER, A. J.
CRAIG, FRANCES.   FRASER, H. A.

University of Illinois (2), *Champaign.*

McGEE, W. S.   McLANE, C. D.

Wheaton College (2), *Wheaton.*

DOW, ELSIE S.   HARRIS, Prof. ROSS A.

Woman's Medical College (2), *Chicago.*

McGREGOR, Miss K. M.   STAUFFER, EMMA.

INDIANA.

Butler College (1), *Irvington.*

LACY, W. F.

Coates College (1), *Terre Haute.*

DOAK, ELEANOR.

DePauw University (6), *Greencastle.*

ERICKSON, C. T.   JACKMAN, FLORENCE. TAKASUGI, J.
GREEN, LILLIE.   NORTON, R. C.   WISE, W. H.

State Normal School (2), *Terre Haute.*

COOPER, EFFIE.   STENNINGER, S. D.

Union Christian College (1), *Merom.*

PENROD, C. TENA.

Wabash College (1), *Crawfordsville.*

CHRISTIAN, W. F.

IOWA.

Cornell College (2), *Mount Vernon.*

ADAMS, GRACE.   BALLZ, JAMES.

Drake University (2), *Des Moines.*

CAMPBELL, G. A.   CARTER, C. O.

Iowa College (1), *Grinnell.*

WEATHERLY, ARTHUR L.

Iowa Wesleyan University (1), *Mt. Pleasant.*

HUENE, G. B. F.

Parsons College (2), *Fairfield.*

KISER, A. E.   KING, MARY.

Penn College (2), *Oskaloosa.*

HADLEY, J. H.   WOODY, CLARENCE E.

Simpson College (1), *Indianola.*
LAUCK, ADA J.
State Normal School (1), *Cedar Falls.*
HOWE, ANNA.
State University (1), *Iowa City.*
BRASTED, FRED.
Western College (1), *Toledo.*
KROHN, W. O.

KANSAS.

Baker University (1), *Baldwin.*
PEARSON, PEARL M.
College of Emporia (1), *Emporia.*
ENYART, F. C.
Kansas Normal School (1), *Fort Scott.*
WELLS, C. B.
Ottawa University (1), *Ottawa.*
KINGSLEY, F. W.
University of Kansas (1), *Lawrence.*
FOGLE, W. C.

KENTUCKY.

Georgetown College (1), *Georgetown.*
BRONSON, RAY.
Kentucky University (4), *Lexington.*
FORREST, W. M.   STEVENS, E. S.   TAYLOR, W. B.
SPICER, E. V.

MAINE.
Cobb Divinity School (1), *Lewiston.*
HAMLEN, GEO. H.
Colby University (1), *Waterville.*
SLOCUM, J. B.

MASSACHUSETTS.
Amherst College (1), *Amherst.*
NORTON, C. D.

Andover Theological Seminary (1), *Andover.*
STEARNS, E. R.

Boston University School of Theology (1), *Boston.*
NAYLOR, S. W.

Harvard University (2), *Cambridge.*
SEARS, WM. R.   SHAPLEIGH, A. L.

Massachusetts Agricultural College (2), *Amherst.*
FELT, E. P.   SHORES, H. T.

Mt. Hermon School (2), *Mt. Hermon.*
MOODY, A. E.   WATSON, R. L.

Mt. Holyoke College (1), *South Hadley.*
CLEVELAND, MARY.

Newton Theological Institute (1), *Newton Centre.*
BARSS, J. HOWARD.

School for Christian Workers (3), *Springfield.*
CORBETT, D. WATSON.   COWLES, E. B., Jr.   LUNBECK, A. W.

Wellesley College (2), *Wellesley.*
JONES, LAURA A.   STERNBERG, AMALIE.

Williams College (1), *Williamstown.*
LUCE, FRANK L.

MICHIGAN.

Adrian College (1), *Adrian.*
CLARK, Rev. H. V.

Albion College (2), *Albion.*
FILLIO, U. H.   PALMER, HELEN E.

Battle Creek College (2), *Battle Creek.*
MAGAN, PERCY T.   ROSSITER, FRED M.

Battle Creek Sanitarium (4), *Battle Creek.*
FOY, Mrs. M. S.   WHITNEY, Mrs. E.   WHITNEY, JEAN C.
LOPER, A. N., M.D.

Hillsdale College (5), *Hillsdale.*
COPP, Prof. JOHN S.   MOODY, LIZZIE.   TRACY, LAURA.
COPP, MABEL.   PELTON, B. H.

Hope College (2), *Holland.*

HUIZINGA, H.   VANDERPLOEG, H.

Olivet College (9), *Olivet.*

BINKHORST, HARRY.   COLE, A. C.   LEE, A. L.
BLISH, W. H.   COURTRIGHT, Miss M.   MEADE, CORA.
BRIGGS, W. A.   FROST, M. A.   WESTRATER, Miss M.

University of Michigan (12), *Ann Arbor.*

ALLEN, Miss M.   GARDNER, F. M.   SANDERSON, MARY.
BLAKELY, WM. A.   GARDNER, Mrs. F. M.   SMITH, L. A.
BOGOFSKY, U. L.   HURD, FANNIE B.   WAPLES, F. A.
BROWN, HUGH.   KING, ELLA.   WOOD, LILLIS A.

MINNESOTA.

Carleton College (1), *Northfield.*
KRAUSE, F. O.

MISSOURI.

Central College (1), *Fayette.*
RANSFORD, C. O.

Park College (3), *Parkville.*
DEMUTH, MAGGIE.   McCLAIN, ALBERT M.   TOWER, FRED J.

Missouri Valley College (1), *Marshall.*
MADDEN, L. W.

Westminster College (2), *Fulton.*
BOVING, C. B.   HICKMAN, W. L.

William Jewell College (1), *Liberty.*
EUBANKS, M. D.

NEW HAMPSHIRE.

Dartmouth College (1), *Hanover.*
POTTER, ELMER C.

NEW JERSEY.

College of New Jersey (4), *Princeton.*
DENMAN, C. H.   RIGGS, C. T.   STREET, IRVING W.
HARRIS, WM.

Drew Theological Seminary (1), *Madison.*
SCHILLING, G. J.

Princeton Theological Seminary (3), *Princeton.*

SAILER, T. H. P.   SPEER, ROBERT E.   WILLIAMS, C. S.

Rutgers College (1), *New Brunswick.*

SCUDDER, WALTER T.

NEW YORK.

Auburn Theological Seminary (1), *Auburn.*

BANCROFT, F. E.

Cazenovia Seminary (1), *Cazenovia.*

HADLEY, C. ARTHUR.

City Mission Training School (2), 129 *East Tenth Street, N.Y. City.*

BEYER, ALIDA.   JEFFERSON, Miss A. M.

Colgate Academy (2), *Hamilton*

CLARE, D. H.   VINTON, S. R.

Colgate University (3), *Hamilton.*

CASE, C. D.   CREGO, H. P.   DEWOODY, CHAS.

Cornell University, Ithaca.

BRAY, WM. L.   HASBROUCK, MAUDE E. KELLOGG, ROBERT J.
BURRAGE, HERBERT F. HAWLEY, SARAH H.

General Theological Seminary (1), *N.Y. City.*

SMITH, WM. WALTER.

Hamilton College (5), *Clinton.*

BROCKWAY, T. CLINTON. FELTUS, GEO. N.   STOELOFF, PANO S.
BUDD, GEO. S.   FLETCHER, ORVILLE T.

Hamilton Theological Seminary (3), *Hamilton.*

GRINNELL, CLAYTON.   HIBBARD, GEO. L.   STANTON, WM. A.

International Medical Missionary Institute (2), *N.Y. City.*

HALL, WM. J.   HENDERSON, A. H.

Rochester Theological Seminary (1), *Rochester.*

MCGUIRE, JOHN.

Union Theological Seminary (15), *N.Y. City.*

CAMPBELL, C. D.   FRYLING, WILLIAM.   MOORHEAD, MAX W.
CLARK, WALTER J.   HASTINGS, W. W.   MORRISON, C.
CORNWELL, G.   IBUKA, Rev. K.   SWIFT, BENJAMIN.
FAIRLY, EDWIN.   JONES, T. J.   THOMAS, J. M.
FRENCH, C. H.   KERR, F. M.   WILDER, ROBERT P.

University of Rochester (1), *Rochester.*
SWEET, F. J.

University of Syracuse (2), *Syracuse.*
FOOTE, ANNA.　　　　　　　WOOD, F. H.

NORTH CAROLINA.

Guilford College (1), *Guilford College.*
REYNOLDS, HERBERT W.

OHIO.

Adelbert College (about 35), *Cleveland.*
Names not taken.

Baldwin University (11), *Berea.*

FISHER, ELMER K.	SIGRIST, C.	STEMM, JACOB.
HAGERMAN, E. W.	SIGRIST, LENA.	STEVER, FRED'K S.
HARRIS, NELLIE.	SIMESTER, JAMES.	VANDEREN, RUTH.
MEYER, Mr.	SHREVE, J. T.	

Dennison University (5), *Granville.*

BRUMBACK, A. M.	PACKER, E. B.	WILKIN, W. A.
MASON, G. L.	TANNER, C. H.	

Farmington College (2), *West Farmington.*

HEAPES, W. J.	TOWNSEND, GEO. B.

Heidelberg University (5), *Tiffin.*

ALSPACH, E. E.	BRUGH, C. W.	ROHRBAUGH, C. M.
BELSER, J. W.	CULVER, WM. H.	

Hiram College (23), *Hiram.*

ALLEN, C. A.	CRAFT, LAURA.	RAGAN, G. A.
ALLEN, E. W.	DEAN, ALLIE M.	RICE, P. J.
BARTLETT, S. H.	FORREST, J. D.	RYDER, C. C.
BARTLETT, Mrs. S. H.	FROST, Miss A. G.	SCOTTA, L. O. E.
BEAMAN, CARRIE A.	LYON, Miss M. A.	SHEPARD, Miss.
BECK, BLANCHE.	MAHORTER, J. H.	SMOOTZ, C. E.
CALVIN, W. D.	MOORE, W. J.	WAGNER, D. G.
CLARK, JOSEPHINE.	NEWTON, J. T.	

Lake Erie Seminary (25), *Painesville.*

BENTLEY, Miss L. P.	HOUGH, Miss K. M.	PRESCOTT, Miss L. T.
BROOKS, BESSIE.	LAWRENCE, Miss M. E.	REED, Miss E. W.
CONGER, Miss B.	LEMON, Miss C. H.	RICHEY, Miss A. G.
EASTMAN, LILLIAN.	LEMON, Miss G.	SARVER, Miss M.
EVANS, MARY.	MACKEY, Miss L. A.	SERATA, Mrs. NOBU.
FISHER, Miss E. F.	MASON, JESSIE A.	SMITH, BERTHA.
HALL, CLARA.	MERSHON, Miss C. L.	WHITE, Miss G.
HIGBEE, EDITH.	MUNGER, Miss M. A.	WILLIAMS, Miss F.
HIGBEE, MARY.		

Lane Theological Seminary (1), *Cincinnati.*

SMITH, A. N.

Marietta College (5), *Marietta.*

ADDY, ARTHUR R. COLE, JAMES M. HUBER, A. T.
BARTLETT, CHAS. W.

Miami University (1), *Oxford.*

KROM, A. E.

Mt. Union College (2), *Mt. Union.*

FOWLER, H. B. KEELER, MYRTA.

Muskingum College (2), *New Concord.*

GLENNON, J. E. MARTIN, Miss JOSE.

Oberlin College and Seminary (81), *Oberlin.*

ALBERTSON, RALPH. GILLIS, MILLIE S. NORTON, HELEN G.
ATWATER, Mrs. E. R. GREENE, C. W. OBENHAUER, H. F.
BEARD, WILLARD L. HASKELL, E. B. PARSONS, Miss E. C.
BLACKSTONE, FLORA L. HASKELL, H. J. PENDLETON, CLARA L.
BRECKENRIDGE JUANITA. HICKS, IDA M. PENNIMAN, IRA B.
BREED, M. A. HINMAN, GEO. W. PHELPS, FLORA B.
BREED, Mrs. M. A. HINMAN, SUSAN F. PIERCE, WILLIAM.
BRINTNALL, W. A. IRELAND, F. A. PINCHA, JOHN.
BROWN, H. E. IRELAND, W. F. ROSS, H. S.
BROWNING, C. H. JANES, T. I. SEVERANCE, A. D.
BURROUGHS, C. H. JOHNSTON, W. J. R. SIMPSON, SAMUEL.
CHILD, B. V. JONES, ALICE I. SINCLARE, C. E.
CHITTENDEN, A. H. JUDKINS, W. L. SMITH, LAURA C.
CHITTENDEN, CARRIE E. KINNEY, MABEL R. STANLEY, E. H., Instr'r.
CHURCH, A. A. KIRKPATRICK, C. C. STANLEY, Miss G. W.
COLBY, S. L. KRIEBEL, O. S. STOUGH, H. W.
COWLEY, EDITH C. LYALL, J. L. VAN BURK, JOHN.
DALZELL, C. O. LYMAN, HENRY J. WALKER, Mrs.
DODGE, E. G. MANLEY, M. ELLA. WALTERS, JAS. J.
DRUMM, JOHN. McCORD, MARY E. WATERHOUSE, E. C.
DUTTON, C. F., Jr. McCORD, J. B. WAUGH, W. M., Jr.
ELLIS, J. T. McLAUGHLIN, ROB'T. WEBSTER, C. S.
FIFIELD, J. W. McROBERTS, T. R. WILDER, GEO. D.
FRENCH, E. G. MEADE, G. W. WILLIAMS, G. L.
FROST, Prof. W. G. MELLEN, GRACE S. F. WISE, JOHN H.
GADSBY, GEO. MILLER, MARTHA H. WOOD, S. R.
GARVER, R. C. MOON, M. ALICE. WRIGHT, G. W.

Ohio University (1), *Athens.*

WESTERVELT, W. A.

Ohio Wesleyan University (12), *Delaware.*

CURTIS, E. H.	HAMMOND, E. S.	RITCHARDSON, G. L. C.
FREY, LULA	JOHNSON, F. I.	SCOTT, W.
GROSS, T. W.	MILLER, S. D.	WISMAN, J. P.
HALLOWELL, IDA.	MORGAN, MINNIE.	WOMER, P. P.

Shepardson College (1), *Granville.*

VAN CLEEF, LILLIAN.

Union Biblical Seminary (5), *Dayton.*

BONEBRAKE, P. O.	ROBERTS, J. T.	TOMAY, MRS. J. B.
KERR, J.	TOMAY, J. B.	

Wittenberg College and Seminary (10), *Springfield.*

BECKER, O. A.	GOTWALD, FRED G.	MOHLER, MARION M.
BRAMKAMP, JOHN M.	HADLEY, M. J.	SIGMUND, WILL S.
DELO, FRANK S.	LIEBERT, E. R.	WEAVER, H. J.
DERR, C. E.		

Wooster Seminary (39), *Wooster.*

ADAMS, LORA L.	FLATTERY, F. L.	NEWELL, WM. R.
ALLEN, C. B.	GREEN, E. F.	PENDLETON, E. M.
AUGELL, J. W.	JONES, M. J.	POLLOCK, KATE.
BABCOCK, BERT E.	KENNEDY, E. B.	PORTER, M. P.
BECK, E. A.	KING, IRA.	SHERMAN, G. D.
BELL, F. W.	LEWIS, A. B.	SKINNER, J. E.
BICKERSTAPH, G. L.	LINHART, S. B.	SPEER, J. S. V.
BUCKLEY, MABEL.	LYON, ABBIE M.	SNYDER, S. S.
BULLARD, F. L., Jr.	LYON, D. W.	TOENSMEIER, E. S.
CAVE, W. L.	MARSHALL, C. P.	TYNDAL, J. W.
CULBERTSON, M. L.	McGAW, A. G.	WHITE, ANNA.
ELDER, JAS. F.	MITCHELL, W. T.	WRIGHT, M. E.
FITCH, ROBERT F.	NEWELL, MARY.	YOUNG, J. W.

Western Female College (3), *Oxford.*

BROWN, BESSIE.	CROWTHER, ELIZABETH.	McKEE, LEILA S.

Western Reserve Academy (3), *Hudson.*

GRANT, W. S.	McVEY, C. Y.	REINHOLD, F. P.

PENNSYLVANIA.

Bucknell University (3), *Lewisburg.*

DAVIS, RAYMOND J.	FRETZ, T. S.	PAULING, E. C.

Evangelical Lutheran Seminary (1), *Gettysburg.*
WIEAND, H. E.

Grove City College (4), *Grove City.*
BLEAKNEY, W. H. KELLEY, J. C. RITCHIE, W. S.
CAMPBELL, HOWARD.

Lafayette College (1), *Easton.*
LAIRD, J. B.

Pennsylvania College (1), *Gettysburg.*
BALL, J. W.

Theological Seminary of Reformed Church in United States (1),
Lancaster.
MUIR, W. J.

United Presbyterian Theological Seminary (9), *Alleghany.*
ANDERSON, W. T.| McFARLAND, K. W. WELSH, J. M.
FULTON, W. K. McNARY, D. S. L. WHITE, J. S., M.D.
McCLURE, R. E. POLLOCK, J. B. WISHART, J. E.

Washington and Jefferson College (3), *Washington.*
JOHNSON, W. C. KNANER, F. G. LEWIS, CHARLES.

Western Theological Seminary (2), *Alleghany.*
LEYENBERGER, JAMES P. SWAN, CHARLES W.

RHODE ISLAND.

Brown University (1).
BEERS, W. L.

TENNESSEE.

Cumberland University (3), *Lebanon.*
DONNELL, JOHN T. HOLISTER, MOSES K. MONTGOMERY, L. M.

Vanderbilt University (3), *Nashville.*
COOK, O. F. NANCE, W. B. PERRY, J. W.

VERMONT.

University of Vermont (2), *Burlington.*
EVANS, JOHN M. PITKIN, GEO. F.

VIRGINIA.

Pantops Academy (2), *Charlottesville.*
TAYLOR, Prof. WM. P. TAYLOR, Mrs. W. P.

Richmond College (1), *Richmond.*

CHAMBERS, R. E.

Roanoke College (2), *Salem.*

GREEVER, W. H.   SHENK, E. A.

Theological Seminary of Virginia (1), *Fairfax Co.*

MEEM, JOHN G.

Union Theological Seminary (1), *Hampden-Sidney.*

JOHNSON, CAMERON.

University of Virginia (1), *University of Va.*

TAYLOR, J. SPOTTISWOOD.

WEST VIRGINIA.

Bethany College (12), *Bethany.*

BALDWIN, MARY.	FOX, EVANGELINE.	PORTER, MAY.
CAMPBELL, LOUISA.	JENKINS, B. A.	WHITE, CLARA.
CHAPMAN, A. L.	McGAVRAN, JOHN G.	WILFLEY, EARLE A.
FORTIER, GRACE.	MUCKLEY, O. K.	WILLIAMSON, MINNIE.

WISCONSIN.

Beloit College (3), *Beloit.*

JACOBS, H. H.   SHUMAKER, F. W.   WHEELER, E. C.

Lawrence University (1), *Appleton.*

ALLEN, E. D.

Ripon College (2), *Ripon.*

BETHEL, H. O.   McDERMID, MARY.

State University (1), *Madison.*

BEFFEL, J. M.

Wayland Academy (1), *Beaver Dam.*

WHYTE, J. P.

Total students,	558.
Total delegates,	680.

Missionary Literature.

In response to many inquiries for the best missionary books, the Corresponding Secretary has given no little time to the preparation of the following list of best available missionary books. Moreover, as these books are not handled by any one dealer (having been selected from the publications of over a score of firms), the Executive Committee have determined, for the convenience of the Volunteers, to undertake to carry a small stock of the books named below. While intended primarily for Volunteers, all who wish may avail themselves of the reduced rates offered.

A uniform discount of twenty per cent. (one-fifth off) is allowed on the list prices which are given after each book. Carriage — postage or expressage — must be paid by the purchaser, except on libraries offered below, or on purchases of $15 or more. In ordering by mail, add postage to four-fifths of list price. In ordering by express, send simply four-fifths of list price, and expressage will be collected on receipt of books.

Only the books named are carried in stock, but inquiries for others will receive prompt attention.

A CLASSIFIED LIST OF SELECTED MISSIONARY BOOKS.

I. GENERAL WORKS.

(a) *Encyclopedic.*

1. **The Encyclopedia of Missions.** A Thesaurus of Facts, Historical, Statistical, Geographical, Ethnological, and Biographical, with Maps, Bibliography, and Statistical tables. Edited by Rev. Edwin Munsell Bliss, late Assistant Agent American Bible Society for Levant. Two volumes. Over 1,700 pages, with elaborate maps, etc. 1891. $12.00. Postage, 40 cents.
   The most recent and complete work on missions. It should be in the library of every pastor and within the reach of every student.

(b) *Historical.*

2. **Short History of Christian Missions,** from Abraham and Paul to Carey, Livingstone, and Duff, by George Smith, LL.D., F. R. G. S. 1890. $1.00. Postage, 7 cents.
   An exceedingly valuable hand-book on the history of missions. It should be in the hands of every Volunteer and every student of missions.

3. **Outline of the History of Protestant Missions** from the Reformation to the Present Time. A Contribution to Church History, by Dr. Gustav Warneck. Translated from the second edition, by Thos. Smith, D.D. 1882. $1.25. Postage, 9 cents.
   Especially valuable to students.

4. **Moravian Missions.** Twelve Lectures by Augustus C. Thompson, D. D. 1882. $2.00. Postage, 11 cents.
   A well written and instructive history of these leaders in missionary effort.

5. **The Dawn of the Modern Mission,** by the Rev. Wm. Fleming Stevenson, D.D. 1886. $1.00. Postage, 6 cents.
   A very readable account of early missions, especially in India.

(c) *Surveys of the World-Field.*

6. **The Crisis of Missions,** or, The Voice out of the Cloud, by Rev. Arthur T. Pierson, D. D. 1886. Paper, $0.35; cloth, $1.25. Postage, 9 cents.
   An inspiring survey of the trials and triumphs of missions, with reference to their urgent claims upon the Church.

7. **Protestant Foreign Missions :** Their Present State. A Universal Survey, by Theodore Christlieb, D.D., Ph. D. Translated from the fourth German edition by David Allen Reed. 1880. $1.00. Postage, 8 cents.
   A valuable review of missions down to 1880.

8. **Christian Missions in the Nineteenth Century,** by Rev. Elbert S. Todd, D.D. 1890. $1.00. Postage, 7 cents.
   A brief study of Christianity in its relations to heathenism, commerce, statesmanship, etc.

9. **Around the World Tour of Christian Missions.** A Universal Survey, by William F. Bainbridge. 1881. $2.00. Postage, 16 cents.

    A very readable account of travel, with many practical observations on missions. Illustrated.

10. **Report of the Centenary Conference** on the Protestant Missions of the World, held in London, June, 1888, edited by the Rev. Jas. Johnston, F.S.S. Two volumes. 1888. $2.00. Postage, 27 cents.

    Contains much valuable information for the use of students.

11. **The Missionary Year-Book** for 1889–90, containing historical and statistical accounts of the principal Protestant Missionary Societies in America, Great Britain, and the Continent of Europe. 1889. $1.25. Postage, 11 cents.

    Useful to students and pastors.

12. **The Great Value and Success of Foreign Missions,** proved by Distinguished Witnesses, by Rev. John Liggins. 1888. Paper, $0.35; cloth, $0.75. Postage, 7 cents.

    A choice collection of testimonials useful to speakers on missions.

13. **The Evangelization of the World,** A Missionary Band. A Record of Consecration and Appeal, by B. Broomhall, Secretary of the China Island Mission. Second edition. 1887. $1.50. Postage, 16 cents.

    A rare collection of short chapters and paragraphs on a great variety of missionary topics. A storehouse for students.

14. **Mission Stories of Many Lands.** A Book for Young People. With three hundred and fifty illustrations. 1885. $2.00. Postage, 21 cents.

    A very interesting and instructive book, covering almost the entire world.

    (d) *Religions not Confined to One Country.*

15. **Present Day Tracts on the Non-Christian Religions of the World.** Comprising : The Rise and Decline of Islam, by Sir William Muir ; Christianity and Confucianism compared in their Teaching of the Whole Duty of Man, by James Legge ; The Zend-Avesta and the Religion of the Parsis, by J. Murray Mitchell ; The Hindu Religion, A Sketch and a Contrast, by J. Murray Mitchell ; Buddhism, A Comparison and a Contrast between Buddhism and Christianity, by Rev. Henry R. Reynolds, D.D. ; Christianity and Ancient Paganism, by J. Murray Mitchell, M. A., LL. D. $1.00. Postage, 8 cents.

16. **Islam and Its Founder,** by J. W. H. Stobart, B. A. 1876. $1.00. Postage, 6 cents.

    The best concise study of Mohammed and his teachings.

17. **The Coran,** its Composition and Teaching, and the Testimony it bears to the Holy Scriptures, by Sir William Muir, K. C. S. I., LL.D. 1878. $1.00. Postage, 6 cents.

    Especially valuable to all who are preparing to come into contact with Mohammedanism.

18. **Buddhism.** Being a Sketch of the Life and Teachings of Gautama, the Buddha, by T. W. Rhys Davids, M. A., Ph. D. $1.00. Postage, 6 cents.

    A brief, standard work.

19. **The Light of Asia and the Light of the World.** A Comparison of the Legend, the Doctrine, and the Ethics of the Buddha with the Story, the Doctrine, and the Ethics of Christ, by S. H. Kellogg, D. D. 1885. $2.00. Postage, 13 cents.

    A careful comparison of Buddhism and Christianity.

209

(e) *Biographies Covering the World-Field.*

20. Pioneers and Founders, or, Recent Workers in the Mission Field, by Charlotte M. Yonge. 1871. $1.75. Postage, 9 cents.

Concise and graphic biographies of John Eliot, David Brainerd, Christian F. Schwarz, Henry Martyn, William Carey, and John Marshman, the Judson Family, three Bishops of Calcutta, Samuel Marsden, John Williams, Allen Gardiner, and Charles Frederick Mackenzie.

21. American Heroes on Mission Fields. Brief Missionary Biographies, edited by Rev. H. C. Haydn, D.D. 1890. $1.25. Postage, 12 cents.

Brief biographies of thirteen missionaries — eight of them located in Turkey and Persia : Mrs. Clara Gray Schauffler, Henry Sergeant West, M.D., David Tappan Stoddard, Asahel Grant, M.D., William Goodell, Titus Coan, H. G. O. Dwight, S. Wells Williams, Elijah Coleman Bridgman, Miss Julia A. Rappleye, Adoniram Judson, William G. Schauffler, and John Eliot.

22. Master Missionaries. Chapters in Pioneer Effort throughout the World, by Alex. Hay Japp, LL. D. 1880. $1.00. Postage, 8 cents.

Brief biographies of Jas. Oglethorpe, David Zeisberger, Samuel Hebich, William Elmslie, Geo. W. Walker, Robert Moffat, Dr. Jas. Stewart, Dr. Wm. Black, John Coleridge Patteson, and John G. Fee.

(f) *Medical Missions.*

23. Medical Missions, Their Place and Power, by John Lowe, F.R.C.S.E. 1890. $1.50. Postage, 11 cents.

The standard work on medical missions.

24. The Healer-Preacher. Sketches and Incidents of Medical Mission Work, by George Saunders, M.D., C.B. 1884. $1.25. Postage, 10 cents.

An account of medical mission work in London, containing many interesting incidents.

25. Medical Work of the Woman's Foreign Missionary Society, Methodist Episcopal Church, by Mrs. J. T. Gracey. 1888. $0.50. Postage, 7 cents.

In India, China, Japan, and Korea.

(g) *Miscellaneous Works.*

26. Foreign Missions, Their Place in the Pastorate, in Prayer, in Conferences. Ten Lectures by Augustus C. Thompson, D. D. 1889. $1.75. Postage, 13 cents.

Especially useful to the home pastor. Highly commended.

27. Missionary Addresses, by Rev. J. M. Thoburn, D.D. 1888. $0.70. Postage, 7 cents.

Contains much wise and helpful advice for the prospective missionary.

28. Women of the Orient. An Account of the Religious, Intellectual, and Social Condition of Women in Japan, China, India, Egypt, Syria, and Turkey, by Rev. Ross C. Houghton, A.M. 1877. $1.25. Postage, 12 cents.

A most entertaining book. Fully illustrated.

29. The Ely Volume, or, The Contributions of our Foreign Missions to Science and Human Well-being, by Thomas Laurie, D.D. 1881. $2.00. Postage, 22 cents.

An exhaustive treatise on the contributions of A. B. C. F. M. Missionaries to science. Full of useful facts and illustrations.

30. **Modern Missions and Culture ;** Their Mutual Relations, by Dr. Gustav Warneck. Translated by Thomas Smith, D. D. 1882. $1.35. Postage 12 cents.

A good book for all desiring a broad, philosophical view of missionary effort.

31. **The Indo-British Opium Trade** and its Effect. A Recess Study, by Theodore Christlieb, D. D., Ph. D. Translated by David B. Croom, M. A. 1879. $0.70. Postage, 4 cents.

A brief, incisive resume of this deadly traffic down to 1879.

32. **Maritime Discovery and Christian Missions,** Considered in their Mutual Relations, by John Campbell. 1840. $1.75. Postage, 18 cents.

Deals largely with the South Sea Islands.

33. **Memoirs of Rev. David Brainerd,** edited by J. M. Sherwood, D.D. 1884. $1.50. Postage, 13 cents.

Highly recommended for intense spiritual tone.

II. AFRICA.

(a) *Historical and Descriptive.*

34. **The New World of Central Africa,** with a history of the first Christian Mission on the Congo, by Mrs. H. Grattan Guinness. 1890. $2.00. Postage, 17 cents.

A graphic description of the Congo Free State, its history, people, etc., with a full account of the first twelve years of the Livingstone Inland Mission. Very entertaining and recent.

35. **Garenganze,** or, Seven Years' Pioneer Mission Work in Central Africa, by Fred. S. Arnot. 1889. $1.25. Postage, 10 cents.

A narration of the thrilling adventures and patient trials of a devoted Christian explorer.

36. **The Story of Madagascar,** by the Rev. John W. Mears, D.D. 1873. $1.25. Postage, 8 cents.

A full account of the persecution of Christians from 1839–61, with notices of earlier and later history down to 1871.

37. **Africa's Mountain Valley,** or, The Church in Regent's Town, West Africa, by Maria Louisa Charlesworth. $1.50. Postage, 8 cents.

A most interesting and instructive chapter in the missionary history of Africa.

(b) *Biographical.*

38. **The Personal Life of David Livingstone, LL. D., D. C. L.,** chiefly from his unpublished journals and correspondence in the possession of his family, by William Garden Blaikie, D.D., LL. D. $1.25. Postage, 14 cents.

Best personal biography of Livingstone.

39. **David Livingstone.** His Labours and His Legacy, by Arthur Montefiore, F. R. G. S. $0.75. Postage, 6 cents.

A brief but comprehensive sketch of his life and labors.

40. **Alexander M. Mackay,** Pioneer Missionary of the Church Missionary Society to Uganda, by his Sister. 1890. $1.50. Postage, 12 cents.

One of the most absorbing missionary biographies. Valuable hints on the industrial phase of foreign missionary work.

41. **The Lives of Robert and Mary Moffat,** by their son, John S. Moffat. 1888. $1.75. Postage, 15 cents.

A well-written story of the trials and successes of missionary life, containing inner glimpses of domestic experience and trials.

42. **James Hannington,** First Bishop of Eastern Equatorial Africa. A history of his life and work, 1847–1885, by E. C. Dawson, M.A., 1886. $1.25. Postage, 12 cents.

A vivid sketch of a remarkable active and useful life and a tragic death.

43. **Samuel Crowther,** the Slave Boy who became Bishop of the Niger, by Jesse Page. 1888. $0.75. Postage, 6 cents.

A brief and entertaining record of a remarkable life and work.

III. ALASKA.

44. **Alaska,** and Missions of the North Pacific Coast, by Rev. Sheldon Jackson, D. D. 1883. $1.50. Postage, 11 cents.

A profusely illustrated description of Alaska, its people, customs, and missions down to 1883.

45. **Life in Alaska.** Letters of Mrs. Eugene S. Willard, edited by her sister, Mrs. Eva McClintock. 1884. $1.25. Postage, 9 cents.

Contains touching glimpses of the trials and joys of missionary life.

IV. BURMAH.

46. **The Life of Adoniram Judson,** by his son, Edward Judson. 1883. $1.50. Postage, 17 cents.

An inspiring and entertaining biography of Burmah's great missionary.

47. **Rivers in the Desert,** or, The Great Awakening in Burmah, by the Rev. John Baillie. $1.50. Postage, 8 cents.

A narrative of the wonderful work of God in that country, with memoirs of the Judsons and of their fellow-laborers.

V. CHINA.

(a) *Historical and Descriptive.*

48. **The Middle Kingdom.** A Survey of the Geography, Government, Literature, Social Life, Arts, and History of the Chinese Empire and its Inhabitants, by S. Wells Williams, LL. D. Two volumes. 1882. $9.00. Postage, 50 cents·

The standard work on China.

49. **China and the Chinese.** A General Description of the Country and its Inhabitants; its Civilization and Form of Government; its Religious and Social Institutions; its Intercourse with other Nations; and its Present Condition and Prospects. By the Rev. John L. Nevius, D. D. 1882. $1.50. Postage, 11 cents.

A thorough presentation of China and its people, with particular reference to missions and methods.

50. **In the Far East.** Letters from Geraldine Guinness in China, edited by her Sister. 1889. Board, $1.00; cloth, $1.50. Postage, 12 cents.

A most intensely fascinating account of life in China. Graphic description, tender pathos, and unusual depth of spirituality place this book in the very front rank. Handsomely illustrated.

51. **The Dragon, Image, and Demon**, or, the Three Religions of China, Confucianism, Buddhism, and Taoism, by Rev. Hampden C. DuBose. 1886. $2.00. Postage, 17 cents.
Fully illustrated and well arranged. Confined to religions.

52. **The Religions of China.** Confucianism and Taoism Described and Compared with Christianity, by James Legge. 1880. $1.50. Postage, 10 cents.
A work by a recognized authority.

53. **Confucianism and Taouism**, by Robert K. Douglas. $1.00. Postage, 7 cents.
Brief but thorough studies of these two systems.

54. **The Chinese Classics.** A Translation, by Jas. Legge, D.D. $0.60. Postage, 12 cents.
Translations of the principal works of Confucius and Mencius.

55. **China**, by Robert K. Douglas. 1885. $1.50, Postage, 13 cents.
In popular form. Christian missions very briefly noticed.

56. **Among the Mongols**, by the Rev. James Gilmour, M. A. 1888. $1.00. Postage, 11 cents.
Account of the pioneer travels of a medical missionary in Mongolia.

(b) *Biographical.*

57. **Robert Morrison**, the Pioneer of Chinese Missions, by William John Townsend. $0.75. Postage, 7 cents.
An interesting sketch of China's pioneer missionary.

58. **Griffith John**, Founder of the Hankow Mission, Central China, by William Robson. 1889. $0.75. Postage, 7 cents.
A sketch of the life and work of the pioneer missionary to central China.

VI. COREA.

59. **Corea, the Hermit Nation.** Ancient and Medieval History; Political and Social Corea; Modern and Recent History. By William Elliot Griffis. 1888. $2.50. Postage, 20 cents.
The standard work on Corea.

60. **Corea, Without and Within.** Chapters on Corean History, Manners and Religion, by William Elliot Griffis. 1885. $1.25. Postage, 9 cents.
A popular description of country and people, condensed from foregoing.

VII. INDIA.

(a) *Historical and Descriptive.*

61. **India**, Country, People, Missions, by J. T. Gracey, D. D. 1884. $1.00. Postage, 8 cents.
A brief study of the needs of India and the success of Christianity in that country.

62. **A Brief History of the Indian People**, by Sir William Wilson Hunter. 1888. $1.50. Postage, 6 cents.
Exceedingly valuable for conciseness and accuracy.

63. **Seven Years in Ceylon.** Stories of Mission Life, by Mary and Margaret W. Leitch. 1890. $0.75. Postage, 11 cents.
Richly illustrated and very entertaining.

64. **Hinduism**, by Sir Monier M. Williams. $1.00. Postage, 6 cents.
A brief but exhaustive study by the leading authority on Hinduism.

65. **India,** by Fannie Roper Feudge. 1880. $1.50. Postage, 12 cents.
Very readable, but Christian missions are very briefly noticed.

66. **The Land of the Veda.** Being Personal Reminiscences of India, its People,
Castes, etc., etc., by Rev. William Butler, D.D. 1871. $3.50. Postage, 28 cents.
Treats of history of Methodist Episcopal missions in India to 1872. Valuable also for narration of events connected with Sepoy Rebellion.

67. **Native Life in South India.** Being Sketches of the Social and Religious
Characteristics of the Hindus, by Rev. Henry Rice. $1.00. Postage, 8 cents.
Brief but comprehensive.

68. **A Woman's Talks About India,** or, The Domestic Habits and Customs of
the People, by Harriet G. Brittain. 1880. $0.90. Postage, 6 cents.
Intended especially for children.

69. **Indian Missionary Manual.** Hints to Young Missionaries to India, compiled
by John Murdoch, LL. D. 1889. $2.00. Postage, 12 cents.
Valuable hints to missionaries to India on a great variety of subjects, but
useful to all missionaries to tropical climates.

(b) *Biographical.*

70. **The Life of William Carey, D. D.,** Shoemaker and Missionary, by George
Smith, LL. D. 1885. $3.00. Postage, 15 cents.
An exceedingly interesting and exhaustive memoir.

71. **William Carey,** The Shoemaker who became "The Father and Founder of
Modern Missions," by John Brown Myers. 1887. $0.75. Postage, 7 cents.
A brief but comprehensive view of Carey's life and work.

72. **The Life of Alexander Duff, D.D., LL. D.,** by George Smith, LL. D.
Two volumes in one. 1879. $2.00. Postage, 17 cents.
A well written and complete life of the great missionary teacher.

73. **My Missionary Apprenticeship,** by Rev. J. M. Thoburn, D. D. 1884.
$1.50. Postage, 10 cents.
A most instructive and interesting account of missionary experience
in India.

VIII. JAPAN.

74. **The Mikado's Empire.** History of Japan from 660 B. C. to 1872 A. D.,
and Personal Experiences, Observations, and Studies in Japan, 1870-1874, by
William Elliot Griffis, A. M. With supplementary chapters. 1890. $4.00.
Postage, 23 cents.
A standard work on Japan.

75. **The Sunrise Kingdom,** or, Life and Scenes in Japan, and Woman's Work
for Woman there, by Mrs. Julia D. Carrothers. 1879. $2.00. Postage, 13 cents.
A familiar description of native life in Japan by a missionary.

76. **Unbeaten Tracks in Japan.** An account of Travels on Horseback in the
Interior, by Isabella L. Bird. Two volumes in one. 1880. $2.50. Postage,
18 cents.
Graphic narration of travels in Japan.

77. **A Budget of Letters from Japan.** Reminiscences of Work and Travel in
Japan, by Arthur Collins Maclay, A.M., LL.B. 1888. $2.00. Postage, 15 cents.
Experiences and observations of an American teacher in government
schools from 1873-1878.

78. **The Land of the Morning.** An Account of Japan and its People based on Four Years' Residence in that Country, by William Gray Dixon. 1881. $2.00. Postage, 17 cents.
     A very readable book, though not recent.

IX. MEXICO.

79. **The Mexican Guide,** by Thos. A. Janvier. 1890. $2.50. Postage, 10 cents.
     A standard repository of information on Mexico, though not containing much on missions.

X. PERSIA.

80. **Historical and Descriptive Account of Persia** from the Earliest Times, by Jas. B. Fraser. 1833. $0.75. Postage, 6 cents.
     A concise but thorough study, down to 1833, with chapter on Afghanistan.

81. **Persia and the Persians,** by S. G. W. Benjamin. Illustrated. 1886. $4.00. Postage, 34 cents.
     An account of this country as seen and studied by the United States Minister to Persia.

82. **Persia, the Land of the Imams,** by Rev. James Bassett. 1886. $1.50. Postage, 12 cents.
     An account of missionary travels during eleven years' residence in Persia.

83. **Faith Working by Love,** as Exemplified in the Life of Fidelia Fiske, by D. S. Fiske. 1868. $1.50. Postage, 11 cents.
     A beautiful and inspiring picture of woman's work as seen in the life of a most devoted woman.

XI. SIAM.

84. **Siam,** or, the Heart of Farther India, by Mary Lovina Cort. 1886. $1.00. Postage, 11 cents.
     An entertaining and comprehensive sketch of the people and customs of Siam, with an account of the missions.

85. **Siam and Laos,** as seen by our American Missionaries. 1884. $1.85. Postage, 13 cents.
     Interesting papers on Siam and phases of missionary work in it. Illustrated.

XII. SOUTH AMERICA.

86. **The Capitals of Spanish America,** by William Eleroy Curtis, late Commissioner from the United States to the Governments of Central and South America. 1888. $3.50. Postage, 26 cents.
     Very interesting and instructive. Fully illustrated.

87. **Brazil,** by C. C. Andrews. 1890. $1.50. Postage, 12 cents.
     Contains much recent information, though not treating missions exhaustively.

XIII. SOUTH SEA ISLANDS

(a) *Historical and Descriptive.*

88. **Missionary Enterprise in the South Sea Islands,** by John Williams.
1888. $1.00. Postage, 10 cents.

The story of the wonderful work of the martyr-missionary, John Williams,
among the South Sea Islands, 1817-39.

89. **The New Hebrides and Christian Missions.** by Robert Steel, D. D.
1880. $2.75. Postage, 13 cents.

A comprehensive view of missions to these Islands, with a sketch of
the Labor Traffic.

90. **Among the Cannibals of New Guinea,** by Rev. S. McFarlane, LL. D.,
F. R. G. S. 1888. $0.75. Postage, 6 cents.

A graphic account of the early history of the New Guinea Mission of the
London Missionary Society, 1871-88.

91. **At Home in Fiji,** by Miss C. F. Gordon Cumming. 1878. $1.25. Postage,
11 cents.

A record of life in Fiji, with considerable mention of missionary work.

92. **Six Months Among the Palm Groves, Coral Reefs, and Volcanoes of
the Sandwich Islands,** by Isabella L. Bird. 1876. $2.50. Postage, 10 cents.

A vivid description of travel and adventure.

(b) *Biographical.*

93. **John G. Paton,** Missionary to the New Hebrides. An Autobiography, edited
by his Brother. Two volumes. 1889. $3.00. Postage, 21 cents.

" The most fascinating narrative of missionary adventure and heroism and
success that we have ever met."— *A. T. Pierson.*

94. **James Calvert,** or, From Dark to Dawn in Fiji, by R. Vernon. 1890. $0.75.
Postage, 7 cents.

A brief but graphic account of the work of missions in Fiji from 1835 to
the present. Fully illustrated.

95. **Bishop Patteson,** the Martyr of Melanesia, by Jesse Page. $0.75. Postage,
7 cents.

The record of a noble student-life, an active young manhood, and a
tragic death.

96. **Life of John Coleridge Patteson,** Missionary Bishop of the Melanesian
Islands, by Charlotte Mary Yonge. Two volumes. 1873. $5.00. Postage,
20 cents.

An interesting and complete memoir.

97. **Memoir of the Life and Episcopate of George Augustus Selwyn, D.D.,**
Bishop of New Zealand, 1841-69, and Lichfield, 1867-78, by the Rev. H. W.
Tucker, M.A. Two volumes. 1879. $5.00. Postage, 17 cents.

A narrative of the Christianization of New Zealand.

98. **John Williams,** the Martyr Missionary of Polynesia, by Rev. Jas. J. Ellis.
1889. $0.75. Postage, 7 cents.

A brief but interesting biography of this pioneer missionary.

XIV. TURKEY.

(a) *Historical and Descriptive.*

99. **Among the Turks,** by Cyrus Hamlin. 1877. $1.50. Postage, 10 cents.
Interesting observations during thirty-five years' residence in Constantinople as a missionary.

100. **The Romance of Missions,** or, Inside View of Life and Labor in the Land of Ararat, by Maria A. West. 1876. $1.50. Postage, 13 cents.
Very entertaining; with glimpses of the peculiar trials and joys of missionary life.

101. **The Women of the Arabs,** with a Chapter for Children, by Rev. Henry Harris Jessup, D.D. 1873. $1.25. Postage, 10 cents.
An account of work for Woman in Syria to 1873, with a most interesting chapter for children.

102. **Ten Years on the Euphrates,** or, Primitive Missionary Policy Illustrated, by Rev. C. H. Wheeler. 1868. $1.25. Postage, 8 cents.
Labors in Harpoot, Turkey, and vicinity.

(b) *Biographical.*

103. **Forty Years in the Turkish Empire,** or, Memoirs of Rev. William Goodell, D.D., by E. D. G. Prime, D.D. 1875. $1.50. Postage, 11 cents.
Full of interesting incidents, and especially helpful in understanding present status of Christian Work in the Turkish Empire.

104. **Autobiography of William G. Schauffler,** for Forty-nine Years a Missionary in the Orient, edited by his Sons. 1887. $1.00. Postage, 11 cents.
A most readable narrative of the varied experiences of this remarkable man.

LIBRARIES.

While it is hoped that each purchaser will make his own selection, yet, as few have the books at hand for examination, the following collections are suggested for those who wish to order in this way.

Should any wish to omit any books suggested, others of equal value will be inserted at their request.

The Volunteer's $15 Missionary Library. Includes Nos. 2, 6, 12, 27, 38, 40, 40, 50, 61, 70, 73, 93, and 100. Sent expressage paid.

The Young People's $10 Missionary Library. Includes Nos. 6, 14, 28, 39, 40, 49, 50, 61, 63, 71, and 94. Sent expressage paid.

The Minister's $15 Missionary Library. Includes Nos. 2, 6, 10, 11, 12, 13, 26, 28, 38, 46, 49, 61, and 93. Sent expressage paid.

The College $15 Missionary Library. Includes Nos. 2, 6, 12, 28, 34, 40, 49, 52, 61, 62, 74, 84, and 94. Sent expressage paid.

The College $35 Missionary Library. Includes Nos. 2, 6, 12, 16, 18, 23, 28, 29, 34, 38, 40, 46, 48, 50, 59, 61, 62, 64, 70, 74, 84, 86, and 93. Sent expressage paid.

The College $50 Missionary Library. Includes, in addition to the $35 library, Nos. 1, 20, 49, 89, and 99. Sent expressage paid.

Send money by postal or express money order, check or draft. By no means send silver, as it is very liable to be lost, and endangers all mail sent to the same address. Address all communications to

WALTER J. CLARK,

97 BIBLE HOUSE,

New York City.

Student Volunteer Series.

No. 1. The American Student Uprising, by John R. Mott. Exhausted; but its place temporarily supplied by "The Report of the Executive Committee presented at the International Convention at Cleveland."

No. 2. Shall I Go? by Miss Grace E. Wilder. Fifth edition exhausted.

No. 3. The Volunteer Pledge, by Robert P. Wilder.

No. 4. The Volunteer Band, by Robert E. Speer.

No. 5. Not yet issued.

No. 6. Not yet issued.

No. 7. The World's Need, by John N. Forman. Almost exhausted.

No. 8. An Appeal from China, by Miss Geraldine Guinness. Almost exhausted.

No. 9. An Appeal from India, by Miss Grace E. Wilder.

No. 10. An Appeal to Christian Medical Students, by W. J. Wanless.

No. 11. An Appeal from Japan, by C. A. Clark.

Missionary Tracts.

In addition to the Student Volunteer Series, the following missionary tracts are commended, and can be obtained from the Student Volunteer Movement office.

A Bird's Eye View of the Foreign Mission Field. Second edition. 10 cents per dozen ; 65 cents per hundred.

Facts on Foreign Missions. (Revised.) Compiled by W. J. Wanless, M. D. 2 cents ; 20 cents per dozen ; $1 per hundred.

A Mute Appeal on Behalf of Foreign Missions, with diagram exhibiting the actual and relative numbers of mankind classified according to their religion. 30 cents per hundred.

Trifling with a Great Trust, with diagram illustrating the annual expenditures in the United States compared with gifts to foreign missions. 30 cents per hundred.

A Comparative View of Christian Work in the Home and Foreign Fields, with diagrams. 30 cents per hundred.

Medical Missions. Facts and Testimonies to their Value and Success, compiled by W. J. Wanless, M. D.

American Missionary Periodicals.

A few of the leading Missionary Magazines and Periodicals are given, trusting that every Volunteer will subscribe for one or more. The list might easily be quadrupled. All are monthly.

The **Missionary Review of the World**, $2 ; $1 to Volunteers. Funk & Wagnalls, 18 and 20 Astor Place, New York City. [Undenominational.]

The **Missionary Echo**, 50 cents ; to students and ministers, 25 cents. The Willard Tract Depository, Yonge and Temperance Streets, Toronto, Ont. [Undenominational.]

The **Medical Missionary Record**, $1 ; to students at reduced rates. Geo. D. Dowkontt, M.D., 118 East 45th Street, New York City. [Undenominational.]

China's Millions, 50 cents. 30 Shuter Street, Toronto, Ont. With American Supplement. [China Inland Mission.]

The **Baptist Missionary Magazine**, $1. Tremont Temple, Boston, Mass. [Bap.]

The **Missionary Herald**, $1. Congregational House, 1 Somerset Street, Boston, Mass. [Cong.]

The **Gospel in All Lands**, $1.50. Hunt & Eaton, 150 Fifth Avenue, New York City. [M. E.]

The **Spirit of Missions**, $1. 22 Bible House, New York City. [P. E.]

The **Church at Home and Abroad**, $1. Presbyterian Board of Publication and Sunday School Work, 1334 Chestnut Street, Philadelphia, Pa. [Pres. North.]

The **Missionary**, $1. Whittet & Shepperson, 1001 Main Street, Richmond, Va. [Pres. South.]

Appendix

EARLY HISTORY OF THE STUDENT VOLUNTEER

✠✠

I. Origin

IN THE EARLY DAYS of this century, partly as a result of the wonderful spirit of revival which was then sweeping through the Eastern colleges, and partly as a result of reading the record of the heroism and sacrifice of the pioneer representatives of the first missionary societies of England, a deep interest in foreign missions began to develop among the students of New England. It first assumed a practical form in 1808 when Samuel J. Mills and a little group of his fellow students secretly organized at Williams College the Society of Brethren. "The object of this society," in the words of its constitution, "shall be to effect in the persons of its members a mission or missions to the heathen." The main reason for secrecy, doubtless, was the possibility of failure, because in those days there was comparatively no sentiment in favor of such an enterprise. It will be remembered that there was then no missionary society on this continent which had a station on a foreign field. Obviously one great problem which confronted these students was so to affect public opinion as to lead to the formation of an aggressive foreign missionary society. By publication and circulation of two strong addresses on missions, by correspondence with leading clergymen, and by personal work with them during vacations, much was accomplished. The center of activity was then transferred to Andover Seminary. Here some of the men who had come from Williams were joined by Nott, Judson, and others, whom they were surprised to find filled with the same idea and spirit. As a result of their combined labor and influence in the seminary, in the colleges, and in the churches, wherever they spoke, they achieved their purpose; for this missionary movement led by students of the New England colleges furnished the occasion for the formation of the American Board of Commissioners for Foreign Missions.

The leaders in this student missionary movement were anxious to accomplish another important object. Not only did they recognize the importance of educating and arousing the Church to send forth and sustain missionaries, but they also clearly discerned that something must be done to awaken and maintain an active interest in missions among college men, in order that there might be a sufficient and constant number of candidates for foreign service. To make this possible they sought by correspondence and visitation to have missionary societies formed in the different colleges. So much in earnest were they that, it is said, some of the members of the parent society at Williams left that institution and entered other colleges, in order to spread the missionary spirit. Their strong desire was to bind the colleges together in an intercollegiate missionary movement. While their labors resulted, in a few years, in planting societies in several institutions, and in raising up a considerable number of missionaries (including some of the most distinguished who have gone out from America), they failed to realize their chief aim—the formation of a widespread, permanent student missionary movement. Their failure in this respect appears to have been due to lack of organization, and more especially to the low spiritual condition of many of the colleges at that time, notwithstanding the fact that in others there had recently been marked revivals of religion. To the American and Canadian students, nearly three quarters of a century later, was left the realization of this hope and purpose.

A memorable conference of college men was held from July 6 to August 1, 1886, at Mount Hermon, overlooking the Connecticut River, in the state of Massachusetts. Two hundred and fifty-one students from eighty-seven colleges, representing all parts of the United States and Canada, had come together at the invitation of Mr. Moody to spend several weeks in Bible study. Ten days passed before the subject of missions was even mentioned in the sessions of the Conference. A few young men, however, like Wilder of Princeton, Tewkesbury of Harvard, and Clark of Oberlin, had come with the deep conviction that God would call from that large gathering of college men a number who would consecrate themselves to foreign missions. They called together all who were thinking seriously of spending their lives on the foreign field. Although several of them had not definitely decided the question, twenty-one students answered this call. This little band of consecrated men began to pray that the spirit of missions might pervade the Conference, and that the Lord would separate many of the delegates unto this great work. In a few days they were to see their faith rewarded far beyond what they had dared to claim.

On the evening of July 16, Dr. Arthur T. Pierson gave a thrilling address on missions. He supported by the most convincing arguments the proposition: "All should go, and go to all." He pressed upon the consciences of his hearers that their relation to missions was after all "only a matter of supreme loyalty to Jesus Christ." He sounded the keynote which set many men to thinking and praying.

A week passed. On Friday night, July 23, a meeting was held which may occupy as significant a place in the history of the Christian Church as the Williams Haystack Prayer-meeting. It is known as the "Meeting of the Ten Nations." It was addressed by sons of missionaries in China, India, and Persia, and by seven other young men of different nationalities—an American, a Japanese, a Siamese, a German, a Dane, a Norwegian, and an American Indian. These men in pithy, burning, three-minute speeches each made one dominant point, namely, the need in his country of more workers from the body of students assembled in that Conference. After the appeals were given, each speaker, during a most impressive silence, repeated in the language of the country which he represented the words, "God is love." Dr. Ashmore, after a few sentences, left with the students the searching challenge, "Show, if you can, why you should not obey the last command of Jesus Christ." The meeting closed with a season of silent and audible prayer, which will never be forgotten by those who were present. The people left the hall in silence. That night was preeminently a night of prayer.

On Tuesday morning, July 27, Dr. William Ashmore of China (who had, as soon as he learned of this Conference on arriving in the country, canceled his engagements for over a week in order that he might attend and lay upon the students the claims of China) added fuel to the flame. He made a ringing appeal to Christians to "look no longer upon missions as a mere wrecking expedition, but as a war of conquest." Mr. Sankey sang with spirit and thrilling fervor, "Tell It Out Among the Nations That the Lord Is King." Mr. Moody prayed earnestly that the missionary spirit might fall upon those present.

By this time the number of volunteers had increased from twenty-one to nearly fifty. During the remaining five days of the Conference the interest became more and more intense. Meetings of the volunteers and those specially interested were held each day. Possibly the most sacred of these was the one held in the parlor of Crossley Hall, from twilight until midnight, on Friday, July 30. Missions became the absorbing topic of conversation wherever the students gathered—in the rooms, in the dining hall, at the swimming wharf, and on the athletic field. Each volunteer became an enlister of others. But the large majority of the decisions were not reached in the presence of others. One by one, the men, alone in the woods or in their rooms with their

Bibles and God, fought out the battle with self, and became obedient to the heavenly vision. Late in the afternoon of the last day the number of volunteers had reached ninety-nine. They assembled for a farewell meeting, during which a man came in and volunteered, making the number at the close of the Conference an even one hundred.

At this final meeting there was a unanimous expression that the missionary spirit, which had manifested itself with such power at Mount Hermon, should be communicated, in some degree at least, to the thousands of students in the colleges and seminaries who had not been privileged to come in contact with it at its source. It was the conviction of the volunteers that the reasons which had led them to decide would influence hundreds of other students, if those reasons were once presented to them in a practical, intelligent, faithful, and prayerful manner. Two days before this the suggestion had come to a few of the volunteers and leaders of the Conference, while on a tramp over the hills near the Vermont border, that a deputation, something like the Cambridge Band, be sent among the colleges. This famous band was composed of seven Cambridge students noted for their scholarship, their prominence in athletics, and above all, their consecration and spirituality. Before going out to China they made a memorable tour among the British universities, creating a great missionary revival among the students—felt also more or less by the entire Church. When this plan was mentioned to the volunteers it was heartily and prayerfully adopted; and a deputation of four students was selected to represent the Mount Hermon Conference and to visit during the year as many institutions as possible.

II. DEVELOPMENT

Of the four men selected for this important mission among the colleges, only one, Mr. Robert P. Wilder, was able to go. After much prayer, Mr. John N. Forman, also of Princeton, was induced to become a member of the deputation. A prominent layman of one of the eastern cities, who was at Mount Hermon during the impressive, closing days, generously offered to bear the expenses involved in the tour, and ever since he has sustained a most helpful relation to the Movement. It would be impossible to estimate the manifold fruitage which has been gathered by the Church as a result of this one man's consecrated giving. Messrs. Wishard and Ober, at that time the international college secretaries of the Young Men's Christian Association, who had selected the members of the deputation, also assumed the responsible duty of facilitating their tour. This first year (1886-1887) may properly be characterized as the year of rapid and wide extension. Messrs. Wilder and Forman visited 176 institutions, including nearly all the leading colleges and divinity schools of Canada and the United States. As a rule they traveled together, but now and then separated in order that they might touch more institutions. Their speeches packed with fresh and telling facts, their arguments firmly anchored in the Scriptures, their unwavering faith in the possibility of evangelizing the world in their generation if the students would but rally around the idea, above all the prayerfulness of their lives, made a lasting impression wherever they went. As a result of their labors the number of volunteers passed from 100 to 2,200 during the year. Even Dr. Pierson in his most sanguine moments had not dared to predict that the Movement would, in so short a time, reach beyond a thousand.

During the second year (1887-1888) the Movement was left to itself. It was unorganized, and had no leadership or oversight whatever. Notwithstanding this fact, and as a result of its inherent life and acquired momentum it continued to expand. The volunteers themselves, by personal work, swelled their number to nearly 3,000. But, on the other hand, like any other vigorous movement left without a guiding hand, it began to manifest certain dangerous tendencies. No particular notice of these was taken until the summer of 1888, when about fifty volunteers from different sections came together at the World's Student Conference at Northfield, and reported the condition of the Movement in their respective institutions. It was then found that there was: (1) A tendency in the Movement at some points to lose its unity. All sorts of missionary societies and bands—with different purposes, methods of work, and forms of constitution—were springing up. It was plain that it would lose much of its power should its unity be destroyed. (2) A tendency to decline in some colleges, because not carefully supervised. (3) A disposition to conflict with existing religious societies appeared in a very few places. All these tendencies were decidedly out of harmony with the original spirit and purpose of the Movement; accordingly it was decided that immediate steps should be taken toward a wise organization. Another consideration helped to influence this decision, and that was a desire to extend the Movement. Thus far it had not touched more than one fifth of the institutions of higher learning on this continent. It was a very critical time in the history of the Volunteer Movement. To Mr. C. K. Ober is due in large measure the credit of safely passing the crisis. He recognized clearly the possibilities of this Movement if properly guarded, developed, and extended; and firmly believed that all the dangerous tendencies would be checked by judicious organization. As chairman of the committee appointed by the volunteers at Northfield for that purpose he suggested, in the main, the flexible yet comprehensive scheme of organization under which the Movement has since been working. Had the counsels of some prevailed at this time, in all human probability the Movement would have disintegrated, and much of the interest have passed away, just as the British delegates at Northfield reported had been the case in their universities after the members of the Cambridge Band and a majority of the men whom they enlisted had gone to the foreign field, and just as the missionary interest waned among the students of New England not long after the pioneer student missionaries had entered upon their lifework in foreign lands. In this connection it is interesting to consider the conditions confronting the Volunteer Movement in the last decade, which differed from those which existed in the colleges in the first decade of the century when the students of Williams College were seeking to form an intercollegiate missionary movement. We have seen that they failed in the effort to accomplish this aim largely because of the lack of Christian organization among the students then, and also because of the low state of spiritual life in many of the colleges. The Volunteer Movement entered a field in which a much larger majority of the students than ever before were Christians. Moreover, it found those Christians peculiarly susceptible to the missionary appeal because of the preparation their minds and hearts had received in Bible classes, in personal work, in country and city missions, and, to a limited extent, in the study of missions, in connection with their Christian Associations. The presence of large intercollegiate Christian organizations not only rendered the spread of the Volunteer Movement a comparatively easy thing, but they also afforded the conditions for making it permanent.

The third year of the history of the Movement (1888-1889) may be called the year of organization. The committee appointed to take this matter in charge decided that the Movement should be confined to students. It was therefore named the Student Volunteer Movement for Foreign Missions. It was noted that practically all the volunteers were members of some one of the four great interdenominational student organizations: the College Young Men's Christian Association, the College Young Women's Christian Association, the American Interseminary Missionary Alliance, and the Canadian Intercollegiate Missionary Alliance. This suggested the plan of placing at the head of the Movement a permanent executive committee composed of one representative appointed by each of these organizations. Thus far the last two organizations named have appointed the same man. This committee is to develop and facilitate the Movement in accord with the spirit and constitutions of the organizations which they represent, and as an organic department of them—thus obviating a new and an unnecessary organization. The plan was first submitted to the College

Committee of the International Committee of the Young Men's Christian Associations, and was heartily approved. They appointed Mr. John R. Mott as their representative. He has held this position ever since. The plan was fully endorsed by the International Committee of the Young Women's Christian Associations, and Miss Nettie Dunn was chosen to represent them. In 1891 she was succeeded by Miss Corabel Tarr. The two Missionary Alliances also favored the plan and named Mr. Robert P. Wilder as their representative. He occupied the position until 1891, when he was followed by Mr. Robert E. Speer, who was succeeded in turn in the spring of 1892 by Mr. D. Willard Lyon. (Mr. Mott was chosen to serve as chairman of the Movement and held that position for over thirty years.) The Executive Committee as first constituted began its work in January, 1889, and soon completed the work of organization. This may be briefly outlined as follows:

The Executive Committee (composed as above) has general supervision and direction of the Movement. It meets on an average of once each month.

The Committee has the following secretaries: (1) A traveling secretary (at times there have been two), whose work consists in organizing, educating, quickening, and setting to work the volunteers in the different institutions and in extending the Movement, not only among previously visited institutions, but also among those as yet untouched. (2) A corresponding secretary, who enrolls and classifies the names of volunteers, tabulates statistics, prepares and distributes printed matter, conducts an extensive correspondence with several hundreds of institutions, and renders such aid to the missionary boards as may be within his power. He also acts as treasurer. Mr. William H. Hannum held this position until shortly before he sailed for India in 1890. Since then Mr. Walter J. Clark has filled the office. (3) An editorial secretary, who aims to keep the Movement before the Church and volunteers. Messrs. R. S. Miller, Jr., E. W. Rand, and Max Wood Moorhead have in turn held this position. Since 1891 it has been unoccupied.

There is an Advisory Committee, with whom the Executive Committee confers about any especially important step in the development of the Movement. It has been composed from the beginning of the following: The Reverend A. J. Gordon, D. D., Bishop M. S. Baldwin, D. D., Miss Abbie B. Child, President Merrill E. Gates, The Reverend George Alexander, D. D., The Reverend A. T. Pierson, D. D.

The Executive Committee, through its traveling secretary, is unable to touch more than one-fifth of the colleges and theological seminaries during the year. It therefore aims to have a corresponding member (or Corresponding Committee) in every state and province in which the extent and condition of the Movement demands it. His work is to carry out the policy of the Committee in his particular field.

In each institution the volunteers are united in what is known as the Volunteer Band. In the colleges this is organized as the missionary department of the College Association. In theological seminaries it is a part of the regular missionary society. These bands hold regular meetings for prayer and for systematic study of missions. Moreover, they seek to spread missionary intelligence, to secure new volunteers, to stimulate systematic giving, and to kindle the missionary spirit in young people's societies and in churches.

While the third year in the life of the Movement has been called the year of organization, it was by no means limited to that. Mr. Wilder was induced to devote this, a second year to work in the field. During that time he touched ninety-three institutions, twenty-five of which had been previously visited, and enrolled 600 new recruits. The larger part of his time, however, he spent in reorganizing the volunteers secured by Mr. Forman and himself on the first tour. During their first year in the work they had favored letting the volunteers form bands independent of the existing religious societies. It was impossible at that time to foresee the result. Two years' observation of the working of these independent bands, however, had completely convinced Mr. Wilder (Mr. Forman in the meantime had gone to India) that it would be far better from every consideration for the volunteers to group themselves together as a part of the missionary department of the existing associations and societies. Within this year, and the one following it, over sixty—or nearly all—of the independent bands merged themselves into these organizations.

The year 1889-1890 will always stand out prominently in the history of the Volunteer Movement as the year of the deepening of its inner life. Mr. Robert E. Speer, of Princeton, 1889, touched 110 institutions, or a larger number than have ever been touched in one year by any other man in the college field. He reached many new colleges, especially in the South and Southwest. Now that the track on which the Movement was to run had been laid down, in the form of wise organization, Mr. Speer saw that its power and efficiency depended on the spiritual life of the individual bands; and so he sought incessantly to bring these groups of volunteers to the great sources of spiritual life and light. Along the pathway of his tour he also gathered 1,100 new volunteers.

The Movement with its principles, purposes, and possibilities was first brought before the Church in a public and an official manner in the year 1890-1891. That was the year of its First International Convention, held from February 26 to March 1, 1891, at Cleveland, Ohio. It constituted the largest student convention ever held, there being about 600 volunteers present from 159 institutions, representing all parts of the United States and Canada east of the Rocky Mountains. In addition to the students there were thirty-three representatives of the leading missionary societies of the United States and Canada, over thirty returned missionaries representing every quarter of the globe, and over fifty other Christian workers. This Convention gave the Movement standing in the eyes of the leaders of the missionary work of the Church. The most conservative among them as they came to understand its methods and spirit gave it the weight of their unqualified approval. During this year the Movement was represented in the field by Mr. W. H. Cossum, of Colgate University, who is now at work in China. Several hundreds of volunteers were added to the roll, and much was done toward making the bands studying and working centers. Miss Lucy E. Guinness, of England, spent nearly three months among the women of our colleges, both in co-educational institutions and in distinctively women's colleges, and enrolled at least 240 volunteers. This tour marked a very successful beginning of special efforts for this class—a phase of work very much neglected up to that time.

The past year (1891-1892) has been a year of education. Mr. J. Campbell White, of the College of Wooster, as traveling secretary, has devoted much of his time, in the 100 institutions which he visited, to the much-needed work of marking out courses of study and lines of work for the volunteer bands. Miss Eloise Mayham has pursued a similar policy in her thorough work among the young women in thirty-five additional institutions. They have been supplemented in this by Mr. Clark, at the office, who has also developed the publication department. Moreover, at the student summer schools, missionary institutes have been established for training leaders of the various volunteer bands. The inauguration of these institutes marked the greatest advance of the year in the development of the Movement. The life and efficiency of the Movement depend chiefly on the life and efficiency of the individual bands; and that in turn depends principally upon the life and efficiency of the leaders of the bands. There was also carried on during the year a thorough investigation into the exact condition and problems of the Movement. This involved a complete examination of the records of all the volunteers as filed in the office, and a careful inquiry into the status of the bands themselves. As the result of a better understanding of the tendencies of the Movement several changes in its methods and policy were made.

The most important of these possibly was the change in the wording of the volunteer pledge or, as it is better called in Great Britain, the volunteer declaration. This was effected on July 14, 1892, at the close of the World's Student Conference at Northfield in a joint meeting of members of the Executive Committees of the Volunteer Movement in Great Britain, and in the United States and Canada. The old wording was: "I am willing and desirous, God permitting, to become a foreign missionary." As changed, it reads: "It is my purpose, if God permit, to become a foreign missionary." The former wording has, as a rule, where it has been carefully explained, been understood to mean simply purpose. At the same time experience had proved that it had been difficult for some men who had employed the old declaration to make its real meaning clear, and moreover, that in some cases, even when clearly presented, it had been misunderstood. It was believed by the two Committees that the new form of declaration would be much more easily explained, and, therefore, much less likely to be misinterpreted. It was decided that the new declaration should be signed only by students who might volunteer after its adoption.

III. ACHIEVEMENTS

Several thousands of students have been led by the Volunteer Movement to take the advanced step of consecration involved in forming the purpose to become foreign missionaries. In the large majority of instances this decision has been formed in the spirit of prayer, and solely as unto God. The Biblical argument has influenced far more men than even the vivid presentation of the needs of the fields. The most powerful consideration has been the thought of loyalty to Jesus Christ by obedience to His last command. Well might Dr. McCosh ask before the Movement was two years old: "Has any such offering of living young men and women been presented in our age, in our country, in any age, or in any country, since the day of Pentecost?"

Over 500 volunteers have already gone to the foreign field under the various missionary agencies, and fully 100 more are under appointment. A noted foreign missionary, while at a conference in this country three years ago, said that not more than 2 per cent of those who volunteered in a missionary revival ever sailed. But already, 7 per cent of the members of this Movement have sailed, and fully 10 per cent of the Canadian contingent. Moreover, a large majority of the volunteers are still in the various stages of preparation. The following list of countries in which volunteers are already working indicates their wide distribution: North, East, West, and South Africa; Arabia, Burma, China, Korea, India, Japan, Persia, Siam, and Laos; Syria and Turkey; Bulgaria and Italy; Central America and Mexico; Brazil, Chile, and the United States of Colombia; and the South Sea Islands.

By means of this Movement, missionary intelligence, methods, enthusiasm, and consecration have been carried into 300 colleges on this continent. In 1885, there was comparatively no interest in missions, save in a few of these institutions. Now the missionary department of the College Young Men's and Young Women's Christian Associations is probably the best developed and certainly one of the most influential departments in their entire scheme of work. Today there are nearly six times as many students in these colleges who expect to be foreign missionaries as there were at the inception of the Movement. At least one fifth of the officers of the Christian Associations are volunteers, although the volunteers constitute but one fifteenth of the active membership. Another important fact should not be lost sight of, and that is that every volunteer who sails means more than one missionary. He stands for a large constituency who are interested in the work because he goes. Who can measure the importance of thus enlisting the intelligent sympathy and co-operation of thousands who are to remain at home, in the great missionary undertakings of the Church?

Missionary interest has also been intensified in forty-five theological seminaries. Special missionary statistics concerning the seminaries show that the number of prospective missionaries has been greatly increased during the past few years. Before 1886, it has been stated that one ordained minister out of seventy-seven had gone into the foreign field. Since then, over 11 per cent of the seminary undergraduates have volunteered for foreign service. A more comprehensive study of missions is being carried on by seminary men. As a result of such study, and of the object lesson of so many devoting their lives to the cause of missions, the men who are to enter the home pastorate are realizing as never before their special responsibility to the world field. The Movement is thus rendering an invaluable service. One of the veteran missionary secretaries of America recently said that the great need today is that of a generation of missionary pastors to supplement the missionary volunteers by spreading missionary intelligence and keeping the conscience of the Church sensitive on the subject of the divine claims of foreign missions.

When this Movement began its work in the institutions of higher learning it found fewer than a dozen collections of missionary books which were abreast of the times. Extended search now and then revealed a few of the old class of missionary biographies and broken files of missionary society reports. In very few cases could there have been found in the reading room a missionary periodical. For seven years the representatives of the Movement have been emphasizing in season and out of season the importance of continued study of the best and latest missionary books and papers. Through their influence carefully selected missionary libraries have been introduced into fully seventy-five institutions; and, in the aggregate, several thousands of dollars' worth of the most helpful and stimulating books have been scattered throughout the student field. It would be difficult now to find an institution where there are not now two or more missionary periodicals on file. Some of the best missionary works of Great Britain have, through the influence of the Movement, been introduced into wide and general circulation.

The plan for colleges and theological seminaries to support their own missionaries under their respective boards has been promoted. The seminaries have been led to treble their contributions, and the colleges, which before 1886 were giving practically nothing to missionary work, have for several years been giving over $10,000 each year. It should be stated that this amount comes from only about one tenth of the institutions. The importance of having students acquire the habit of giving systematically to the cause of missions cannot be overestimated. They will not abandon it after they leave the college and the seminary, but as leaders in their churches they will do much to solve the financial problem of missions.

It may truthfully be said that the Volunteer Movement has done more than all other agencies combined to emphasize the idea that each church should support its own missionary. Volunteers have elaborated the plan and have also printed and circulated a pamphlet clearly setting it forth. Moreover, they have actually introduced it in many churches of different denominations with the most gratifying results. A large number of strong testimonials have been collected. The following given by the secretaries of the Foreign Mission Board of the Presbyterian Church, U.S.A., is a striking recognition of the importance of this work:

> We have before us a long list of testimonials from pastors who have tried the experiment with most gratifying results; and we are assured that if this method should become general throughout the churches, it would mark a new era of progress in foreign missions, while, by its reflex influence at home, it would bring one of the greatest blessings that the Church has experienced in a generation.
>
> . . . We gladly recognize the influence which has been exerted along these lines by the Student Volunteer Movement in our colleges and theological seminaries. . . . And we recognize with equal clearness and satisfaction the large part which this Movement has had in arousing churches, Young Men's Christian Associations, Christian Endeavor Societies, etc., to a new interest and to a more adequate contribution of means. . . . The interest which they (the volunteers) create and the funds which they raise are a clear gain. . . .
>
> So far as the Presbyterian churches are concerned, we most heartily commend the work.

F. F. ELLINWOOD,
ARTHUR MITCHELL, } Secretaries
JOHN GILLESPIE,

NEW YORK, November 6, 1890   WILLIAM DULLES, Treasurer

The success of the Volunteer Movement in the United States and Canada has been so marked that its influence has already been strongly felt in British and Continental universities. The delegates who have come from these insitutions from year to year, have been particularly impressed by this student missionary uprising, and have done much to carry back its methods and spirit. Messrs. Forman, Reynolds, Wishard, and McConaughy have also at different times done not a little toward bringing its principles to the attention of European students. To Mr. Wilder is due in large part the credit of actually organizing the Movement in Great Britain and Scandinavia. For two years students from these countries had urged the Executive Committee to send some representative to Europe. Mr. Wilder was induced to undertake this mission while on his way to India in 1892. An organization to direct the work among the universities of Great Britain was perfected in April, at Edinburgh. It was modeled very closely after the organization which has worked so successfully on this side. The organization of the Movement in Scandinavia is just now taking definite shape. A striking fact is the recent introduction of the Movement in three institutions of South Africa. This resulted from reading accounts of the Movement in this country. Miss Rose J. Sears, a Wellesley volunteer, teaching in the Huguenot Seminary at Wellington, Cape Colony, united and organized the three groups of volunteers.

Another thing achieved by the Movement, while not as tangible as some of the other points named, has been nevertheless just as real and important, and that is the emphasis which it has constantly given to the idea of *the evangelization of the world in this generation.* In over 400 centers of learning this keynote has been sounded year after year in the ears of those who are soon to be the leaders of the different evangelical church agencies. At hundreds of conventions, in all parts of Canada and the United States, it has been proclaimed with convincing power. In thousands of churches it has appealed to the loyalty of Christians, and evoked a sympathetic response. It has differentiated the Volunteer Movement from every other missionary movement undertaken by students. It constitutes at once its ultimate purpose and its inspiration. More and more as the volunteers prayerfully look through the doors of faith opening today unto every nation, ponder the last command of Jesus Christ, and consider the resources of His Church, they are convinced of the necessity, duty, possibility, and probability of realizing their watchcry.

IV. Present Status

During the past year an extensive correspondence has been instituted with the volunteers for the purpose of receiving information for statistics. A large proportion of the volunteers have responded, and the following figures, based upon the returns, all are considered safe estimates.

Distribution of volunteers, according to section where enrolled:

CANADA,   480

| New Brunswick | 15 | Ontario | 325 |
| Nova Scotia | 45 | Quebec | 95 |

NEW ENGLAND STATES,   650

Connecticut	95	New Hampshire	25
Maine	60	Rhode Island	25
Massachusetts	430	Vermont	15

MIDDLE ATLANTIC STATES,   1440

| Maryland | 45 | New York | 630 |
| New Jersey | 340 | Pennsylvania | 425 |

SOUTHERN STATES,   845

Alabama	10	South Carolina	25
Arkansas	15	Tennessee	190
Georgia	25	Texas	45
Kentucky	140	Virginia	270
North Carolina	80	West Virginia	45

CENTRAL STATES,   2345

Illinois	805	Michigan	390
Indiana	185	Ohio	740
	Wisconsin	225	

WESTERN STATES,   1680

Iowa	460	Missouri	315
Kansas	450	Nebraska	255
Minnesota	185	South Dakota	15

PACIFIC STATES,   60

| California | 35 | Oregon | 20 |
| | Washington | 5 | |

Total number of volunteers 7500

Distribution of volunteers according to stages of preparation:

IN INSTITUTIONS OF LEARNING,   2900

Academies	540	Colleges	1600
Normal schools	125	Medical colleges	110
Theological seminaries	425	Training schools	100

Out of Institutions (because of state of health, insufficient means, etc.)	950
Graduates (postgraduates, special students, etc.)	500
Ready to go	125

Acceptable by some Foreign Missionary Society... 100
Hindered by outward surroundings or health, but still wanting to go... 625
Unknown or lost (a majority of them lost track of before Movement
    was organized) 775
Rejected by some Foreign Missionary Society... 75
Renounced—would not go if conditions were favorable............................ 650
Deceased during preparation.. 90
Sailed to engage in foreign missionary work.. 510
Non-students affiliated with voluntary bands.. 200

Distribution of volunteers according to age:

Under 20 years..	10 per cent.
Over 20 years and under 25 years............................	48 " "
Over 25 years and under 30 years............................	31 " "
Over 30 years..	11 " "

Distribution of volunteers according to sex:

Male, 4875	65 per cent.
Female, 2625	35 " "

Distribution of volunteers according to denomination:

Presbyterian, (8 branches)...........................	28 per cent.
Methodist, (10 branches)...............................	27 " "
Baptist, (3 branches)...................................	18 " "
Congregational	15 " "
Other denominations	12 " "

V. PURPOSE

The Student Volunteer Movement seeks to enroll volunteers in the colleges and theological seminaries in numbers sufficient to meet all the demands made upon it by the foreign missionary agencies on this continent.

This Movement aims to carry the missionary spirit into every institution of higher learning in the United States and Canada, and to co-operate with similar movements in other lands. The power which will thus come from uniting the Christian students of the world to carry out the last command of Jesus Christ will be irresistible.

Not only does the Movement plan to enlist volunteers, but also to guard and develop them until they pass beyond its proper sphere of influence. This involves the organizing of the volunteers into bands; outlining courses of study for them; enlisting them in active work for missions on educational, financial, and spiritual lines; making the bands praying and self-perpetuating centers; and, finally, helping to bring the volunteers into touch with the various missionary societies or boards.

Since the financial problem is one of the most serious which today confronts every missionary agency, the volunteers propose to do all within their power to hasten its solution. An effort is being made to have each volunteer before sailing secure a financial constituency, and so to cultivate it as to ensure his support on the field. The plan of having each church support its own missionary will be introduced as widely as possible. Moreover, recognizing the wonderful possibilities of the various young people's societies of the day, the Volunteer Movement is making a special effort to secure their active co-operation. These two great movements, called into being during the same decade, are destined to supplement each other in their service to world-wide evangelization.

By far the greatest need of modern missions is that of united, definite, importunate prayer. This alone will lead the Church in this time of times to lift up her eyes and behold the fields. Moreover, the Christians of the two wealthiest nations on the face of the earth will never give as they should until selfishness and practical unbelief in the great designs of God are swept away by the prayers of men who believe in God. And beyond all this, the thousands of consecrated students who have given themselves to this work will never reach the great harvest fields of the world until there is absolute compliance with the human condition laid down by the Lord in His command: "Pray ye, therefore, the Lord of the harvest that He send forth laborers into His harvest." Each volunteer band, therefore, is urged to become a "school of prayer"; and each volunteer wherever he goes should have as his greatest burden the deepening of the prayer life of the Church.

Underlying all these forms of purpose is that ultimate and fundamental object of the Student Volunteer Movement—the evangelization of the world in this generation. This is the watchcry of the volunteers. What does it mean? It does not mean the conversion, or the Christianization, or the civilization of the world, no matter how much the volunteers may believe in each of these. It does mean that the Christians of this generation are to give every person of this age an opportunity to accept Jesus Christ. The volunteers believe that this is an awful necessity, because without it millions will perish. They believe that it is a solemn duty because Christ has commanded it. They believe that it is a possibility because of the inspired object lesson of its achievement by the early Christian Church under far more adverse circumstances than those which confront the Church of the nineteenth century. They believe that it is a probability because of the reasonableness of the demands made by the missionaries themselves that this may be accomplished. Within the last few years, in the two most densely populated and in many respects most difficult fields in the world, large conferences of missionaries have declared with confidence that this can be done. The volunteers say, if they at the front sound the battle cry, should we at the rear beat a retreat? The convocation of missionaries in India, whose estimate corresponds with that of the conference in China, maintained that at least one foreign missionary would be needed for every 50,000 people in unevangelized lands. This means then that 20,000 missionaries are needed in order to "preach the gospel to every creature" within this generation. To say nothing of the great student centers of Great Britain and Scandinavia, is that too large a number to ask for and to expect from the colleges and seminaries of the United States and Canada? There are two states in this country each of which has in its institutions of higher learning more than 20,000 students. Over 2,000,000 young men and women will go out from the institutions of Canada and America within this generation. The foreign field calls for only *one one-hundredth* of them. But where will the money come from to send and support them? It would take less than one six-hundredth of the present wealth of the Christians of America. Stated in another form, it would easily be secured should each of the over two millions of members of our many young people's Christian organizations raise but three cents each day.

There are men and women enough to spare for this grandest mission of the ages. There is money enough to spare to send them. May the spirit of Christ lead His Church to pray the prayer of faith, and to consecrate her men and money to the carrying out of His last command!

Speaker Index

SELECTED MISSIONS BOOKLIST
1979

ALL LOVES EXCELLING (Women in Missions), Beaver, Eerdmans	$3.95
CALL TO MISSION, Neill, Fortress	$3.95
COMMITTED COMMUNITIES, Mellis, William Carey Library	$4.95
CRUCIAL DIMENSIONS IN WORLD EVANGELIZATION, Glasser, et al, William Carey Library	$7.95
DEATH OF A GURU, Maharij, Holman	$3.15
GIVE UP YOUR SMALL AMBITIONS, Griffiths, Moody	$1.95
THE GOSPEL AND ISLAM, McCurry, MARC	$9.00
GREAT COMMISSION FOR TODAY, Howard, Inter-Varsity	$1.35
HIDDEN PEOPLES 1980 (2' x 4' Chart), William Carey Library	$1.50
A HISTORY OF CHRISTIAN MISSIONS, Neill, Penguin	$4.95
HUDSON TAYLOR AND MARIA, Pollock, Zondervan	$4.95
LORDS OF THE EARTH, Richardson, Regal	$5.95
ONCE MORE AROUND JERICHO: THE STORY OF THE U.S. CENTER FOR WORLD MISSION, Winter, William Carey Library	$1.95
OPERATION WORLD: A HANDBOOK FOR WORLD INTERCESSION, Johnstone, STL	$4.95
PENETRATING THE LAST FRONTIERS (Booklet), Winter, William Carey Library	$1.25
SIX ESSENTIAL COMPONENTS OF WORLD EVANGELIZATION (Booklet), Winter, William Carey Library	$ .75
SO THAT'S WHAT MISSIONS IS ALL ABOUT, Coggins, Moody	$1.95
STOP THE WORLD I WANT TO GET ON, Wagner, William Carey Library	$3.95
THAT EVERYONE MAY HEAR (Reaching the Unreached), Dayton, MARC	$2.50
THE 25 UNBELIEVABLE YEARS, Winter, William Carey Library	$3.95

UNDERSTANDING CHURCH GROWTH, McGavran,
  Eerdmans $4.95
UNDERSTANDING LATIN AMERICANS, Nida,
  William Carey Library $3.95
THE WORLD CHRISTIAN MOVEMENT: 1950-1975
  (Booklet), Winter, William Carey Library $ .75
  Pack of ten $7.50
WORLD CHRISTIANITY - MIDDLE EAST,
  McCurry, MARC $6.00
YOU CAN TELL THE WORLD - A MISSION READER,
  Inter-Varsity $2.50

HOW TO ORDER

Send orders to William Carey Library, 1705 N. Sierra Bonita
Avenue, Pasadena, California 91104 (USA). Please allow four
to six weeks for delivery in the U.S.